Womanist Ethics

Black Religion / Womanist Thought / Social Justice
Series Editors Dwight N. Hopkins and Linda E. Thomas
Published by Palgrave Macmillan

"How Long this Road": Race, Religion, and the Legacy of C. Eric Lincoln
Edited by Alton B. Pollard, III and Love Henry Whelchel, Jr.

White Theology: Outing Supremacy in Modernity
By James W. Perkinson

The Myth of Ham in Nineteenth-Century American Christianity: Race, Heathens, and the People of God
By Sylvester Johnson

African American Humanist Principles: Living and Thinking Like the Children of Nimrod
By Anthony B. Pinn

Loving the Body: Black Religious Studies and the Erotic
Edited by Anthony B. Pinn and Dwight N. Hopkins

Transformative Pastoral Leadership in the Black Church
By Jeffery L. Tribble, Sr.

Shamanism, Racism, and Hip Hop Culture: Essays on White Supremacy and Black Subversion
By James W. Perkinson

Women, Ethics, and Inequality in U.S. Healthcare: "To Count Among the Living"
By Aana Marie Vigen

Black Theology in Transatlantic Dialogue: Inside Looking Out, Outside Looking In
By Anthony G. Reddie

Womanist Ethics and the Cultural Production of Evil
By Emilie M. Townes

African American Religious Life and the Story of Nimrod
Edited by Anthony B. Pinn and Allen Callahan
(forthcoming)

Whiteness and Morality: Pursuing Racial Justice through Reparations and Sovereignty
By Jennifer Harvey
(forthcoming)

Black Theology and Pedagogy
By Noel Leo Erskine
(forthcoming)

Womanist Ethics and the Cultural Production of Evil

Emilie M. Townes

First published in 2006 by
PALGRAVE MACMILLAN™
175 Fifth Avenue, New York, N.Y. 10010 and
Houndmills, Basingstoke, Hampshire, England RG21 6XS
Companies and representatives throughout the world.

PALGRAVE MACMILLAN is the global academic imprint of the Palgrave Macmillan division of St. Martin's Press, LLC and of Palgrave Macmillan Ltd. Macmillan® is a registered trademark in the United States, United Kingdom and other countries. Palgrave is a registered trademark in the European Union and other countries.

ISBN-13: 978-1-4039-7272-9 hardback
ISBN-10: 1-4039-7272-9 hardback
ISBN-13: 978-1-4039-7273-6 paperback
ISBN-10: 1-4039-7273-7 paperback

Library of Congress Cataloging-in-Publication Data

Townes, Emilie Maureen, 1955–
    Womanist ethics and the cultural production of evil / Emilie M. Townes.
        p. cm.— (Black religion, womanist thought, social justice)
    Includes bibliographical references and index.
    ISBN 1-4039-7272-9 (alk. paper)—ISBN 1-4039-7273-7 (alk. paper)
        1. Christian ethics. 2. Womanist theology. I. Title. II. Series.

BJ1278.F45T69 2006
170.82—dc22   2006043253

A catalogue record for this book is available from the British Library.

Design by Newgen Imaging Systems (P) Ltd., Chennai, India.

First edition: October 2006

10 9 8 7 6 5 4 3 2 1

Printed in the United States of America.

Transferred to Digital Printing in 2009

Write the vision; make it plain upon tablets, so those may run who read it. For still the vision awaits its time; it hastens to the end—it will not lie. If it seem slow, wait for it; it will surely come, it will not delay.

Habakkuk 2: 2–3

You should never carry around your own prison.

Ronne Hartsfield
December 11, 2001

All of us have a tremendous capacity for evil. All of us . . . But that is not the end of the story. We also have an extraordinary capacity for good.

Archbishop Desmond M. Tutu
February 6, 2002

for

Oliver McClean and George F. Moore

Contents

Preface

On Memory

i begin with memory
    a particular memory
i am still young—7 or 8 or 9 years old
    i walk from my school—fayetteville street elementary
    up the street to the biology building at ncc
        at that time it had no "u"
    the biology building is where my mother works
i sit outside her class room
    cross-legged
    listening to her teach
        marveling at the *sound* of her words
        as i also learn biology
listening to her lecture
    captured by the precision of her enunciation
        the ease of her movement through technical biological tidbits
        the rapid-fire give and take of questions and answers
        the prodding of creativity about life and its meaning as it lay
        before students in the death of the dissecting table
    knowing without a doubt
        that she loves not only talking about amoebas and the
        glycerinerated stalks of the vorticella
        but also wanting students to learn to love biology
            but more importantly
            learn to love learning
                its potent legacy
this little emilie memory
    resides in me deeply
    because it was sitting outside my mother's classroom
        that i first learned about teaching and learning
it is, in fact, both a precious memory and a demanding memory
    because although i do not want to be my mother

i do want to teach and learn as she did
and did until her death
it is this act of loving what she did
that i want to remember and enact in my own teaching and scholarship
i want to create, with a good bit of help from students and colleagues
an atmosphere that truly cherishes teaching and learning
to care not only about ideas
but the consequences of holding them
of living them
of losing them
of gaining them
such is the power of memory
rooted in me
rooted in all of us
living . . .

Preface

This work is classic Emilie Townes. It is poetic and prophetic, words dance as they coax, berate, and persuade. And always we not just discover but encounter hope directly in the arguments and artistic prose, but sometimes hope comes through her writing side ways. If one is not alert, one can miss the blessing. Clearly this book is dancing words and, moreover, a thinking book. Actually, it stands (dances?) within the courageous and creative tradition of enslaved African Americans who approached the Bible as a talking book. They could not read, at least the majority of the ancestors—Emilie Townes's ancestors. So they listened for the words to dance from a speaker's mouth into their ears and hearts. For them and for Townes the deployment and crafting of words mean something for life and death. We imagine that Townes somehow listens as she writes. She hears with the head and spirit of an audience long gone, crossed over but whose souls linger on this side. She hears with her own head and spirit as the audience who is listening back to her talking book that the reader has before us. There is a lot of dancing, talking, and hearing back in this text. The power of the presentation can only be further enhanced by performing the chapters of this work. Writing, here, is fighting and loving and visioning that a better world is possible whether in the U.S.A. or Brazil. Has anyone in the academy ever choreographed a text?

Townes knows her womanist self. That is why the writing is so powerful and so meaningful and so challenging. Out of her self and her community's context, universality emerges with the force of a hungry bear ending a hibernation. Black women folk in the U.S.A. can paint a canvass with the evils experienced by them in this world, and the impact on them, their children, adopted children, and the men in their lives, too. And this is what this book is about: the cultural production of evil. Evil is spirit but it is also principalities and powers on earth. Evil invades and warps our memory, both historical memory and the site of memory. What happens when evil is so terrible that one fears the telling? Is this what stunts the dancing of the words on a page or a community's gathering to dance like psalmist David or the West African derived drum-based Candomble of Brazil? Or maybe evil is the popular stereotype of the African North American woman. Sometimes she is depicted as the mammy who is super (black) woman—taking charge of the master's house, nursing his children, running his affairs, keeping other black folk in line, and, above all as Malcolm X said, loving the master and his offspring more than the black woman loves herself. Or maybe it is the color caste, unspoken everyday reality in the black community and church where high yellow trumps charcoal black, even in the silence of the grins and "we are all the same African American people" mantras.

But evil is as long as evil has the last say. Thank goodness Townes poeticizes and prophesizes the reader into her paths of justice and hope. This journey weaves us and encourages us and rallies us toward the ethics of life over the ethics of death. Along the way, we want to learn about and change the evils of unpaid black labor in the U.S. public policy while black woman's moral autonomy provide a model for dancing in justice and hope. And we see a concrete theoretical way to take apart this evil in community and in solidarity with all. And just as culture spews up evil, counterculture or people's culture can articulate the ethics of imagining a newness. We invite the reader to join Townes's as she dances with her words in that unique and engaging black woman's dance. Here for her, there are some new steps in the key of womanist ethics.

Emilie Townes's book represents one definite dimension of the Black religion/womanist thought/social justice series—pioneering conceptual work and boundary-pushing effort. The series will publish both authored and edited manuscripts that have depth, breadth, and theoretical edge and will address both academic and nonspecialist audiences. It will produce works engaging any dimension of black religion or womanist thought as they pertain to social justice. Womanist thought is a new approach in the study of African American women's perspectives. The series will include a variety of African American religious expressions.

By this we mean traditions such as Protestant and Catholic Christianity, Islam, Judaism, Humanism, African diasporic practices, religion and gender, religion and black gays/lesbians, ecological justice issues, African American religiosity and its relation to African religions, new black religious movements (e.g., Daddy Grace, Father

Divine or the Nation of Islam), or religious dimensions in African American "secular" experiences (such as the spiritual aspects of aesthetic efforts like the Harlem Renaissance and literary giants such as James Baldwin, or the religious fervor of the Black Consciousness movement, or the religion of compassion in the black women's club movement).

Dwight N. Hopkins,
University of Chicago Divinity School
Linda E. Thomas, Lutheran School of Theology at Chicago

Acknowledgments

There are many people who helped me think through this book. First, I must thank The board of directors of Union Theological Seminary and President Joseph C. Hough and Academic Dean Rosemary Skinner Keller for supporting and granting me a sabbatical year for 2001–2002. Also, I thank Dean Harold W. Attridge of Yale Divinity School, my new home, for his willingness to have me depart for sabbatical soon after my arrival in July 2005. From 2001–2002 I found an incredible supportive home that year in the Women's Studies in Religion Program at Harvard Divinity School. The director of the program, Ann Braude and the administrative assistant, Martha Kay Nelson gave us a rich environment and a room of our own to work and to discuss our work. The research associates for that year, Joan Branham, Anne Lapidus Lerner, Vijaya Nagaran, and Michelene Pesantubbee were tremendous colleagues and are fine scholars who listened and prodded me to clarify my thoughts and encouraged me in this project. From 2005–2006, the Association of Theological Schools selected me as a Henry Luce III Fellow in Theology. I thank both the Luce Foundation and its president, Michael Gilligan, and program director for theology, Lynn Szwaja, and the selection committee, director of leadership education and accreditation, William R. Myers, and executive director of the Association of Theological Schools, Daniel O. Aleshire. The Luce Fellows program is an incredibly collegial and interdisciplinary one that fosters lively conversations, good food and drink, and a space to think through the implications of our ideas in a community of scholars who listen hard to each other and push one another toward excellence.

Several groups of students have engaged me in this manuscript as well. Two generations of the Theological and Social Ethics Methods Seminar and the Political Economy of Misery course at Union Theological Seminary, Harvard Divinity School, and Yale Divinity

School; and the Metaphors of Evil course at Yale Divinity School brought new insights to my work and also endured tough sledding as we peeled back the onion of evil together. As I have lectured from various chapters in this book, students from Auburn Theological Seminary, Bangor Theological Seminary, Barry University, Episcopal Divinity School, Escola Superior de Teológia, Faculdade Baptista Brasiliero, Instituto de Educação Teológia da Bahia and the YAMI collective, Lewis University, Luther Seminary, Lutheran Theological Southern Seminary, Núcleo de Estudos Teológico da Mulher nas América Latina collective of the Universidade Metodista de São Paulo, Seminario Teológica Baptista do Nordeste, United Theological Seminary of the Twin Cities, University of New Hampshire, Wake Forest University Divinity School, and Wartburg Seminary have engaged my ideas and help me refine my thought. My colleagues in the Womanist Approaches to Religion and Society Group of the American Academy of Religion and the Society of Christian Ethics provide a firm counterbalance at all times. I have been enriched through my conversation with the Black Clergywomen of the United Methodist Church and the Women in Leadership in Theological Education of the Association of Theological Schools in the United States and Canada. My most challenging and critical audiences have been church gatherings of various sorts and community public lectures. In these settings, I found a very active and engaged audience who pushed me to clarify what I was saying and helped me appreciate the implications of my ideas for their lives.

My colleagues near and far read drafts and talked through ideas with me. Each, a sterling colleague in her or his own right, has created for me a great cloud of witnesses in my work: Linda Barnes, Katie G. Cannon, Kelly Brown Douglas, C Dale Gadsden, Siobhán Garrigan, Cheryl Townsend Gilkes, Claudia Highbaugh, Serene Jones, Belva Brown Jordan, Charles Long, Joan Martin, Peter Paris, Larry Rasmussen, Marcia Riggs, Tex Sample, Diana Swancutt, and Renita Weems. Peter T. Nash took great care in reading the drafts of this manuscript and also heard me lecture on parts of it in both English and Portuguese. In the latter language, he had the challenge of being my translator at times—something he did with patience, care, and good humor. To him I owe a special debt of gratitude. Peggy and Tex Sample provided the wonderful hammered copper dinner table on which I finished this book. Their southern sense of hospitality and love is always a marvelous thing.

I must say a special word about Larry Rasmussen. As I was finishing the first draft of this manuscript, he was preparing to retire from Union Theological Seminary. I was mourning his impending retirement, as well as that of Rosemary Keller and Delores Williams. Larry was and remains a remarkable colleague for the years I taught at Union. He is, true enough, Minnesota nice, but he's also a fine human being and an excellent ethicist. I missed his leaving more than he can know but I celebrate his coming years as he will now have the time and space to do more of things he likes in a much warmer climate than New York. The one great bonus for me is that I can now visit him and Nyla in Santa Fe where he assures me that I can play golf to my heart's content.

As always, I end with thanks to my family. In 2003, a great soul left this side of the Jordan. Mom was mentor and mother in ways that are lasting. I miss her wit and wisdom each and every day. However, the legacy she left for my sister Tricia and me is a lasting and good one. She taught us the value of telling the truth, listening more than you talk, and the importance of learning how to truly look at and see what is going on around you. She was, as her students used to say, "a little piece of leather who was well put together." My aunts Agnes Moore and Helen McLean and my uncles Oliver McClean and George Moore continue to provide the wisdom of "old souls" through their humor and in their humanity. It is to my uncles, who have been waiting for me to dedicate a book to them that I say a particular thank you. They are good people—even Uncle What's His Name.

The Womanist Dancing Mind: Cavorting with Culture and Evil

There is a certain kind of peace that is not merely the absence of war. It is larger than that. The peace I am thinking of is not at the mercy of history's rule, nor is it a passive surrender to the status quo. The peace I am thinking of is the dance of an open mind when it engages another equally open one—an activity that occurs most naturally, most often in the reading/writing world we live in. Accessible as it is, this particular kind of peace warrants vigilance. The peril it faces comes not from the computers and information highways that raise alarm among book readers, but from unrecognized, more sinister quarters.[1]

—Toni Morrison, *The Dancing Mind*

This quotation is taken from Morrison's acceptance speech for the National Book Foundation's Medal for Distinguished Contribution to American Letters in 1996. As such, Morrison focuses on the dangers, the necessities, and the pleasures of the reading/writing life in the late twentieth century. For her, the dangers are captured in two anecdotes. In one, it is the danger that, in her words, "our busied-up, education-as-horse-race, trophy-driven culture poses even to the entitled." In the second, she teases out "the physical danger to writing suffered by persons with enviable educations who live in countries where the practice of modern art is illegal and subject to official vigilantism and murder."

It is in the dancing mind that many of us meet each other more often than not. It is in the books and essays and lectures and papers that those of us who are not womanists most often meet us those of us who are womanists for the first, if not the only time and way. It is in this dancing mind—where we tease through the possibilities and the realities, the hopes, the dreams, the nightmares, the terrors, the critique, the analysis, the plea, the witness—that womanist work is done in the academy, in the classroom, in the religious gatherings of our various communities, in those quiet and not so quiet times in which we try to reflect on the ways in which we know and see and feel and do.

This womanist dancing mind is more than my attempt to make sense of the worlds surrounding us—sometimes enveloping us, sometimes smothering us, sometimes holding us, sometimes birthing us. It is more than my desire to reconfigure the world and then invite others to come and inspect the textures, the colors, the patterns, the shapes, the sizes of this new order, this new set of promises.

No, the womanist dancing mind is one that comes from a particular community of communities yearning for a common fire banked by the billows of justice and hope. As such, this particularity marks us with indelible ink. My task is to explore the twists and turns of the communities from which we spring and have our very life and breath. It is to be very particular about the particular—and explore the vastness of it.

The womanist dancing mind—the one that weaves in and out of Africa, the Caribbean, Brazil, the United States (South, North, East, and West); the Christian, the Jewish, the Muslim, the Candomblé, the Santeria, the Vodun, the Native American, the caste of color, the sexuality, the sexual orientation, the socioeconomic class, the age, the body image, the environment, the pedagogies, the academy—has before it an enormous intracommunal task. One in which we are trying to understand the assortments of African American life. If I do this task well, I will realize the ways in which Black life is not my life alone, but a compendium of conscious and unconscious coalitions with others whose lives are not lived solely in the Black face of United States life.

This is an important quest for this discussion of evil. I argue that a key way to understand the arithmetic of misery that evil invokes and provokes is to concentrate on particularities rather than universals. In this womanist dancing mind, the expansiveness of womanist ethics must be the absolutely last methodological consideration. I am interested in exploring the *depths* of African American life—female and male. For it is in exploring these depths, in taking seriously my particularity—not as a form of essentialism, but as epistemology—where I can meet and greet others for we are intricately and intimately interwoven in our postmodern culture.

In this particularity, I explore the ways in which human lives and cultures have become commodities that are marketed and consumed in the global marketplace. I must stand toe-to-toe with the damaging and destroying effects of the made-in-America color-caste hierarchy that remains largely unacknowledged and explored. I explore connections between empire and reparations as linked phenomena that spew genderized and racialized moralizations into the global marketplace. I explore the need for recognizing women's moral autonomy within communities as an important factor in developing public policy in the United States.

This particularity challenges me to explore gender—sexuality, sexual orientation, sexism—to get at not only my hope for wholeness, but also to understand the ways in which age and body image, and a history that contains the ultimate mammy, the emasculating bitch, the tragic mulatta, the castrating matriarch, and the pickaninny continue to ooze from the pores of videos and magazines and television and radio and music and the pulpit. These images of Black women and girls rest solidly in the imagination of U.S. culture and must be deconstructed and understood for the awful impact they have on how a stereotype is shaped into "truth" in memory and in history. This is an important task in this book.

Because I sit in the academy, the church, the classroom, and the community, I must explore socioeconomic class and globalization as it moves in and out of Black life with blazing speed—taking the poor *and* the wealthy out of sight. Because we all have to live somewhere, the environment, is something I cannot forget to call back continually into my consciousness and work—to broaden the Black community's understanding of what is at stake in the atmosphere we breathe in, an atmosphere beyond the pristine and irrelevant images of Sierra Club calendars that rarely, if ever, put people in nature. Part of my task is to help us understand that postmodern culture and the air it spews will kill us if we do not start paying attention to and then strategizing for a healthier environment for all of us to live in.

This focus on particularity invites a more expansive awareness and vision for womanist ethical reflection. I am challenged to deromanticize the African continent by coming to know its peoples on their terms, not mine. I am compelled to search out and recover my Caribbean and Brazilian streams of consciousness and memory to understand the different ways in which Black folk have survived (or not survived) our own diaspora and the different manifestations of the latent Middle Passage in

our historic and contemporary lives. I must listen to the different
rhythms of blackness that come from the different geographies that
shape peoples bodies and health. I am drawn, sometimes with enormous
reservation and circumspection, to understand the different ways in
which the religious—beyond my own Christian identity—has shaped me
and my communities, and to understand what is at stake when we have
lost, forgotten, or been stolen away from the rich medleys of the religious
in Black life. As I reach further into my particularity, I am brought face-
to-face with the tremendous loss of touch with Native American peoples.

Much of this journey is not overtly found in this book. I give you,
the readers, a sense of the terrain I understand this book to be a part
of. However, parts of the journey are here. I believe that it is through
the particularity of the womanist dancing mind that I can meet and
greet those parts of myself that have been lost through neglect, ignorance, well-practiced amnesia, or malicious separation. I am challenged to look at those instances wherein the "isms" that I impose on
others are turned back at me and I am asked to see myself through the
eyes of those whom I would and do reject. It does not matter that this
rejection is not intentional or malevolent. What does matter is that if I
say, as a womanist, that I am engaged in an integrated and interstructured analysis, then I must face those places within myself and within
my work that ignore the ways in which that interstructuring takes
place.

Exploring evil as a cultural production highlights the systematic
construction of truncated narratives designed to support and perpetuate structural inequities and forms of social oppression. Thus, this
interdisciplinary study of dismantling evil as a cultural production
seeks to understand the interior material life of evil through these narratives. This has its roots in my childhood. As a child, I was trans-
ported to Troy by Homer and I devoured all I could about Greek and
Roman mythology. The idea of gods seemed quite novel to one who
was growing up to "Jesus loves me this I know . . ." Apollo and
Athena took me out of my daily musing on Jesse Helms and fire hoses.
I could enter, through Homer's prompting, a different time and place
where I learned that maybe the holy could be capricious and not
always stern. Throughout my life, I have always learned a great deal
from writers and poets. I speak, primarily, of those who do not deal
with dense theoethical discourse and reflection, but of writers such as
Elizabeth Alexander, Tina McElroy Ansa, Nikky Finney, Alice Walker,
William Faulkner, Ernest Hemingway, Ayn Rand, Carson McCullers,
Gabriel Garcia Marquez, Jorge Amado, Chinua Achebe, . . . the list

goes on and on. Fine writers help us "see" things in tangible ways and "feel" things through intangible means. Their ability to turn the world at a tilt, to explore our humanity and inhumanity challenges me in ways that theories and concepts do not.

Given my Niebuhrian roots, I realized that I would be bound in untenable and unproductive ways if I approached a study of theodicy solely through the realm of concepts and theories. From John Hick's classic study of evil, Arthur McGill, and John Douglas Hall to more recent works by Wendy Farley, David Ray Griffin, Marjorie Suchocki, and Terrence Tilley—the deep interior material life of evil and its manifestations were missing. Instead, I thought, "What has the writing life taught me?" What have writers such as James Baldwin, Patrick Chamoiseau, June Jordan, Toni Morrison, Sonia Sanchez, and Harriet Beecher Stowe said about the struggles and joys of humanity that I could use to understand evil? Perhaps they can share with all of us an ongoing and abiding hope. Perhaps it will be pessimistic love or jaded faith. What I hope most, is that they will remind me that to simplify the complex is to neuter richness and defame the marvelously complex gift of life found pulsing ubiquitously around us.

Good writers teach me that there is a world in our eye, but it not the only one. We can and must consider the eyes, the worlds, of others. In allowing these worlds to dance or collide with one another has always caused me to grow and to change my angle of vision from the straight and narrow to akimbo. The project responds to this, in part, because it engages writers who furnish an entrée to understanding evil and who are different conversation partners than those whom we traditionally engage in Christian social ethics. Further, once I gain access to the interior life of evil, I seek to offer suggestions on how to dismantle it through the intersection of ethical commitment and social location.

Throughout the course of this book, I also engage in a conscious dialogue/interaction among the self, the community, and the society within a global culture. This has been a theoethical as well as sociopolitical and cultural endeavor. Such engagement is necessary to draw the outlines of what it will take to dismantle structural evil. In many ways, I have been engaging in H. Richard Niebuhr's responsibility ethics[2] as I have tried to discern his basic question "What is going on?" by looking at identity as property, uninterrogated coloredness, empire and reparations, and religious values and public policy. These are only parts of systemic evil and the difficulty in exploring them points to a key reason why I use the present participle "ing" with dismantle. To eradicate evil is a process, not an event.

The other parts of Niebuhr's ethic—interpretation, accountability, and social solidarity—are evident throughout the book as well. In making use of Niebuhr's understanding of interpretation, I have tried to make sense of structural evil by categorizing and looking for the pattern and meaning of life as we have currently constructed it. Accountability or anticipating the consequences of my viewpoints and opinions in this book has been a constant companion. I have sought consistency and continuity in my analysis and reflections. Finally, the most pressing part of Niebuhr's ethic is his sense of social solidarity. For me, life and wholeness (the dismantling of evil/the search for and celebration of freedom) is found in our individual interactions with our communities and the social worlds, peoples, and life beyond our immediate terrains.

This last part of Niebuhr's schema may well be the most challenging. As I have argued for an understanding of the common good that recognizes and respects our diversity, Niebuhr's understanding of social solidarity provides a bit of a rub. For him, responsibility is possible if all the members of a community of moral agents maintain a relatively consistent scheme of interpretations of what is going on. Here, Neibuhr's ethic may be tempted to slide into a form of positivist epistemology with its emphasis on common cause and reciprocal loyalty. However, Niebuhr is clear that a key feature of social solidarity is its relational nature.

The interplay between forms of structural evil, stereotype of Black womanhood, and literary guide that frames this book serves as a way to encourage the dialogue that Niebuhr so wished to engage in with moral decision-making. He believed, as I do, that we must pay attention to what is happening around us and look long beyond (both above and below) the surface of events, theories, or positions. Candidly put, we *do not* live in a seamless society. We live in many communities—often simultaneously. This makes us a deeply historical people although the mood of our times pushes us toward ahistoricism.

Topsy and the other stereotypes I deal with point out that our failure to live an engaged and responsible life often produces fractured stories that serve to maintain a grasping social order that consumes us in its drive to possess and control creation itself. If we refuse to engage in dismantling systemic and intentional structural evil, we only leave a parched and desolate land for generations to come.

The movement of the book is more straightforward than my methodology. In the second chapter, I draw on Toni Morrison's essay "The Site of Memory." For Morrison, truth is the key ideal to seek, for facts can exist without human intelligence but truth cannot. As Morrison explores the interior life of people, I want to explore the interior material life of evil. To examine the interior worlds of those who endure evil as well as the interior worlds of evil itself to discover what truths may be found there, I begin by addressing the interplay of history and memory. Rather than replicate the traditional paradigm of history as scientific and memory as subjective, I join Jacques Le Goff and Matt Matsuda by working from the perspective that history and memory are subjective. This expansion of French historian Pierre Nora's work in his influential essay "Between Memory and History," as he searched for the origins of the French past, coupled with Morrison sets the context for two key aspects of my project: first, is to recognize the subjective nature of history and memory so that these traditional categories can be expanded to consider how they can be both preserved and broadened to represent the diversities that shape us. An increased awareness, appreciation, and respect for these diversities, I believe, can guide us down theoethical pathways that can dismantle systematic evil—evil as cultural production—by providing us with even more articulate resources and strategies to tackle such a large task. We no longer depend on ourselves alone, but lean into a richer and more diverse web of creation. Second, to understand evil as a cultural production is to recognize, from the outset, that the story *can* be told another way. It can be told in such a way that the voices and lives of those who, traditionally and historically, have been left out are now heard with clarity and precision. Even more, these voices can then be included into the discourse—not as additive or appendage— but as resource and codeterminer of actions and strategies. Yet this is not a crass teleological world, but one that acknowledges the intimate humanity of our plurality and works with as much precision as possible to name its textures.

Using the interplay of history and memory as a critical frame, I turn to consider how the imagination works within this to create images that buttress evil as a cultural production. Combining Michel Foucault's understanding of the imagination and Antonio Gramsci's use of hegemony, I develop how the imagination—the fantastic hegemonic imagination—"plays" with history and memory to spawn caricatures and stereotypes. I turn to five stereotypes that continue to have profound influence in our social order—Aunt Jemima, Sapphire, the Tragic Mulatta, the Welfare Queen, and Topsy—to explore how a manifestation of evil as a cultural production is embodied. Aunt Jemima opens up identity as property and commodity. Sapphire explores uninterrogated coloredness. The Tragic Mulatta embodies empire and empire building. The Welfare Queen unpacks how religious values play a part in public policy formation. Topsy presents a more complex and nuanced understanding of the kind of solidarity needed to address the cultural production of evil. From the task of dismantling evil, I now turn to the notion of countermemory. This expansion of Michel Foucault through the work of George Lipsitz and Gramsci's understanding of counterhegemony seeks to open up the subversive spaces of counterhegemony. I argue for a reconstitution of history such that we begin to see, hear, and appreciate the diversities in our midst as flesh and blood rather than as cloying distractions within the hegemonic imagination. Countermemory begins with the particular to move into the universal and it looks to the past for microhistories to force a reconsideration of flawed (incomplete or vastly circumscribed) histories. This focus on localized experiences of oppression in countermemory allows me to recenter dominant narratives into a reframing of what constitutes the universal—thus getting into the interior life of evil to unhinge its underpinnings.

Chapter 3 pairs the stereotype of the Mammy with James Baldwin's essay "Many Thousands Gone." With the rise of massive global market capitalism, human lives and their cultures have become commodities that are marketed and consumed in the global marketplace. This chapter explores the structural matrix that supports this phenomenon by looking at how the marketing icon Aunt Jemima was used to sell not only pancake mix, but also Black life in the first successful national marketing campaign in the United States.

Chapter 4 returns to Morrison's work and her essay "Unspeakable Things Unspoken." The Sapphire stereotype is the conversation partner in this chapter where I argue that race is an ill-conceived and arbitrary notion. This chapter explores the notion of race consciously, suspiciously, and analytically in academic, economic, ethical, social, theological, and political arguments. Ultimately, my aim is to incorporate the entire color spectrum—from whiteness to blackness—into a discussion of race and racism within the U. S. context.

In chapter 5, the Tragic Mulatta is paired with notebook entries from Patrick Chamoiseau's novel *Texaco* to contextualize the U.S. reparations debate within the reality of empire. The "almostness" of the Tragic Mulatta is a helpful figure in understanding the ways in which history and memory do a strange dance within reparations talk as I explore the history and the reality of 40 acres and a mule and what that means in today's milieu.

Chapter 6 draws on poet Sonia Sanchez's "haiku 6" and the stereotypes of the Black matriarch and the Welfare Queen. I begin with an
exploration of the Calvinist roots of the protestant work ethic and the
emergence of the autonomous self. This chapter focuses on the presence, or the lack, of recognition given to women's moral autonomy
that is actualized in communal formations as an important factor in
developing public policy that considers the sociocultural and economic
matrix that embodies U.S. life—social and religious.

Chapter 7 speculates about the challenges of solidarity in the midst
of differences when addressing social evils such as these that are, in
fact, cultural productions. This is a hardheaded look at the elements
necessary for a tough-minded society that does not romanticize or sen-
timentalize the high-walled barricades that can prevent genuine and
enduring acts of justice in the face of structural evil. I draw on two
authors for this chapter that features the stereotype of the pickaninny.
Harriet Beecher Stowe's *Uncle Tom's Cabin* and June Jordan's "Of
Those So Close Beside Me, Which are You?" serve as guides and prods
in this discussion.

The final chapter offers a framework for dismantling the cultural
production of evil. I focus on the fantastic hegemonic imagination to
do so. Congresswoman Barbara Jordan's speech before the house judiciary committee during the Watergate hearings in 1974 provide the
touchstone for this work. Her insistence that the United States live into
the fullness of "We the people" provides both an individual and communal outline for the tools it will take to unhinge the underpinnings of
evil as a cultural production.

While dealing with evil, it is not time to dumb down or take cover.
Evil does not hide from us nor does it come in pristine forms. Like
goodness, it is messy and rather confusing. Writers often appreciate
this more than ethicists I think. And so I engage these writers as mentors and guides. Yet, like mentors and guides, they can only go so far
and then I must make the journey on my own. I attempt to provide a
set of lenses for examining and understanding the structural nature of
evil. In the process, imagination, memory, and history dance through
my analysis as Macbeth's three witches—"Fair is foul, and foul is fair."[3]

Sites of Memory: Proceedings too Terrible to Relate

In her essay "The Site of Memory" Toni Morrison explains how her work can be situated within the genre of the memoir. Her essay helps introduce several major themes of this chapter and the book as a whole: imagination, history, the fantastic, the power of images, and memory. She begins her discussion with slave narratives that, she notes, say two things: "This is my historical life—my singular, special example that is personal, but it also represents the race" and "I write this text to persuade other people—you, the reader, who is probably not black—that we are human beings worthy of God's grace and the immediate abandonment of slavery."[1]

Morrison finds it difficult to understand why slave narratives were attacked as "biased," "inflammatory," and "improbable" in contrast to the reception given to the autobiographical narratives of church martyrs that were read for their messages and their experiences of redemption. Morrison contends that the writers of slave narratives knew they faced a sternly suspicious White audience and so wrote to appear as objective as possible. This meant, in Morrison's words, "whatever the level of eloquence or the form, popular taste discouraged the writers from dwelling too long or too carefully on the more sordid details of their experience."[2]

With piercing insight, Morrison observes that slave narratives do not mention the interior lives of the enslaved because the writers shaped their narratives to be acceptable—"they were silent about many things, and they 'forgot' many other things." Because of this, Morrison's job becomes "how to rip that veil drawn over 'proceedings too terrible to relate.' The exercise is also critical for any person who is black, or who belongs to any marginalized category, for, historically, we were seldom invited to participate in the discourse even when we were its topic."[3]Memories are important for this work also, but Morrison finds that neither they nor recollections give her total access to the unwritten interior lives of the enslaved—only imagination can do so. Noting that her work is often classified in the literary genre of the fantastic, Morrison is uncomfortable with this label because she sees that her utmost responsibility "is not to lie."[4] She then makes an important distinction between truth and fiction: "It [truth] may be excessive, it may be more interesting, but the important thing is that it's random—and fiction is not random." Then she explains,

> . . . the crucial distinction for me is not the difference between fact and fiction, but the distinction between fact and truth. Because fact can exist without human intelligence, but truth cannot. So if I'm looking to find and expose a truth about the interior life of people who didn't write it . . . then the approach that is most productive and most trustworthy for me is the recollection that moves from the image to the text. Not from the text to the image.[5]

I mirror this methodology. I take Morrison's probing distinction between truth and fact seriously. Rather than argue for a simplistic notion of history as fact, I am more interested in getting into the interior worlds of those who endure structural evil as well as the interior worlds of structural evil itself to discover what truths may be found there. This, I argue, is the proper realm of womanist discourse based on an interstructured analysis that includes class, gender, and race within the framework of social ethics. It provides a helpful framework to do the necessary critical and analytical work that can expose the ways in which a society can produce misery and suffering in relentlessly systematic and sublimely structural ways. This is what I call the cultural production of evil.

As Morrison remarks, I have found that to take on the task of engaging in such an analysis and critique of structural evil in order to begin the process of dismantling it would mean that "the image comes first and tells me what the 'memory' is about."[6] Memory for Morrison points to the truth of proceedings that may have been too terrible to relate but must be told nonetheless. Through a sometimes subtle, at other times not so subtle, interplay between such images of Black women as Aunt Jemima (the Black Mammy), Sapphire, the Tragic Mulatta, the Black Matriarch (Welfare Queen), and Topsy (pickaninny), there is a productive entrée into the different manifestations of systematic and structural evil I consider in this book. These images act as conductors and seeresses. They evoke not only memory but also history and countermemory as tools and possible strategies for discovering the truths found in the interior life of evil—how it is created, shaped, maintained, dismantled. I turn, now, to history, memory, the fantastic hegemonic imagination, and countermemory to ground the discussion and to introduce strategies that can aid in dismantling the cultural production of evil.

"This is My Historical Life"

The traditional paradigm of history and memory is that history is a discipline and memory is subjective. Memory is a personal activity corrupted by the teller's choice of words and her or his sense of how to shape the story. As Geneviève Fabre and Robert O'Meally point out so well, memory is often viewed as "a created version of an event snatched away from the chaos of the otherwise invisible world gone by."[7] History, however, is often viewed as closer to a "scientific" field where the historian plies proofs and corroborating evidence as the twin guardians for an objective, balanced analysis. Therefore, memory is impressionistic and history is knowledge.

Rather than travel down the ultimately unproductive path that views history as scientific and memory as subjective, the work of French historian Pierre Nora challenges this traditional paradigm. In his landmark essay "Between Memory and History: Les Lieux de Mémoire," Nora is concerned about the impact of democratization, globalization, and the rise of mass media in France. He sees these contemporary features of modern/postmodern life as engines leading to the disintegration of societies based on memory and reproduction (sociétés-mémoire). For Nora, historical continuity has been broken and it survives only in residues or in what he calls sites of memory. These sites of memory replace what Nora considers real living memory that was with us for ages but has now ceased to exist.

In Nora's view, this constructed history replaces true memory, which means that sites of memory are artificial and deliberately fabricated. They exist to help us recall the past. Nora sees history, then, as static ("how our hopelessly forgetful modern societies, propelled by change, organize the past") and memory as dynamic ("open to the dialectic of remembering and forgetting").[8] History is a reconstruction of what no longer exists and calls for analysis and criticism. This makes history both problematic and incomplete for Nora. Memory, however, is life, always carried by living societies, and therefore, it remains in permanent evolution, open to the dialectic of remembering and forgetting, unconscious of successive deformations, vulnerable to all appropriations and manipulations, susceptible to long periods of latency and sudden revitalizations.

In the Hegelian dialectic that frames the essay, Nora believes that memory oozes out of a group and, evoking the work of Maurice Halbwachs discussed in greater detail below, he argues that there are as many memories as there are groups.[9] Memory is multiple but also specific; collective and plural but also individualized. History belongs to everybody and to nobody, which gives it the veneer of the universal. Memory is life itself and is almost sacred, absolute, and rooted in "spaces, gestures, images, objects."[10] History is only interested in temporal continuities, and in the relationships between things. Memory is an absolute, and history only knows the relative.[11]

In essence, Nora believes that memory is unconscious reproduction whereas history is a conscious effort to reproduce. Sites of memory are created because of the impression that memory is lost: "They are the bastions against which we lean. But if what they defend was not threatened, we would not need to construct them."[12] For Nora, memory becomes a tool to regain and reconstruct both the past *and* history: "the quest for memory is the search for history." Ultimately, Nora argues for *sites* of memory instead of real environments of memory (*milieux de mémoire*). Sites of memory are the places where memory "crystallizes and secretes itself."[13] These include archives, museums, cathedrals, palaces, cemeteries, and memorials; concepts and practices such as commemorations, generations, mottos, and all rituals; objects such as inherited property, commemorative monuments, manuals, emblems, basic texts, and symbols.[14]

For Nora, a constructed history replaces true memory. Sites of memory are artificial and deliberate inventions. They exist to help us recall the past that helps us live in our contemporary world in meaningful ways. The purpose of sites of memory is "to stop time, to block the work of forgetting," and they all share "a will to remember."[15]

In our modern pluralistic societies, Nora provides a theoretical framework for the ways in which the idea of a total history supported by global memory is seriously and rightly challenged by the microhistories within these societies and the multiplicity of memories they entail.[16] In contrast to revisionist history that more conservative forces often denounce, microhistories are the ignored or forgotten or discounted histories of real people experiencing the ebb and flow of their societies and their cultures. They are microhistories only because the larger society selects certain markers of the past and invests them with symbolic, political, and theological significance while ignoring others.[17] Put more bluntly, the histories of dominant cultures and societies have most often bolstered ruling ideologies, philosophies, or states that run roughshod over competing ideologies that do not carry commensurate abilities to exert coercion and/or force.

In a similar vein with Nora, Werner Sollors notes that the term "history" can infer motives of "aggressively willful exclusion." One example of this for Sollors is Hegel's arrogant assertion that America and Africa had not yet entered "the true theater of History."[18] Sollors suggests that memory may become a kind of counterhistory that "challenges the false generalizations in exclusionary, 'History.' "[19] Sollors' key point is that the polarization of history and memory is not necessary or inevitable. Indeed, for oppressed or subjugated peoples, memory may serve as a corrective to dominant sociocultural portrayals of history. However, it is when they are polarized and then drawn along the color lines of Black and White, Sollors observes, that history usually becomes the terrain of Whites. It is objective, rational, and true. Memory is the terrain of Blacks. It is subjective, emotional, and suspect.

Perhaps the wisest words come from Carolyn Walker Bynum. In her introduction to her collection of essays, *Fragmentation and Redemption: Essays in Gender and the Human Body in Medieval Religion*, Bynum writes,

> . . . historians can never present more than a part of the story of history and that these parts are true fragments, not microcosms of the whole; but such a conception of the historian's task does not, after all, preclude making each fragment as comprehensible and self-contained as possible . . . the writing of history must come to terms gracefully with the incomplete, . . . I suggest that the pleasure we find in research and in storytelling about the past is enhanced both by awareness that our own voices are provisional and by confidence in the revisions the future will bring.[20]

For Bynum, the task of the historian forestalls wholeness. Instead, she asserts the comic mode, noting that it is "not necessarily the pleasant, or at least it the pleasant snatched from the horrible by artifice and with acute self-consciousness and humility."[21]

A comic stance knows there is, in actuality, no ending (happy or otherwise)—that doing history is, for the historian, telling a story that could be told in another way. For this reason, a comic stance welcomes voices hitherto fore left outside, not to absorb or mute them but allow them to object and contradict. Its goal is the pluralist, not the total. It embraces the partial as partial. And, in such historical writing as in the best comedy, the author is also a character. Authorial presence and authorial asides are therefore welcome; methodological musing—even polemic—is a part of, not substitute for, doing history.[22]

These extended quotations point to two key aspects of my project: first, is to recognize the subjective nature of history and memory. In doing so, these traditional categories can be expanded to consider how they can be both preserved and broadened to represent the diversities that shape us. An increased awareness, appreciation, and respect for these diversities, I believe, can guide us down theoethical pathways that can eradicate systematic, structural evil by providing us with even more articulate resources and strategies to tackle such a large task—we need no longer depend on ourselves alone, but lean into a richer and more diverse web of creation. Second, to understand structural evil is to recognize, from the outset, that the story *can* be told in another way. It can be told in such a way that the voices and lives of those who, traditionally and historically, have been left out are now heard with clarity and precision. Even more, these voices can then be included into the discourse—not as additive or appendage, but as resource and codeterminer of actions and strategies. Yet this is not a crass teleological world. Rather, it acknowledges the intimate humanity of our plurality and works with as much precision as possible to name this plurality in its vicissitudes.

In reality, both history and memory can be ideologically constructed. Maurice Halbwachs' understanding of collective memory as being socially constructed is apt.[23] Collective memory endures and draws strength from individuals as group members who are drawing on the cultural and sociopolitical contexts of the group to remember. Collective memory is held together by the confidence found in association and is a constructive and reconstructive process through such cultural forms as music, dance, fiction, poetry, historical scholarship, and theoethical musings. Therefore, rather than *a* collective memory sitting as monolith, there are as many collective memories as there are groups and institutions in a society. For Halbwachs no memory is possible outside the social frameworks used by people living in society.[24]

Like Nora, Halbwachs believes that this art of memory points to the fact that throughout history we preserve memories that help give us a sense of identity. Halbwachs notes the complex nature of memory in that he sees collective memory as repetitions that, even at the moment of reproducing the past, involve our imagination that is influenced by the present social milieu—construction and reconstruction in dynamic interaction.[25] In noting the constraints that modern societies impose on people, Halbwachs argues, somewhat pessimistically, that "memory gives us the illusion of living in the midst of groups that do not imprison us, that impose themselves on us only so far and so long as we accept them."[26] For him, the mind reconstructs its memories under the pressures of society. Further, memories are coded in language that is ultimately a social fact and not an individual or group's choice. In short for Halbwachs, we create and recreate narratives in response to ever-changing political and social circumstances.

What Halbwachs helps bring to the fore is the fact that we are located in history and its ever-changing social frameworks and relationships. For him, we occupy definite positions in society and we are subject to their constructs. This puts us within sets of relational dynamics that involve human will and our ability or inability to impose that will on others. This multiplex character of agency shifts within history; and as we engage in the process of collective memory, we are in dynamic tension between the past, the present, and the future.

Drawing on Bynum, Halbwachs, and Nora, it seems that it is a truly silly exercise to engage in debates over that which is better or more accurate or more scholarly—history or memory. In terms of this book, both sit as potential tools and resources to aid us in understanding and dismantling structural evil. By looking at the particular lives of Black folk, or more specifically, particular manifestations of Black lives in the United States through the stereotyping of Black femaleness, I suggest that there is a window into understanding the dynamic of systematic, structural evil in our societies.

From the various perspectives that shape the moral landscapes of Black life, the polarization of memory and history is neither necessary nor inevitable. Memory may serve as a corrective to dominant sociocultural and theological portrayals of history. Memory can help Black folk deal with the reality of America, as Charles Long says, that is "impenetrable, definite, subtle, and *other*—a reality so agonizing that is forces us to give up our innocence while at the same time it sustained us in humor, joy, and promise." For Long, it reveals instead a " 'nitty-gritty' pragmatism" that enables us to understand a history—both real and imagined—that touts an America forged *solely* on hard work and moral fortitude.[27] Rather than debate over which concept or method is better, I work from the stance that memory and history are natural dance partners. They sweep and dip across the American (U.S.) imagination in a centuries-long Quickstep.[28]

"We Are Human Beings Worthy of God's Grace"

When cast in an ethical framework with the multilegacies (microhistories) that form the United States, Nora's sites of memory vibrate memory *and* history. This pushes ethical thought to consider the very construction of history and memory in shaping and maintaining structural forms of evil. I take this tact because I believe that the bulk of theoethical analysis and critique of structural evil tends to focus on the rational mechanisms that hold forms of oppression and misery in place. I contend that this can only take us so far as structural evil is also maintained by more heuristic forces that emerge from the imagination as emotion, intuition, and yearning. What can emerge from this possibility is recognizing that when memory and imagination impersonate history they are fruits of the fantastic hegemonic imagination. This blending of Michel Foucault's use of fantasy and imagination and Antonio Gramsci's understanding of hegemony[29] pushes the boundaries of Foucault's perception of the return of the medieval sense of the imagination. Foucault argues "for centuries Western literature sought to ground itself on the natural, the plausible, on sincerity, on science as well—in short on 'true' discourse."[30] This meant that the imagination was subordinated to the accepted moral landscape and its rules and sociopolitical and cultural realities. The imagination had to express and refer to those rules and realities because it was acceptable only if tied to a particular scientific, political, or sociological rationality.

In challenging this sense of the imaginary, Foucault incorporates the fantastic. In his essay "Fantasia of the Library," he argues that the "domain of phantasms" is no longer found solely in dreams or "the sleep of reason, or the uncertain voice that stands before desire." The fantastic "arises from the black and white surface of printed signs, from the closed dusty volume that opens with a flight of forgotten words; fantasies are carefully deployed in the hushed library."[31] Dreams are summoned in reading and a true image is the product of learning—amassing facts. The imaginary is not formed in opposition to reality, but grows in the intervals between books. Foucault's sense of the fantastic is that of other worlds, nonmaterial existences.

> The imaginary now resides between the book and the lamp. The fantastic is no longer a property of the heart, nor is it found among the incongruities of nature; it evolves from the accuracy of knowledge, and its treasures lie dormant in documents. Dreams are no longer summoned with closed eyes, but in reading; and a true image is now a product of learning: it derives from words spoken in the past, exact recensions, the amassing of minute facts, monuments reduced to infinitesimal fragments, and the reproductions of reproductions . . .[32]

I want to push the boundaries of Foucault's perception of the imaginary as that which is found in books. In building from this aspect of Foucault's thought, I argue that the fantastic is not limited to the worlds of literature but goes beyond to form a part of the cultural production of our realities—it is in the very fabric of the everyday. The fantastic lives in those moments of uncertainty when it is not clear if what we perceive or experience is an illusion of the senses (which makes it a product of the imagination and the laws of the world remain intact) and when we detect that the event has actually taken place but laws unknown to us control reality.[33] The fantastic is the hesitation experienced by a person who knows only the laws of nature confronting an apparently supernatural event—it is defined in relation to the real and the imaginary.

Yet the fantastic is even more. It is also being comfortable with the supernatural or what may seem supernatural to others. In other words, the fantastic may be the everyday for those who *live in it*. They may not find the presence of ghosts or shifted realities unusual. Therefore, they need no explanation. Only those of us who sit outside these worlds must ponder what they "see," "feel," "know" because *our* realities are challenged in the face of the fantastic as it emerges from other, sometimes more sinister, sources.

However, it is not only ghosts and shifted realities that comprise the fantastic. It may also be structures of domination and subordination. This is not to suggest or advocate a subtle or not so subtle determinism. It is, however, to suggest that the cultural production of evil can and does entrap many if not most of us. We often operate out of structurally determined limits that do, at points, offer some creativity and autonomy—but these are controlled and managed by hegemonic forces. Selected individuals may prosper in conditions of domination, so would selected groups. However, this is a limited prosperity that never threatens the framework and structure of society. It only creates an austere marginal space that can lull many of us into a false but oh-so-deadly consciousness that contours our imaginations.

I also nuance Gramsci's basic understanding of hegemony as ideological domination that is moral, political, and cultural and is transmitted by language. In breaking with economistic versions of Marxism that emphasize economic factors as the major cause of change, Gramsci argues that dominant groups secure the consent of subordinate groups to their rule by persuasion and coercion—and force, if necessary. In "Notes on Italian History," Gramsci writes

> . . . that the supremacy of a social group manifests itself in two ways, as "domination" and as "intellectual and moral leadership." A social group dominates antagonistic groups, which it tends to "liquidate," or to subjugate perhaps even by armed force; it leads kindred and allied groups. A social group can, and indeed must, already exercise "leadership" before winning governmental power . . . it subsequently becomes dominant when it exercises power, but even if it holds it firmly in its grasp, it must continue to "lead" as well.[34]

Essentially, hegemony is the set of ideas that dominant groups employ in a society to secure the consent of subordinates to abide by their rule. The notion of consent is key, because hegemony is created through coercion that is gained by using the church, family, media, political parties, schools, unions, and other voluntary associations— the civil society and all its organizations. This breeds a kind of false consciousness (the fantastic in neocultural and sociopolitical drag) that creates societal values and moralities such that there is *one* coherent and accurate viewpoint on the world. It is important to stress that hegemonies exist throughout history and within our society. For example, Christianity, Islam, Judaism, conservatism, liberalism, and so forth can be seen as hegemonic in particular societies. Those who practice hegemony are not always "they," it is often "we."

Gramsci is clear that revolutionaries who want to break hegemony must build up counterhegemony. For Gramsci, hegemony does not mean there is only one universally valid position for all time. Rather, other worldviews—in any given stage of historical development—can provide the major way of interpreting and perceiving the world. This opening provides the intellectual and sociopolitical space from which Gramsci argues that changing the popular consensus and the ways in which institutions work is possible. It creates a space that allows questioning the right of leaders to rule in their current way. The success of counterhegemony, for Gramsci, is that it permeates society with a new system of values, beliefs, and morality.

My blending of Foucault and Gramsci is meant to direct our energies to advocate an interstructured consideration of class, gender, and race in this process of domination by using the strategy of countermemory. Building on the notion of counterhegemony, countermemory seeks to open up not only the subversive spaces of counterhegemony, it argues also for a reconstitution of history such that we begin to see, hear, and appreciate the diversities in our midst as flesh and blood rather than as cloying distractions within the fantastic hegemonic imagination. As I shall argue, it is the resource and strategy that enacts Gramsci's understanding of counterhegemony.

The fantastic hegemonic imagination traffics in peoples' lives that are caricatured or pillaged so that the imagination that creates the fantastic can control the world in its own image. This imagination conjures up worlds and their social structures that are not based on supernatural events and phantasms, but on the ordinariness of evil. It is this imagination, I argue, that helps to hold systematic, structural evil in place. The fantastic hegemonic imagination uses a politicized sense of history and memory to create and shape *its* worldview. It sets in motion whirlwinds of images used in the cultural production of evil. These images have an enormous impact on how we understand the world, as well as others and ourselves in that world. Subjugation and consent sashay to deadly images that are largely unchecked until they lose their force and are replaced by more deadly and sinister images such as the movement from the Black Matriarch to the Welfare Queen.[35] It is most important to note at this point that the fantastic hegemonic imagination is in all of us. It is found in the privileged and the oppressed. It is no respecter of race, ethnicity, nationality, or color. It is not bound by gender or sexual orientation. It can be found in the old and the young. None of us naturally escape it, for it is found in the deep cultural codings we live with and through in U.S. society.

For marginalized groups such as Black folk in the United States, part of challenge is to enact memory and history in culture without crumbling under the hegemonic demand that all these groups must display a heavily romanticized and impossible "genuineness" in a society founded on miscegenation, assimilation, and a discrete autonomous self that is independent and self-directing. In other words, the challenge is to resist measuring Black realities by the ideological stereotypes, the denigrating myths, of the fantastic hegemonic imagination. As literary theorist Susan Willis notes that a "mass-media-generated postmodern culture, whose fascination with diversity requires that the entirety of the world's 'ethnic' populations represent themselves in authentic 'native' music and costumes . . . [is the] only culture not required to be authentic, to replicate its past in its present, is the invisible, never stated, but all-powerful central void of the dominant culture."[36]

Willis illustrates a feature of collective memory and the reconstruction of the past that Halbwachs describes. For Halbwachs, people form affectional ties with each other as we also compete with each other. For some, the painful (read oppressive) aspects of human history in relationship are "forgotten." However, this is not the kind of strategic forgotteness Morrison speaks of regarding slave narratives. It is a studied, malicious amnesia that is calculating and precise in obscuring the decimation of large parts of humanity and nature and the unctuous images that are its lethal tools. The power of the fantastic hegemonic imagination is also very much alive in Halbwachs' understanding of collective memory. More to the point, Halbwachs argues that "society obligates people not just to reproduce in thought previous events of their lives, but also to touch them up, shorten them, or to complete them so that we give them a prestige that reality did not possess . . . this is done despite however convinced we are that our memories are exact."[37]

From the Image to the Text

This act of controlling and manipulating human lives through processes of domination and subordination are not, as Gramsci points out, inevitable or unanswerable. The fantastic can also open up subversive spaces within the status quo rather than ghettoizing fantasy by encasing it within currish linear or deterministic thought or strategies. The fantastic can retain its subversive qualities without capitulating to narrow categorization or classification designed to tame or make the fantastic sensible. One such subversive place/space is countermemory.

George Lipsitz notes (and womanist ethical reflection also advocates) that countermemory is that which seeks to disrupt ignorance and invisibility. It is a way of "remembering and forgetting that starts with the local, the immediate, and the personal."[38] Countermemory begins with the particular to move into the universal and it looks to the past for microhistories to force a reconsideration of flawed (incomplete or vastly circumscribed) histories. This focus on localized experiences of oppression in countermemory allows us to refocus dominant narratives touting narrow lenses into a reframing of what constitutes the universal.

In essence, countermemory is another way to talk about particularity in womanist moral discourse. Particularity *begins* with a narrowed focus on the lives of Black folk, particularly Black women, to pry open teleological ruminations that often demand closure while seeking to discipline life's uncertainties to conform to a future structured by the fantastic hegemonic imagination. Womanist thought begins with this radical particularity that quickly finds that the story of Black women's moral lives cannot be told in a vacuum. It is a story that can only be understood in relation to other stories—this is the universal or the first dawning of it.

Countermemory can open up subversive spaces within dominant discourses that expand our sense of who we are and, possibly, create a more whole and just society in defiance of structural evil. The universal, then, is created in the creolization of discourses, not in the austere terrain of monochromatic abstract conceptualizations spuming from the fantastic hegemonic imagination.

Lipsitz differs from Foucault who believed that countermemory "must record the singularity of events outside of any monotonous finality; it must seek them in the most unpromising places, in what we tend to feel is without history—in sentiments, love, conscience, instincts; it must be sensitive to their recurrence, not in order to trace the gradual curve of their evolution, but to isolate the different scenes where they engaged in different roles."[39] Further for Foucault, countermemory "will cultivate the details and accidents that accompany every beginning; it will be scrupulously attentive to their petty malice; it will await their emergence, once unmasked, as the face of the other."[40] Finally, Foucault believed that countermemory must describe "the endlessly repeated play of dominations."[41] Foucault's relentlessly unnostalgic view of history is an important critique of the hierarchization of history and memory. He maintains a deep skepticism of totalizing narratives and cautions against historical writing that uses language as a tool for its celebration of past and present oppressions as necessary and inevitable.

Lipsitz, on the other hand, argues that any single story must be understood in relation to other stories. He is aware that it may be impossible to create a truly total story that is inclusive of the plurality of experiences on our planet, but he believes that the pursuit of such totality is essential. Lipsitz argues that unless we recognize the collective legacy of human actions and ideas, we will be unable to judge the claims to truth and justice found in any one story.[42]

For Lipsitz, countermemory practices a delicate negotiation between local, immediate, and personal experiences and global, indirect, and social realities.[43] Learning, appreciating, and respecting the microhistories of any society demands, for Lipsitz, a "complex negotiation between the legacy of historical events that affect everyone and the partial and limited accounts of those events that make up the historical record as authored by dominant groups."[44]

Ultimately, countermemory is not a rejection of history, but a reconstitution of it. Barbara Christian captures this dynamic:

> It is the resonance of history that lets us know we are here. Memory not only reproduces the past, it gives us guides by which to evaluate the present, and helps to create the future, which is an illusionary concept unless we know that yesterday we saw the present as future. It is not surprising then that contemporary Afro-American women writers have spent so much energy on reclaiming their history, so disrupted and ignored by both black and white scholarship.[45]

Lipsitz believes that "playing" memory against history is a new synthesis that can offer dignity to all peoples without forcing them into "an imaginary identity constructed from a top-down perspective on human experience."[46] However, for countermemory to succeed as a strategy, it must resonate with the experiences and feelings of those whose microhistories it purports to represent and be an advocate of. It must address the collective memory—however partial and incomplete and socially constructed—of those who have experienced real historical oppressions and memories.

Combining Foucault's lack of nostalgia and Lipsitz's optimism, I suggest that memory *can* be used to create a space or site in historical discourse that has often negated microhistories. It is grim business if the totality of Black folk is collapsed into the stereotypes and myths of Black life and history that often unfold in various forms of media. Indeed, when adding the impact of culture, it is questionable if mass culture offers Blacks or other disenfranchised groups a means of preserving their history and cultural practices over time.[47]

One possible response to such a deadly cultural dumbing down is in the work of W. E. B. Du Bois.[48] Du Bois provides an excellent example of Black countermemory as reconstructive strategy. He was clear that the U.S. historical community subordinated the Black experience to the point of making it virtually unknown. He saw this neglect and prejudice against Black folk as an aspect of a prevailing elitism in dominant history-writing in general.[49] After surveying the contemporary history textbooks of the late 1920s and early 1930s, Du Bois noted that American children were taught that all Negroes were ignorant, lazy, dishonest, extravagant, and responsible for bad government during Reconstruction.[50]

In a moving passage in his mammoth volume, *Black Reconstruction in America*, Du Bois pointedly says, "we have too often a deliberate attempt so to change the facts of history that the story will make pleasant reading for Americans."[51] Halbwachs echoes this observation years later in his observation that unpleasant memories are often forgotten to make palatable the meannesses of history, and the human will and action that comprise it. Du Bois continues,

> One is astonished in the study of history at the recurrence of the idea that evil must be forgotten, distorted, skimmed over. We must not remember that Daniel Webster got drunk and only remember that he was a splendid constitutional lawyer. We must forget that George Washington was a slave owner, or that Thomas Jefferson had mulatto children, or that Alexander Hamilton had Negro blood, and simply remember the things we regard as creditable and inspiring. The difficulty, of course, with this philosophy is that history loses its value as an incentive and example; it paints perfect men and noble nations, but it does not tell the truth.[52]

Du Bois inveighed against separating morality and science because doing so caricatured science. He believed that what is just is also true. While objectivity in the sense of utter neutrality is absurd, he did not believe this ruled out the possibility of describing reality.

> If history is going to be scientific, if the record of human action is going to be set down with accuracy and faithfulness of detail which will allow its use as a measuring rod and guidepost for the future of nations, there must be some standards of ethics in research and interpretation.
>
> If on the other hand, we are going to use history for our pleasure and amusement, for inflating our national ego, and giving us a false but pleasurable sense of accomplishment, then we must give up the idea of history either as a science or as an art using the results of science, and admit frankly that we are using a version of historic fact in order to influence and educate the new generation along the way we wish.[53]

For Du Bois, the historian must "make clear the facts with utter disregard to his own wish and desire and belief . . . we have got to know, so far as possible . . . . the things that actually happened in the world . . . with that much clear and open to every reader, the philosopher and prophet has a chance to interpret these facts; but the historian has no right, posing as scientist, to conceal or distort facts; . . . until we distinguish between these two functions of the chronicler of human action, we are going to render it easy for a muddled world out of sheer ignorance to make the same mistake ten times over."[54]

Our contemporary debates on multiculturalism in education are evidence of this.[55] It is quite odd to hear and read that seeking to educate students about the plurality of the republic is seen as inferior education. The integration of microhistories and *their* ideologies into dominant ideology and history does, to be sure, *challenge* the position of supremacy of a narrow educational sandbox, but it does not make it inferior. To the contrary, it opens up intellectual explorations that can illuminate and better prepare us for the global world in which we are intricately enmeshed.

Du Bois had a profound sense of the right, the just, and held a basic faith in reason and a passionate commitment to achieving the just through the force of reason—this is what Du Bois meant by his use of the word science. His exercise of countermemory in *Black Reconstruction* does not attempt to wipe clean the deeds of the Confederacy, to promote a higher moral ground for the North, or to suggest that Black folks were angels. Rather, Du Bois states,

> I want to be fair, objective, judicial; to make no searing of the memory by intolerable insult and cruelty make me fail to sympathize with human frailties and contradictions, in the eternal paradox of good and evil. But armed and warned by all this, and fortified by long study of the facts, I stand at the end of this writing literally aghast at what American historians have done to this field. . . . No, it is simple to establish the Truth, on which Right in the future may be built. We shall never have a science of history until we have in our colleges men who regard the truth as more important than the defense of the white race, and who will not deliberately encourage students to gather thesis material in order to support a prejudice or buttress a lie.[56]

The theme of forgotteness returns once again in Du Bois. I suggest that this ability of the fantastic hegemonic imagination to forget is both a serious medical condition and an astute strategy of domination.

It is not healthy—not even for the dominant elite—to fail to remember the textures of our common humanity. To ignore, as it were, the vast and varied terrains that comprise not only the strands of our histories but also the concrete materialities of our existence throttles our humanity in creation. It is strategic in that to "forget" is to be able to feign ignorance and lack of agency. It enables the production of pro-duce images that express what we thought was the case rather than to take the time and effort to show genuine respect and come to know each other in significant and more authentic ways. Forgotteness ulti-mately destroys.

As tool and strategy, countermemory challenges images that deni-grate and asphyxiate. Both are slow, methodical processes that sap the sense of life and well-being out of us. The imagination that produces these images is linked to memory and history. It is the product of a withering fantastic that does not invite very many of us to "participate in the discourse even when we [are] its topic."[57] However, as Morrison notes, there are other images linked to memory and history as well—those that spring from an imagination seeking to distinguish fact from truth. This distinction, made by Morrison, recognizes that "fact can exist without human intelligence, but truth cannot."[58] As illusive as truth may be (much like quests for the authentic, the real, the natural), countermemory insists that to deconstruct and eradicate systems of evil demands that we engage in exposing the truth of the multiplicities that form us—nationally and globally—with as much precision as we can. This, I believe, follows both Hebrew Bible and New Testament images of pilgrims whose goal is not nearly as important as the journey.

In the final analysis, my use of countermemory throughout this book does not view memory and history as suspect. Rather, they too are natural dance partners—moving from Quickstep to Jitterbug.[59] The images of Aunt Jemima, Sapphire, the Welfare Queen, the Tragic Mulatta, and Topsy are countermemory. They unsettle and disrupt notions of identity as property, uninterrogated coloredness, repara-tions and empire, religious values in public policymaking, and solidar-ity. They challenge the images of the fantastic imagination that celebrate noxious stereotypes of Black women, children, and men. They also provide an alternative and more creative or "real" space to better understand who we are in our diversity. Rather than assume that such knowledge will destroy our ways of living, it offers the pos-sibility that they will, in fact, enhance our lives—all our lives. It is to *begin* the work of dismantl*ing* evil.

3

Vanishing into Limbo: The Moral Dilemma of Identity as Property and Commodity

Part 1: Mammy: Conflation of Memory, Myth, and History

. . . what it means to be a Negro in America can perhaps be suggested by an examination of the myths we perpetuate about him.

Aunt Jemima and Uncle Tom are dead, their places taken by a group of amazingly well-adjusted young men and women, almost as dark, but ferociously literate, well-dressed and scrubbed, who are never laughed at, who are not likely ever to set foot in a cotton or tobacco field or in any but the most modern of kitchens. There are others who remain, in our odd idiom, "underprivileged"; some are bitter and these come to grief; some are unhappy, but, continually presented with the evidence of a better day soon to come, are speedily becoming less so. Most of them care nothing whatever about race. They want only their proper place in the sun and the right to be left alone, like any other citizen of the republic. We may all breathe more easily. Before, however, our joy at the demise of Aunt Jemima and Uncle Tom approaches the indecent, we had better ask whence they sprang, how they lived? Into what limbo have they vanished?[1]

—James Baldwin, "Many Thousands Gone"

In this 1955 essay, Baldwin explores Richard Wright's novel *Native Son* to illuminate what it means to be a Negro in America. For Baldwin, this is visceral. He is tired of Black folk being treated as mere social agendas rather than as flesh and blood. He notes that dehumanization is never a one-way street, that the loss of identity—be it stolen, borrowed, denied, or annihilated—has consequences far beyond those who are the immediate victims. For Baldwin, our crimes against ourselves echo and haunt and damn and eviscerate us. It is not enough (not in 1955 when the essay was published, not today) to think that we can leave our memories checked at some dismal door of gerrymandered elections or xenophobic nationalism or sycophantic equalities. Indeed for Baldwin, the story of Black folk is the story of Americans, one that is not, in his words, "a very pretty story."[2] This is a story of shadows, or a series of shadows that are for Baldwin "self-created, intertwining." And, sadly, Black folk do not exist except in "the darkness of our minds."

What strikes me in bold fashion are the ways in which Baldwin's 1955 essay sounds much like contemporary progressive social observations on Black lives. For, as Baldwin goes on to note, so much of Black history and our interrelationships with the rest of U.S. life have been made a social project—not the story of flesh and blood and spirit and emotion. It is, for Baldwin and for us, a matter of looking at Blacks as a set of "statistics, slums, rapes, injustices, remote violence; it is to be confronted with an endless cataloguing of losses, gains, skirmishes; it is to feel virtuous, outraged, helpless, as though [our] continuing status among us were somehow analogous to disease—cancer, perhaps, or tuberculosis—which must be checked, even though it cannot be cured."[3]

This harsh assessment is one I bring into a twenty-first century conversation on evil and its peculiar impact on identity. It also illuminates an irksome problem of our time. This problem has not materialized out of the mists, but it is one that has tracked human history with deadly precision—treating our identity as property and commodity. When placed within the larger context of the cultural production of evil, it takes on different textures, shapes, tones, and tastes. To accentuate this claim, I turn to a familiar cultural and marketing icon— Aunt Jemima. She is a ubiquitous figure in U.S. life. As such, her story prompts us to consider Baldwin's trenchant observation that Blacks are "a social and not a personal or a human problem." I argue, that Blacks are not the only ones damned by treating identity as property. To be sure, there are winners and losers in this deadly commodification. However, the ways in which we have produced this weary state of affairs have been a group project in American life. We have used memory and myth and history to deceive ourselves—all of us.

However, the smell of blood and dirt and catastrophe are ripe within our nostrils if we recall; if we allow memory and the power of memory to weave other stories of the American Dream—not different, not separate, not oppositional, not subversive—simply other stories. Not "the Other" as a social problem or an object of too many Derridas, Foucaults, or Spivaks;[4] but the folks who are really just round the corner—but we act as if we do not know them because this is what we have been trained to do as "natural." Frankly, this use of "the Other" is neither liberatory nor transformative. In postmodern America, discourse on "the Other" often becomes an excuse to remain ignorant and arrogant about our illiteracy of other peoples—their thoughts, their religions, their politics, their values, their social structures, their moral landscapes—their isness/ontology—both mundane and radical.

We practice this highly suspect brand of progressivism as import and export. What remains "natural" is hegemony that is now prettified with neat word games and mental masturbations. All that we really achieve with many postmodern categories is the production of constructs such as "center" and "periphery" that reveal our vexing fixation on making a complex world simplistic and on the messiness of diversity neat and pristine when it is really a mash pit of realities. Hence, we remain the same people who want to do justice but demand safety; who want to be prophetic but fret over status and position; who search for truth but grasp at nettling shadows.

Aunt Jemima has her origins in the Mammy image of U.S. history and culture. From slavery through the Jim Crow era (1877–1966), the Mammy image served the economic, political, and social interests of White ideology and history in the United States. Her caricature was used to prove that Black women (and by extension children and men) were happy with their enslavement. In fact, Mammy became a central figure in the plantation legends of the Old South.[5]

Along with her evil twin Jezebel, the Mammy image was and remains an extremely contested site of memory and history.[6] The image is, in short, a prime example of the history of dominant culture resorting to denigrating myths to maintain the status quo. The Mammy is a myth that has taken on reality and then moved on to become a stereotype. Her construction is a response to abolitionist claims that slave owners sexually exploited their female slaves, especially the light-skinned ones. Mammy is constructed as an ugly antidote to such charges. After all, who would abuse a desexualized, fat, old Black woman when the only other morally viable alternative was the idealized White woman? Mammy was not sexual or sensual—she was and is completely deeroticized and safe. However, this safety did not extend to White women of the plantation South or Black women, children, and men. The Mammy provided safety for an idealized patriarchal White family structure—she provided safety for White men.

The Mammy image is a fantastic facade for the sexual exploitation of Black women by White men during the antebellum period. She is "confirmation" that White men did not find Black women sexually attractive or desirable. The image confuses and distracts from the living proof of miscegenation. She is the "super mothering" figure who conveys, as Cheryl Thurber notes, an ambiguous message of Black and White ideals of motherhood: To be the perfect Mammy meant the Black woman must neglect her own family.[7]

The Mammy of slavocracy did not want freedom. She was too busy serving as surrogate mother and grandmother to "her" White families. The prototypical fictional Mammy: asexual, fat, self-sacrificing, excellent cook, excellent housekeeper, self-sacrificing, and above all loyal to her family. In fact, the Mammy was so loyal that she neglected her own family; so much so that when asked to choose between her White family and her own, she opted to be a part of the "better" White family. Regrettably, the antebellum Mammy was glorified in such a way as to praise some Blacks while criticizing other Blacks who did not fit into her subservient and contented ideal. Mammy represented a version of the Black world to "her" White folks—if they knew her, they knew and understood all Blacks.

If we relied on the popular "historical" accounts, we are often led to believe that Mammies existed in legion. However, Catherine Clinton's exhaustive study, *The Plantation Mistress: Woman's World in the Old South*, shows that only a handful of women actually fit the Mammy image.

> The Mammy was created by white Southerners to redeem the relationship between black women and white men within slave society in response to the antislavery attack from the North during the antebellum era, and to embellish it with nostalgia in the post-bellum period. In the primary records from before the Civil War, hard evidence for her existence simply does not appear.[8]

Herbert Gutman's research also reveals that the prevalence of Mammies was completely distorted.[9] He found that there were few older Black women who served the role of Mammies as late as the 1880s when southern memoirs begin to tout her presence and importance. Gutman shows that most domestic workers in White households were young, single girls who did not fit the stereotypical image of a mature Black woman who loved *her* White children more than her own children. In reality, the conditions of slavery rarely allowed for such a large old woman to be in a position to care for the masters' and mistress' children.

> Like the field hands, those black bondswomen who worked indoors were unlikely to be overweight because their food stuffs were severely rationed. They were more likely to be light as dark because household jobs were frequently assigned to mixed-race women. They were unlikely to be old because nineteenth-century black women just did not live very long; fewer than 10 percent of black women lived beyond their fiftieth birthday.[10]

One of the best repositories of the history of the plantation South is the Federal Writers' Project of Works Progress Administration interviews with former slaves. These interviews give little indication of the widespread existence of Mammies. Very few former slaves mentioned older relatives who had the traditional Mammy role in the antebellum era and few said that the role itself afforded any protection or concern from White folks. These interviews do reveal that many former slaves were devoted to the White children they were raised with, but there is little mention of Mammies' devotion to White children. Those who did assist in the care of White children were either children or teenagers—not those with the elderly Mammy image. In addition, many women mentioned working as cooks or maids as adults, but few said that they or their female relatives had been Mammies. Thurber posits that Mammies did exist in the antebellum era, but in much smaller numbers that the mythology indicates.[11]

Du Bois, Foucault, and Nora are instructive at this point. Historical reality may not exist in the Mammy image, but myth does. Indeed the dangers of memory are ripe. However, this is a contested site with memory functioning as myth *and* historical process. The reality is that although the historical Mammy is suspect, the imagined and the mythological that springs from the fantastic hegemonic imagination— the re-membered one—is alive and well. It served the needs of nostalgic White southerners seeking to make sense of and defend slavery and segregation. Interestingly, most of the references to the Mammy in the *Confederate Veteran* magazine appeared in pieces written by women.[12] Instances of these references rose (and reached its peak) from 1906 to 1912 and began to decline in 1918, with little mention of Mammy by the late 1920s. In fact, most of the antebellum evidence for Mammies from Whites does not come from actual evidence but from fictional sources and romanticized memoirs. In later years, the glorification of Mammy happened in the abstract rather than in the more concrete forms of appealing to real people.

The New South movement often used Old South mythology of a utopian harmonious community to promote its cause. This, coupled with increased northern racial tensions fueled by the Black migration from the South, made the Old South mythology attractive because it suggested that the South had solved its racial problems. However, the Mammy was not an uncontested image among Whites. The 1918 *Confederate Veteran* magazine article by Mrs. W. L. Hammond displays both acceptance and rejection of the myth:

> One of the first steps necessary is to bury the old black mammy . . . . Her removal will clear the atmosphere and enable us to see the old soul's granddaughters, to whom we must in just pay something of the debt we so freely acknowledge to her.[13]

The comments of the Honorable Bridges Smith also rejected the myth. Smith's rebuttal in the *Macon Telegraph* was a response to an article in the New York edition of *Sun* that glorified the Mammy.

> Bless your ignorant souls, honey, the old black mammy has been dead and buried these many moons. And if flowers were laid upon her grave and tears were dropped on the mound, it was right and proper. She deserved every flower and was due every tear. We shall never look upon her like again . . . She is dead and long since buried, and she should rest in peace. . . . It was only the imitation, the caricatures, of the devoted, the loyal, the ever-faithful old black mammy that the present generation knows. And this is why the *sun*, in its ignorance of the original, says she is trotted out on so many occasions that she has become a racial type, a political institution, and a good deal of a bore. That the imitation should be got out of the way, the sooner the better, may be all well and good; but as for the old black mammy as we knew and loved her, she is dead beyond resurrection.[14]

During the latter part of the 1800s, many White middle-class households in the United States began to expect to have domestic service. By the early 1900s, in the South, the supply of Black labor was so plentiful that even some White working-class households expected to employ Black women. The heightened glorification of Mammy from 1906 onward corresponded to the changes in the role of women and in race relations. It is questionable that the rise of the Mammy and the ideal of the Southern Belle appearing simultaneously was a mere coincidence. The Southern Belle was traditional, sweet, innocent, beautiful, and White—she emerged with great enthusiasm during the drive for women's suffrage. Mammy was a perfect counterpoint because she implied that Black women were fit to be *only* domestic workers. This rationalized all economic discrimination based on race and gender. During the Jim Crow era, the U.S. race-based and race-segregated job economy limited most Blacks to menial jobs and meager wages. Black women were forced into one job category—the maid. Jo Ann Robinson points out that

> Jobs for clerks in dimestores, cashiers in markets, and telephone opera-tors were numerous, but were not open to black women. A fifty-dollar-a-week worker could employ a black domestic to clean her home, cook the food, wash and iron clothes, and nurse the baby for as little as twenty dollars per week.[15]

During the Jim Crow era, middle-class White women could hire Black domestic workers but these women were *not* Mammies. Mammy was "black, fat with huge breasts, and head covered a ker-chief to hide her nappy hair, strong, kind, loyal, sexless, religious and superstitious."[16] Mammy spoke in bastardized English, did not care about her appearance and was politically and culturally "safe." She was and is largely a nostalgic figment of the White imagination that yearns for a past that never was. She is a mythical construction of the dominant culture that often claims her as historical fact. Real domes-tics of the Jim Crow era were poor Black women who were denied a wide range of economic choices. They performed many duties of the mythological Mammy but they departed company from her when it came to loyalty to their families and resentfulness at their enforced economic status.

As Blacks demanded economic, racial, political, and social equality during the first half of the twentieth century, the Mammy became an increasingly popular entertainment industry figure.[17] The first talking movie, *The Jazz Singer* (1927), featured Al Jolson in Blackface singing "Mammy." In 1934, *Imitation of Life* told the story of a Black maid, Aunt Delilah (played by Louise Beavers), who inherited a pancake recipe. Aunt Delilah gives the recipe to Miss. Bea, her boss, who successfully markets the recipe and offers Aunt Delilah a 20 percent interest in the pancake company.[18]

Beginning in 1910, various suggestions arose for memorials to the Mammy. This ended with the 1923 United Daughters of the

Confederacy proposal to erect a monument to her memory in Washington, DC. This Mammy Memorial movement began in earnest in 1911 when a White newspaper, *Banner* (Athens, Georgia), reported a Southern movement to establish monuments and memorials to the "old Black Mammies of the South."[19] The 1923 proposal from the United Daughters of the Confederacy was met with vigorous Black protests. Some suggested that a "better memorial would be to extend the full rights of American citizenship to the descendants of these Mammies."[20]

It is clear that the physical image of Mammy is heavily influenced by popular culture. The rise of the Civil Rights and feminist movements helped clarify the racist and stereotypical image of the mythological Mammy. Mammy is best understood as the product of plantation legends featuring a bucolic, idyllic society with Mammy waiting upon White children—a representation that among the memories of White childhood never existed as prevalently as legend holds. Despite the facts, the belief that White owners loved their Mammies became ingrained in U.S. culture. Although the Aunt Jemima description does not fit neatly into the early image of the Mammy, today the two characters of Aunt Jemima and Mammy have merged.

Part 2: "I'se in Town, Honey": Marketing Aunt Jemima

We have all seen Aunt Jemima. She began in St. Joseph, Missouri, when Chris L. Rutt (a newspaper reporter) and Charles G. Underwood (a mill owner) bought the Pearl Milling Company in 1888. They began producing the first commercial pancake mix under the generic label "Self-Rising Pancake Flour" that they perfected in 1889. While they were searching for a symbol for their new product, Rutt visited a local vaudeville house and saw a performance by the blackface minstrel team of Baker and Ferrell. The high point of the show was a cakewalk performed to the tune "Old Aunt Jemima." This version was copyrighted in either 1875 or 1876 by the White minstrel James Grace:[21]

> Went to de church de other night,
> Old Aunt Jemima, oh! oh! oh!
> To hear de colored folks sing and pray,
> Old Aunt Jemima, oh! oh! oh!

Old Pomp got tight and Dinah walk along,
Old Aunt Jemima, oh! oh! oh!
And made old Gumbo sing a song,
Old Aunt Jemima, oh! oh! oh!
CHORUS
Car'line, Car'line, can't you dance de peavine,
Old Aunt Jemima, oh! oh! oh!

Dar was a bullfrog dressed in soldier clothes,
Old Aunt Jemima, oh! oh! oh!
He went out to drill dem crows,
Old Aunt Jemima, oh! oh! oh!
But de bullfrog he made such a mighty splutter,
Old Aunt Jemima, oh! oh! oh!
Dat I up wid my foot and kicked him in de water,
Old Aunt Jemima, oh! oh! oh!
(CHORUS)

I carried a hen coop on my knee,
Old Aunt Jemima, oh! oh! oh!
I thought I heard a chicken sneeze,
Old Aunt Jemima, oh! oh! oh!
'Twas nothing but a rooster saying his prayers,
Old Aunt Jemima, oh! oh! oh!
He gave out a hymn, such a getting up stairs,
Old Aunt Jemima, oh! oh! oh!
(CHORUS)[22]

Rutt decided to use the name and a likeness of the southern Mammy on the lithographed posters advertising the act that depicted either Baker or Ferrell dressed as a Mammy. Rutt and Underwood registered the trademark in 1890, but they were unable to raise the necessary capital for advertising. They sold the company to the R. T. Davis Mill and Manufacturing Company that year and Davis, a 50-year veteran of the milling business, designed the first and one of the most successful promotional campaigns ever launched in U.S. marketing history.

There was a world of symbols and history behind the Baker and Ferrell minstrel show. If they followed the pattern of the minstrel shows of their era, the final segment was a plantation skit that relied on slapstick, song, and dance. After the 1850s, these were farces that incorporated Shakespearean drama. The blending of history with memory, and now ridicule, was ironic. When slaves performed the cakewalk during harvest festivals, *they* were ridiculing their *masters'* mannerisms and competed for prizes, one of which was often a cake.[23] The cakewalk Rutt observed was the epitome of the minstrel show as it mocked Black culture (as far as the performers understood it) and it looked back longingly on the idyllic plantation South. Little did Rutt, or any of the other White audience, realize that the minstrel performers were, in fact, mocking themselves. This is precious irony.

Aunt Jemima began when a White man decided that he could be Black and a woman, and so he dressed in drag, put on blackface, and became a part of the minstrel tradition that helped to sing the White man's cares away. Blackface transvestism is, as J. J. Manring points out, almost as old as the minstrel tradition itself. These "women" usually demonstrated the "profane and murderous power of women" in the shows.[24] By the 1880s, the standard Mammy was a fat, cantankerous cook who slaved in southern plantation kitchens.

Davis began to search for a Black woman who epitomized southern hospitality and had the personality to make Aunt Jemima a household name. He chose Nancy Green, a former slave born in Montgomery County, Kentucky, in 1834.[25] Green was not a large woman and did not fit the Mammy stereotype. At the time she signed her contract with Davis, she was the cook and nurse for a White family in Chicago and was already well known for making delicious pancakes. Her contract gave her the right to impersonate Aunt Jemima for the rest of her life. It is important to note that Davis used a caricature of Green on the package until 1917. At that point, Green's caricature was redrawn as the well-known smiling, older, heavyset housekeeper with a bandanna wrapped around her head.[26]

Several other advertising campaigns connected the idyllic South of White elites with a product. In each of these campaigns, Whites were shown celebrating their culture while Black servants worked to make the festivities possible. The Mammy image in these campaigns was used to sell various household items beyond breakfast foods: detergents, planters, ashtrays, sewing accessories, and beverages. In fact, Aunt Jemima was not the first "aunt" in advertising. As early as 1875, Aunt Sally (a Mammy image) appeared on cans of baking powder. Later Mammy images appeared on Luzianne coffee and cleaners, Fun to Wash detergent, and Aunt Dinah molasses. By 1925, Mammy figures appeared on numerous kitchen-related items—Aunt Jemima had a great deal of company.

Aunt Jemima literally came to life from the pens of advertising copy editors and illustrators to "grace" the pages of ladies' magazines. This interstructuring of class, gender, and race with marketing and profit margins accentuates the ways in which history and memory function in U.S. culture and society. Part of Mammy's appeal is that she described an idealized, if not stylized, ante- and postbellum South. It is a bitter coincidence that the same year that Aunt Jemima appeared, Philip Alexander Bruce published his infamous *The Plantation Negro as Freeman*. This wicked compendium of swill linked what he saw as Black male savagery with the failure of Black mothers to instill the proper moral values in their children. He collapsed the nature of motherhood into race as he and others lifted up the specter of Jezebel as the true nature of Black womanhood.[27] Mammy was the perfect counterbalance to Jezebel—she demonstrated the benefits of maintaining the color line and how Black women behaved under proper White control.

With a caricature of Nancy Green on the package, the 1893 World's Columbian Exposition was the launching pad for the Aunt Jemima Pancake Mix. Green was the focus of the exhibit in which she served more than a million pancakes and helped bring in over 50,000 orders for the mix from across the world. Her logo, "I'se in town, honey," became a popular phrase during and after the exposition.[28]

Other real-life Aunt Jemimas toured county fairs and grocery stores and club bake offs to sell the pancake dough of a White advertising industry that understood that images sell. From 1951 to the early 1960s, there were several Aunt Jemimas working simultaneously to promote the pancake mix.[29] Speaking in dialect, the various Aunt Jemimas told "inoffensive" tales of slavery as they gave away samples at fairs, grocery stores, and other public gatherings. These Jemimas made her up—creating legends about her, or was it about them?

Just after the Columbian Exposition, Purd Wright, an advertising executive, wrote the earliest version of Aunt Jemima's "life story," *The Life of Aunt Jemima, the Most Famous Colored Woman in the World*.[30] In 1920, the Aunt Jemima Mills Company authorized another "biography" of Aunt Jemima entitled "When the Robert E. Lee Stopped by Aunt Jemima's Cabin."[31] In this pamphlet, a Confederate general returns to Aunt Jemima's cabin on the Higbee plantation in Louisiana twenty years after the Civil War to thank her for saving his life during the war by feeding him her famous flapjacks. Aunt Jemima is still living and the general repays her kindness with gold pieces and enjoys yet another delicious meal of her flapjacks. The general continues on his way, but a representative of a large Missouri flour mill, who was one of the general's traveling companions, returns to Aunt Jemima's cabin and convinces her to sell him the recipe. Aunt Jemima agrees to go to the mill to oversee the preparation of the ready mix form. Selections from these "biographies" were used in advertising copy. Marketing and property collide in the creation of naming not only a product, but providing (lying, making up) a life story.

Mythical Aunt Jemima revived hundreds of (White) southern soldiers with her pancakes. She had been a slave on colonel Higbee's plantation down on the Mississippi River. Her pancakes saved Colonel Higbee's life when Union soldiers were about to pluck out his mustache at the roots. Mythical Aunt Jemima was freed after the Civil War and she gave up her flapjack recipe to a northern milling representative. This had to be myth to think that a Black woman who knows how to cook would give up *all* of her recipe to anyone. What more proof do we need that she did not spring from authentic Black life than this?

James Webb Young, the manager of the Chicago branch of the J. Walter Thompson Advertising Company, used these and other such phony legends in the advertising campaign. Young added a new twist. He added his experiences of growing up in Covington, Kentucky, as the son of a riverboat captain to the Wright story. With the addition of N. C. Wyeth illustrations, Aunt Jemima, just like Mammy before her, truly becomes an invention of the White imagination. Like chattel slavery, property and commodity are combined. This time, however, identity was added.

Commodification and Property

The Aunt Jemima rag doll was one of the most coveted marketing premiums ever created.[32] Other manufacturers seized on the success of the rag doll and introduced other dolls with the now-familiar Aunt Jemima look: a warm, smiling face in domestic regalia. Unlike Black versions of Barbie and Skipper with darkened European features, these dolls were fat, had thick red lips, and a large pearly white toothed smile. Aunt Jemima began appearing on salt and pepper shakers, cookie jars, plastic and cardboard items, a pottery set of kitchen condiment holders, and a syrup pitcher. By 1910, the Aunt Jemima trademark was known in every state, and by 1918, more than 120 million Aunt Jemima breakfasts were served annually.[33]

The Aunt Jemima marketing campaign intentionally kept the Southern Belle out of the ads. It did not fit the marketers' agenda to show Colonel Higbee with a wife or a daughter who could, in theory, play the role of hostess or supervisor of the slaves. The Thompson Advertising Company targeted women who could not find or afford a household servant. They also could not have the recipe since all that the ads told them was that their only job is to add water. The ads appeared as White women's jobs shifted from domestic work to other forms of paid employment. Manring argues that the southern mistress could not be in the ads because they were designed to have White housewives place themselves in the role of the mistresses (Miss Anns) of their own homes.[34] The ads removed White female domestic labor and replaced it with Black labor—Aunt Jemima—a "real" person and slave. Subtly or otherwise, the ads suggested that although White women could not have Aunt Jemima in the kitchen (or any other hired servant), they could mimic the lifestyle of a southern plantation mistress—they could *possess* Aunt Jemima but not *be* Aunt Jemima. As advertisers reconstructed an idyllic South, they also gave White housewives the ability to reconstruct their worlds.

Aunt Jemima personal appearances continued into the 1960s despite Black hostility toward the product since as early as 1918.[35] Aunt Jemima became such a contestable term in Black life and culture that by the 1940s and 1950s it had become a form of insult to call someone an Aunt Jemima (male or female), and local National Association for the Advancement of Colored People chapters tried to block live appearances by Aunt Jemimas.[36] The ongoing protests by Blacks finally paid off in 1987.

> She lost about 150 pounds, dropped 40 years, got herself a new head-dress and moved from the plantation to New Orleans. It took more than 80 years, but the symbol on the label of the best selling pancake mix made the transformation from freed slave cook to Creole cooking teacher.[37]

The new awareness created by the Civil Rights movement, the Black Power movement, and the feminist movement finally exposed the racist, sexist, classist stereotypes that framed the Aunt Jemima image. Beginning in the 1970s, the mammy-decorated cards and kitchenware disappeared (except as Black memorabilia) and Quaker Oats needed to craft an image of a Black woman who could sell their pancake mix. She moved from being fat and kerchiefed to plump and polka-dot scarfed (1970s) to the scarfless, perm-coiffed woman who could be a housewife or a woman working outside the home (1989 to present). What remains is the strong, Black nurturing woman who can cook—that is, just add water. With her is a 40 percent market share and a product line that accounts for $300 million of Quaker Oats's $5.3 billion in annual sales.

Also present is a resurgence of interest in Black memorabilia. This time, however, more Blacks than Whites are the collectors. Despite this and Spike Lee's soaring indictment, *Bamboozled*,[38] White artists such as Eminem continue to ignore accusations of covert and overt racism and perform postmodern minstrel shows—and become wealthy doing so.[39] These characterizations, stereotypes, are no less demeaning that Aunt Jemima or Mammy in that they never get it right—they are unable to truly hear, let alone experience, the *reality* of Black anger, joy, pain, or protest. The actual blackface may not be rubbed on their skin, but the freakish interpretation of Black culture is no less demeaning, no less a commodification of Black identity.

This is one of the mean sides of hybridity in its postmodern form.[40] Unlike creolization that is a melding of cultures and their ideologies to form a new person or people who then draw on the various streams and histories to become moral agents, hybridity as practiced by Eminem, Christina Aguilera, Milli Vanilli, Elvis Presley, Joss Stone, Vanilla Ice, and others appropriates Black culture with no reciprocity. The agency involved is one in which the bottom line is marketing and the acquisition of wealth and privilege—commodification in its rawest form. This is not the "play" in which we can come to know other peoples and cultures, a "play" that represents one of the positive sides of hybridity. When commodification is afoot, the richness and complexity of cultures and the people that shape and inhabit them are thrown into a shackled subaltern wasteland. Those who appropriate have no desire to *know*, only to *use* the new culture to fit into a profit margin that is most often commercial and sociocultural.

Manthia Diawara argues that instead of freeing Aunt Jemima and other Black stereotypes from the White fantastic imagination, attempts to make stereotypes positive tend to reinforce the immediacy of these stereotypes in our collective imagination.[41] Further, for Diawara, any insistence on positive images only strengthens the negative stereotypes in both the Black and White imaginations. Given the "history" of Mammy and Aunt Jemima, Diawara's critique is to the point: "new interest in blackface stereotypes involves historical, political, and aesthetic implications that are more complex than allowed by the debates over positive and negative images. Every stereotype emerges in the wake of pre-existing ideology that deforms it, appropriates it, and naturalizes it. The blackface stereotype, by deforming the body, silences it and leaves room only for white supremacy to speak through it."[42] For Diawara, blackface stereotypes represent a White retreat from dealing with the brutality of slavery, the demands of the Civil Rights movement, and the lingering call for desegregation into a gothic Old South.

Yoked with the increased interest in Black memorabilia, and appropriation of blackface stereotypes, is the rise in Black memorabilia reproductions (a.k.a. fakes) from slave shackles to Sambo imagery. These reproductions often find their way into the market as authentic period pieces.[43] The authentic Black memorabilia market began to grow in the 1970s when White collectors realized that "No Coloreds" signs and their ilk would soon be scarce. Some authentic memorabilia can command up to $1000 while its reproduction no more than $30. However, by the time many reproductions find their way into thrift and antique shops or swap meets, the labels are often gone, the original packaging is gone, and it becomes difficult to tell the authentic from the fake.

Black identity has been made property and it should leave a sickening weariness in the pit of our collective stomach for property means things owned, possession. On a good day it can mean attribute, quality, or characteristic. On another day it may mean a moveable object used in a dramatic performance.[44] It does not help us that property stems from the Latin proprieties—related to "proper"[45]—that is, pertaining to oneself or itself or a person or thing particularly strictly pertaining; thorough, complete, excellent, fine; specifically adapted from the Latin proprinus (one's own, special, peculiar, problem); from the French pro priuo (as private or peculiar thing); hence properly (appropriate, fitting); property ownership (especially private): thing or things owned; attribute, quality; propriety, portable article for a dramatic performance.

However, there is more than what we can glean from a good day at stake. The modern conception of property considers it an economic resource, deems it friendly to money making, and regards the demands of the state as a drain on resources and a threat to a person's right to do as he or she will with their property.[46] Implicit in this is an understanding of liberty as noninterference from the state. Ownership, then, means rights over resources that the individual can exercise without interference. Indeed, for James Madison, property meant not only external objects and our relation to them, but also those human rights, liberties, powers, and immunities that are important for human well-being. For Madison, these were freedom of expression, freedom of conscience, freedom from bodily harm, and free and equal opportunities to use one's personal faculties.[47]

Frederic Pryor defines property as a collection of rights or a set of relations between people concerning a good, service, or "thing," and also that such rights must have economic value and must be enforced in some manner recognized by society.[48] One aspect of property rights is the right to use a particular good, service, or thing to obtain income other than by means of labor. This is also called ownership. Another aspect is the right to use goods, services, or things in the process of production and exchange. In short, property has content and implies the right to control material resources.

Behind the sterile understanding of property is the Representation Clause of the Constitution; better known as the Three-Fifths Compromise, this clause declared slaves to be only three-fifths of a person.[49] The clause, designed to settle the issue of representation between the North and South, laid down the method that would be used to count slaves for the purposes of taxation and representation. Also in the background is the Fugitive Slave Laws of 1793 and 1850 (repealed in 1864) that provided for the return of escaped Black slaves between the states.[50] It is an unyielding fact that Black bodies were considered property for the better part of the history of the Americas.[51]

The commodification of bodies mutated into the commodification of identity—Black history, Black culture, Black life—Black identity. Black identity as property means that a community of people has been reduced to exchange values that can be manipulated for economic gain—*but rarely by the members of the community themselves*. This manipulation includes merging race with myth and memory to create history. It includes caricaturing Black life, and in some cases Black agony, to sell the product. Even the discipline of Christian ethics causes the willies because of how it has understood property as the goods of this earth given by God so we all must use them in the pursuit of our self-realization.[52] In ethics, though there is a right to own property, it is subordinate to the common right to use property.

Ultimately, property means owning and ownership and possession—be it a moral-philosophical view of ownership or a sociolegal view of ownership, I am caught with a churning in the pit of my womanist theoethical stomach because the arrogance of all these definitions is manifest in the assumption of control and autonomy—being politically, socially, and theoethically free.[53]

I wonder in what space (or spaces) in this country (after living and enduring a grotesque presidential election in 2000 in which massive voter registration drives were countered with massive disenfranchisement, a pliant public and press that often seemed interested only in who would win the game rather than in the morality of its existence) holds the repository for Black autonomy? The sad part is that this is nothing new for poor communities or colored peoples in this country. It is just that this time it was national, it was public, and the same damned thing that usually takes place in some misbegotten metaphorical or actual backwoods happened in broad daylight. In what spaces in this country, then, do Black peoples and our kin have control and autonomy? Most of us are barely in control of our lives and we have almost no control over our commodified bodies. Autonomy is a far away ideal.

How do we grasp a hold of our identity and truly name ourselves instead of constantly looking into some strategically placed funhouse mirror of distortions and innuendos and mass marketing that smacks its lips and rolls its eyes while chanting "mmmm mmmm good?" When Black identity is property that can be owned by someone else, defined by someone else, created by someone else, shaped by someone else, and marketed by someone else, we are chattel dressed in postmodern silks and linens. Our buckboards and dusty trails have been exchanged for one-legged stools by the one-way revolving door of academia and boardrooms. We are told that these canting stools are truly seats at the table, but when we speak, we are not heard; when we scream, they do not listen. We are often left standing on some malformed Gold Dust Twins soap box with auction blocks as our foot stools and the hangman's noose as our lullabies to rock us into the ultimate deep sleep.

Identity and Countermemory

Aunt Jemima—many in my generation grew to despise her or to be embarrassed by her in the 1960s, and we thought we had banished her with raised black gloved fists and self-empowerment and affirmative action and an emerging Black middle class. She vanished, but only into limbo, into an ambiguous oblivion. Baldwin tried to warn us this would happen. We could not vanquish her completely because Black folk never controlled Aunt Jemima or Uncle Tom or Topsy or any of their kin. They are creations of the White imagination—its fears and its terrors and its stereotypes and its unilateral attempts at justice.

If we do not heed Baldwin's warning, if we do not examine the myths perpetuated about us, we will never know our true selves. It should not be surprising that Black and biracial writers did not agree on the Mammy image. Some saw her as the sheltering mother of Black uplift; others saw her as a painful figure of stereotype and death.[54]

What we *will* know are caricatures that sit like so many rows of false teeth molded to fit someone else's head. We will fail to grasp the full impact of what it means to say that Black folk did not and do not own these public identities of Black life. The power in naming things and people such as Mammy is the power to name reality and history—no matter how inaccurately. Like any image, Mammy morphed into Aunt Jemima is a powerful medium of communication. This power, one that springs from the fantastic hegemonic imagination, is the province of caricature and stereotypes. It takes on a life and history of its own. Memory only serves to feed this history for those who seek to (re)create it. White women and men indulged in recalling the Mammy to the point that eventually they had to make her an abstraction because she was not a real person. However, as an abstraction, she did not allow them to develop a full set of teeth that could suck the life blood out of Blacks seeking to name themselves and demand recognition of their humanity.

But Aunt Jemima *is* back—updated, kerchiefless, and with pearls. Popular not only on pancakes (original, complete, buttermilk, buttermilk complete, whole wheat—also available online, buckwheat—also available on line, frozen homestyle and buttermilk and homestyle batter, frozen mini pancakes, and mini syrup pancake dunkers) but also on syrup (original, buttermilk, butter rich, lite, and butter lite) and frozen waffles (homestyle, buttermilk, lowfat, syrup dunkers, and blueberry—actually dried apple parts treated with blue food dye) and frozen French toast (homestyle, cinnamon, cinnamon toast sticks, and syrup dunkers), coffee cake mix, corn bread mix, cornmeal mix (white, yellow, self-rising, preblended), and griddlecake sandwiches. Aunt Jemima is back because limbo returns her to us as more than a relic, more than an updated image of Black womanhood or as collateral to Black manhood. She is back as commodity and property. She is back because she is profitable and identifiable. In a world where you and I are often reduced to digits and statistics, image matters when one is in the business of making money.

Aunt Jemima is back in giveaways and mail-in premiums and in recipe booklets and dishware and with an entire family of character dolls with names and history.[55] If we refuse to use the power of her presence and endurance and to rear up even weary heads to ask this ethical question:

Who Is It that Has Named Aunt Jemima's Family?

Is this some obscene product line from the World Wrestling Federation or Mattel sold at our local Toys-R-Us or KayBees or FAO Schwartz meant to outduel Barney and Beanie Babies and Teletubbies and SpongeBob SquarePants for the favor of little kids who have been shaped into megaconsumers of a megaculture and pseudohistory? Is this Barbie and Ken in Black woman drag electric sliding[56] off boxes of powered flapjacks so that we can dash into the day more efficiently with the promise that we have been well fed by a good cook? If there is no time or space or method in ethical discourse to ask crucial moral questions—Who is naming *any* of us? Who is making our history a denigrating mythological construction?—then we allow others, real others, to carve out hollow legacies for the future generations of all color. This is gross iconization of Black life.

Enter countermemory—not the rejection, but the reconstitution of history.[57] One that is found in the writings of Black folk from Du Bois to Baldwin to Morrison; Crummell to King to Williams and Cannon.[58] Countermemory is the patient and persistent work of mining the motherlode of African American religious life. It is a methodological strategy that helps combat the hollow legacy of this kind of gross iconization of Black identity. Countermemory helps to disrupt ignorance and invisibility. Du Bois notwithstanding, it remains true that countermemory can fail in spectacularly devastating ways. It can leave blanks and fill blanks with mistakes. Memory can be a collaborator with forces that know only suppression and denial of life and wholeness. Countermemories can vanish into limbo (into absolute neglect, into oblivion) only to filter back into our lives as shame or anger or pride or righteousness.

But countermemory can also succeed in deep and profound ways. It can provide hope in the midst of degradation, and strength to continue to put one foot in front of the other in movements for justice. Countermemory has the potential to challenge the false generalizations and gross stereotypes often found in what passes for "history" in the United States. Countermemories can disrupt our status quo because they do not rest solely or wholly on objectivity or facts. They materialize from emotions and sight and sounds and touch and smell.

They come from the deepest part of who we are. Countermemories are dynamic and spark new configurations of meaning. Also present is the recognition of decades-long patterns of meaning-making that remain alive in fallow discourses that can shape the enterprise of history into a dynamic process rather than into a static hegemony where Aunt Jemima and her kin can be found. And if held to a Du Boisian standard of joining morals with science, they keep us on the potter's wheel so that we never rest too comfortably in the knowledge that is, at best, only partial and never ultimately complete.

Limbo returns us to the midst of this socioeconomic, sociopolitical, theoethical struggle where the search is not only for truth (whatever that is) but also for justice (wherever that may be found). This is not solely academic, for wrapped up in the fantastic hegemonic imagination are dominations repeated endlessly until they become fixed in our rituals—social and religious—with meticulous precision that impose rights and obligations in biased and nuanced ways that masquerade as objectivity. Our memories become engraved with illusions and we are no longer able to see them as the figments they actually are because we have no scaffolding in place that can help us see otherwise. We cannot create countermemories that will help us dismantle the stultifying and death-bringing stereotypes created by the fantastic hegemonic imagination that circumscribe our isness.

Nevertheless, we have Baldwin's admonition as watchword and beacon of hope. How is it that we consent to others naming us, commodifying us? How is it that others do so without our assent or knowledge? How is it that we know so little about the world around us that when we hear suspect calls to arms we jump for our battle gear without stopping to think about what this will mean for the next generation or the one following the next? Aunt Jemima helps demonstrate how the fantastic hegemonic imaginings of the Old South can be commodified and sold as history. As Whites imagined themselves into a country that no longer tolerated *de jure* slavery, it allowed them to keep *de facto* segregation firmly in place through the bald-faced lie of Aunt Jemima as the Mammy. She was the collaborator with White society, one who provided sustenance and comfort to them, who told them what to do, and who could keep Black men and children in line. She also enabled White males to keep both Black and White women under control as her "story" told volumes about what White men and women thought (and think?) about each other and Black men.

However, there is countermemory at work here as both a corrective and a critique. The song "Old Aunt Jemima" also had a more popular

version written by the Black minstrel musician Billy Kersands in 1875.[59]
"Old Aunt Jemima" was Kersands biggest hit. By 1877, Kersands was
reported to have sung the song anywhere from 2,000–3,000 times.[60]
By 1880, Kersands improvised the verses as he sang with at least three
versions of the original song.

Kersands is a complex figure. His performances and many of his
songs reinforced anti-Black sentiments and stereotypes. Yet he was
enormously popular with both Black and White audiences. It may be
that Kersands presented a character who was the least of the least—
more ignorant and worse off than anyone in the audience.[61] His Black
audiences "read" his lyrics very differently from his White audiences.
Kersands sprinkled Black folklore throughout his lyrics and coded
them for differing epistemological worlds. Both versions of "Old Aunt
Jemima" from 1875 placed the action in Black worship as did Grace's
version. However, the lyrics in Kersands's 1880 version differs from
the lyrics in Grace's version heard by Chris Rutt as sung by the White
minstrel team of Baker and Ferrell.

> I went to church the other day.
> Old Aunt Jemima, Oh! Oh! Oh!
> To hear them white folks sing and pray,
> Old Aunt Jemima, Oh! Oh! Oh!
> They prayed so long I couldn't stay,
> Old Aunt Jemima, Oh! Oh! Oh!
> I knew the world would come that way,
> Old Aunt Jemima, Oh! Oh! Oh!
>
> The monkey dressed in soldier clothes
> Old Aunt Jemima, Oh! Oh! Oh!
> Went out in the woods to drill some crows
> Old Aunt Jemima, Oh! Oh! Oh!
> The jay bird hung on the swinging limb
> Old Aunt Jemima, Oh! Oh! Oh!
> I up with stone and hit him on the shin
> Old Aunt Jemima, Oh! Oh! Oh!
> Oh! Carline, Oh Carline
> Can't you dance the bee line,
> Old Aunt Jemima, Oh! Oh! Oh!
>
> The bullfrog married the tadpole's sisters
> Old Aunt Jemima, Oh! Oh! Oh!
> He smacked his lips and then he kissed her
> Old Aunt Jemima, Oh! Oh! Oh!

> She says, if you love me as I love you
> Old Aunt Jemima, Oh! Oh! Oh!
> No knife can cut our love in two
> Old Aunt Jemima, Oh! Oh! Oh!
> Oh, Carline, Oh, Carline
> Can't you dance the bee line,
> Old Aunt Jemima, Oh! Oh! Oh![62]

The first verse of the 1880 version places the singer in a White church that he leaves because they "prayed too long." Whites and some Blacks looked down on Black for the ecstatic nature of their worship—seeing it as entertainment. They also criticized enthusiastic worship for not praying properly. However, some Blacks could hear these same lyrics as a critique of sanctimonious Whites and Blacks.

In one of Kersands's 1875 versions of the second stanza, Kersands put himself in the place of the crow, a symbol of Black folk. He also used aggressive action instead of the frustrating kick directed against a symbolic animal, not the Whites. William Toll suggests that this retains the indirection of the Black folk tradition. In the 1880 version, he substituted "monkey" for "bullfrog." Now, both animals are black symbols and, rather than finishing the verse by attacking the monkey, Kersands shifted to the first and last lines of the Grace version of "Old Aunt Jemima."

> The jaybird hung on the swinging limb
> I up with a stone and hit him on the shin.[63]

Another version, performed almost exclusively before Black audiences, explained failed emancipation to the slave:

> My old missus promise me
> Old Aunt Jemima, oh, oh, oh
> When she died she'd set me free
> Old Aunt Jemima, oh, oh, oh
> She lived so long her head got bald
> Old Aunt Jemima, oh, oh, oh
> She shore she would not die at all
> Old Aunt Jemima, oh, oh, oh[64]

Toll notes that the overt protest message and omission of face-saving comic victory for the Black character suggest that this version was original to White minstrelsy.[65] For Toll, the Black minstrel tradition used for Black characters symbolic indirection and "victories" that this verse does not display. Toll goes on to suggest that by the time Kersands used this verse, White minstrels had discarded it but it still had meaning for Blacks. In the above stanza when the slave's mistress goes bald, Kersands could be criticizing the numerous broken promises Whites had made to Blacks *and* laughing at the idea of a bald, White woman. More to the point, however, Manring suggests that the most important reason Black audiences appreciated "Aunt Jemima" was that Kersands had adapted it from a work song that Blacks sang as they carried out their various tasks on a farm or plantation.[66]

The irony of Kersands lyrics can teach us much about how the commodification of Black life occurs and how to contest such commodification. The minstrel tradition was one in which White men in blackface performed a grotesque mockery of Black life and culture. However, because they did not (and do not) know us, they had no idea that by singing authentic Black songs they were also critiquing themselves—their arrogance, their ignorance, and their elitism. They presented a counterfeit imagined version of blackness as truth—complete with Aunt Jemima loosed from her box. However, this kind of thorough-going commodification—one spawned from the complex of myth, memory, and history—is not easily recognized, analyzed, critiqued, or eradicated.

It is small wonder that many of us tried our best to banish Aunt Jemima into limbo, into a crude marginal space. The complex sociocultural matrix of U.S. society and the intracommunal dynamics of African American communities make her a painful reminder of not only slavery but also the very commodification of identities that has become our stock and trade on a global scale.

This process of commodification turns us (let alone our identities) into commodities—economic goods that are bought and sold on a large scale. Our ontologies move via rail and road and plane and Internet and Fed-Ex from place to place. *We* are not there, but our alleged identities are. One quick example of how this works comes from an experience I had in the summer of 2001 in Sâo Leopoldo, Brazil. I presented a paper on race and sex in education at a feminist philosophy conference. After I finished presenting the paper and we moved into the question and answer session, a White Brazilian man in the audience, believing he was backing me up on a point, told me (and the rest of the audience) with utter sincerity that he understood what I meant because his favorite television show was "The Cosby Show." He "knew" and understood Black life in the United States because of this show.

Even in the communities of resistance that seek genuine diversity and equality, Aunt Jemima and her kin (Uncle Ben, Rastus, Old Uncle Tom, Uncle Remus, Mandy the Maid, Preacher Brown, Deacon Jones, Sambo, the Gold Dust Twins, and ol' Mammy) rise up as haunting Black life spectered caricatures created to buy and sell not only products but to siphon off our lives through a sea of big lips, large grins, rolling eyes.

Rather than avoiding the reinscription of conventional oppressive hierarchies of class, gender, and race, Black marginalized communities have often fallen victim to these hegemonic forces of which Aunt Jemima and *all* of us are the casualties. As Kersands' lyrics demonstrate, marginalization, though not desirable, *can* function as a site of resistance. It can birth spaces of respite and judgment:

> Baby Suggs clearing
> Mama Day's lightening powder
> Celie's "till you do right by me"
> Sanchez's lions
> Baby's veil
> Danticat's krik krak[67]

Though marginalization can be a lonely place, it can also be a place that encourages creativity in thought, word, and deed. This space is where counterhegemony has its birthing as the marginalized can begin to develop and enact pithy analysis and trenchant cultural critiques to dismantle the cultural production of evil. The spirituals, gospels, blues, work and protest songs, jazz, R&B, soul, hip hop, all have within them segments that have taken a long, hard look at the nature of subjugations in our lives and have something to say about it and the ways to lessen, if not eradicate, the many wounds inflicted on Black lives on a minute-by-minute basis. Enacting memory and history and myth in a culture while refusing to measure Black realities by ideological stereotypes is to resist the scatological moonshine of the gross commodification of human lives in which peoples are reduced to profit margins or product brand names.

The use of countermemory in ethical reflection helps avoid earlier patterns of essentialism endemic to the fantastic hegemonic imagination. Once again, countermemory is *not* a rejection of history, but its emendation. This extends to the African American culture and history as well. With countermemory, theoethical reflections and sociocultural critiques do not further erase and exclude women in racial analysis,

the multiplicity of sexualities for Black men and women, the socioeconomic stratification within and beyond Black culture, the genuine
valuing of age—young and old, the mélange of African American
religious worldviews sweeping head and heart/body and spirit, the
continuing impact/fall out/beat down of colonial and neocolonial
mentalities on peoples of the African diaspora.

The use of countermemory in ethical reflection helps avoid the earlier patterns of essentialism, endemic to making history and ideology, in
dominant cultures invested in a choked status quo. It also helps avoid
new forms of essentialism in subjugated cultures so that they can
remain true to the struggles of exploited and oppressed groups in their
attempts to critique the dominant structures from positions that give
meaning and purpose to this struggle. Countermemory prompts a necessary and vital intracommunal analysis that is crucial in womanist ethical reflection. This is a conversation *and* a challenge to the forms of
essentialism in African American religious communities, Black theological discourses, and larger Black culture as these locations seek to produce and practice liberatory ethics, that womanist ethical reflections
address its first audiences. Womanist ethical thought does not deny the
importance and power of identity-making and shaping, but it explores
the magnitude and scope of the diversity of Black identities so that *we*
do not commit the gross errors of stereotype and sentimentalization
that are often forced on our communities, in short, it recreates our
commodification over the countermemory. A Du Boisian/Baldwinian
countermemory in womanist ethical analysis cautions us against
neglecting accountability and responsibility within our own communities. It is far too easy to fall into a warped and inarticulate rhetoric of
victimization that does little to craft justice and truth.

In countermemory, the interplay between identity and essentialism
is not only intracommunal, it is intercommunal as well. The challenge
here is to maintain the rigorous pursuit of identity as a form of resistance to the fantastic hegemonic imagination—wherever it is found.
This pursuit of the authentic and varied identities in Black lives in the
United States combines the experiential with the analytical (often in
this order) to question many epistemological and ideological assumptions found in the larger culture and its social institutions, as well as
within Black lives.

There may be times when the assertion of an exclusive essentialism
is a strategy to undercut and destabilize hegemonic forces. Yet great
care must be taken to avoid creating a monolithic identity that fails to
represent the true heterogeneity of Black life in the United States. In

short, it is of little help if, in our cultural and theoethical critiques, womanist thought replaces the forms of supremacy that we know so well with a postmodern Black slow drag of annihilation.

Countermemory enables us to value identity even as we analyze and critique the formation and practice of identity. It is important to remember that Black identity is not a mere commodity formed as a natural by-product of culture and genetics and theological systems. It is also a social reality and socially constructed. This makes it, like Asian, Asian American, Latino/a, Native American, and White identities, open to interpretation and construction by others. Aunt Jemima and Mammy are galling because both figures are often treated as historical artifacts rather than as romantic essentialist constructs that became commodities.

Countermemory is also helpful in questioning the label of essentialism when it is always applied to the people who are dispossessed, yet empowered enough to demand that their personhood is valuable and should be valued.[68] We must ask why is it that the ones who have for decades, if not centuries, practiced hegemony with precision are never guilty of collapsing reality into their own image? If this checkered legacy is what we consider to be normal and whole, then what a misbegotten notion of normal and wholeness we live. May God help us!

The struggle has always been for womanist theoethical reflections to name, analyze, and critique the simultaneous subordinations of class, gender, and race as *lived experiences* and also as theoretical constructs. Further, it is to name the ways in which these forms of subordination and oppression are carried out within the African American community and by men and women in other racial ethnic groups. Within this struggle is the recognition that accountability is paramount. This accountability functions at the individual and at the communal level. Womanist ethicists are held accountable by the African American community for the ethical, theological, social, and political choices we make as we straddle academy, church, and community. In this vein, we can never forget that we stand within a community as active members and participants. The community functions to remind us that there may be lapses within our analysis and critique, lapses that warrant a reassessment of our perspectives.

On the communal level, accountability means being open to the width and breadth of the community. It also means remaining vigilant to the forces of hegemony that can and do co-opt authentic Black life and replace it with stereotypes and innuendoes that pathologize African American resistance struggles against a dehumanizing hegemony concocted from ideologies of elitism and repression. The question, then, is how to implement accountability without reinscribing hierarchies endemic to African American culture and its social institutions. Answering this question is an enduring challenge for womanist ethics and to all forms of ethical and theological reflection that focus on Black religiosity and African American liberation that is spiritual and social. And it does not stop there.

If we breathe genuine life into Aunt Jemima, we begin to see the ways in which countermemory makes it possible to answer Baldwin. In doing so, we also unmask the structural evil that makes her continued existence possible and profitable. However, neither memory nor countermemory alone can help us answer these questions fully. Yet they do not keep us so far away from actual history that we make foolish mistakes with deadly consequences. When identity is commodified, we have been beaten by a willfully narrow history that suppresses the richness of who we are. We have fallen victim to the long fostered habit of belittling and/or forgetting the thoughts and actions of peoples we do not know. To treat identity as property is one form of the cultural production of evil. The task of womanist ethical reflection is to continue to mine the motherlode of memory and history to explore this dynamic. If it does not, then it will collapse into a meaningless drivel of hosannas or inconsequential theological escape hatches that only serve to reify demonic stereotypes in theoethical discourses meant to break the fine rain of death on Black identities and realities.

Aunt Jemima has not vanished into limbo. She has not slipped away into a netherworld. She is here with us and we are her family—*all* of us. We must name ourselves with precise anger and ornery love while churning justice and truth into a new analysis of our ethical dilemma. The dilemma of what it means to shape and name and create an identity forged by the hope found in those who are still here . . . regardless.

Invisible Things Spoken: Uninterrogated Coloredness

Our postmodern culture suffers from the enormous impact of market forces on everyday life. We live in an era where the United States has replaced Europe as the global hegemonist. There is an increase of political polarizations along the lines of nation, race, gender (sex, sexuality, sex roles, sexual orientation, sexism), class, denomination and faith traditions. In our world, culture is sanitized and then commodified. This process of changing aesthetic tastes—domestication of the once exotic or feared other, uncontrolled appropriation, market-driven refiners' fires, mass production, and marketing—is for our enjoyment at the expense of people's lives and shrinking paychecks. Often the solution is placed in the hands of lottery games—games of chance.

Rather than challenge and debunk master narratives such as the United States as the city on the hill, the lone heroic self-made man or woman, or inevitable and unalterable progress as good and civilized, our fashionable narratives are nationalist and xenophobic. They are layered with strong religious, racial, patriarchal, homophobic, hetero-sexist, ageist, and classist overtones and bell tones. In our postmodern culture, the structural inequalities that form the superstructure of U. S. society are alive and well—and they are growing.

Postmodern thought has raised various warnings in its critique of modernity's excessive focus on individualism, universals, ahistorical reason, universal knowledge, the elevation of science as sheer objectivity, the social contract and morality organized around civil rights, and the liberties of the free individual. However, our postmodern culture has, thus far, made only a creative and sociocultural space in which racial, gender, and so-called subclasses now have theoretical entrée into the emerging global marketplace of power, privilege, and pleasure.

This entrée may be imperative for these groups that have been, until recently, among the dispossessed. Yet too many of our postmodern conversations do not take us beyond reform movements to transformations of social systems and practices that model justice for all peoples and a respect for creation beyond human skin color and the violence that circumscribes our lives.

This turn has been taken, in part, because postmodernisms have failed to show, until recently with the development of social postmodernism, concern for institutions, social classes, political organization, political economic processes, and social movements.

It is at this disquieting crossroads that my work as a Christian ethicist seeks to understand the multitude of absurd metaphors encircling our lives. In this crucible, it is crucial to remember that inclusion does not guarantee justice; and access to a social order that is inequitable and grossly maldistributed cannot transform fragmented communities or whole ones. Race is an "interesting" notion to consider in this context.

Willful Oblivion

> . . . invisible things are not necessarily "not there"; . . . a void may be empty, but it is not a vacuum. In addition, certain absences are so stressed, so ornate, so planned, they call attention to themselves; arrest us with intentionality and purpose, like neighborhoods that are defined by the population held away from them. Looking at the scope of American literature, I can't help thinking that the question should have never been "Why am I, an Afro-American, absent from it?" It is not a particularly interesting query anyway. The spectacularly interesting question is "What intellectual feats had to be performed by the author or his critic to erase me from a society seething with my presence, and what effect has that performance had on the work?" What are the strategies of escape from knowledge? Of willful oblivion? . . . Not why. How?[1]

I am tired of talking about Black folks and racism. This time I will talk about whiteness and White people.

Questions of race and racism are two avenues womanists use to articulate the concerns of Black women who are feminists and committed to rigorous theological reflection and the dismantling of evil.

These questions assume and point to the silences found in both traditional theological discourses as well as in Black Theology and Feminist Theology about important elements in Black women's lives and their religious experiences. As the opening quotation from Morrison demonstrates, such silences and absences are not confined to the theological worlds of academic discourses.

These silences include more than race—ethnicity, sexuality, age, social class location—the list goes on and on. There are items on this list that many treat as a threadbare list of gripes. Latter day versions of "what do they want?" or "they get all the jobs, don't they?" abound in our academic musings in print, in professional societies, at dinner parties, at social hours, in the offices of colleagues, and in the halls of our institutions. Somehow, and quite remarkably, relatively few Black women in the theological academy have become akin to Joel's horde of locusts—cutting, swarming, hopping, destroying. For others, we are Joel's relentless army—not swerving, not jostling, not halted, and entering theoethical discourse like thieves.[2]

In dazzling displays of intellectual hubris, orthodox moral discourses ignore the diversities within their (and our) midst in an ill-timed and increasingly irrelevant search for an objective viewpoint that can lead us toward the [T]ruth. Such inquiries have served (and continue) to preserve a moral and social universe that has mean-spiritedness at one end of its ontological pole and sycophancy at the other. A large portion of *noblesse oblige* often acts as filler and buffer for those who seek to maintain or recapture an intellectual and material corpus that reeks of an onerous status quo. This often makes Black women in the academy and in society the invisible visible. We are not alone in this status.

There are a variety of ways to approach this conundrum and in many ways a consequential subaltern of this book is the interstructuredness of such an inquiry. My aim at this point, however, is to focus on race and racism. Morrison's question "Not why. How?" provides the methodological frame. I want to explore how it is that the diversity in our midst is largely ignored in theoethical discourse. I use race and racism as the entrée.

In her essay "Unspeakable Things Unspoken: The Afro-American Presence in American Literature," Morrison notes that race is still a virtually unspeakable notion. She aptly points out a strong movement within the social sciences (left largely unaddressed by the majority of scholars in the theological disciplines) to question the efficacy of race as a helpful category to explore our social order.

> For three hundred years black Americans insisted that "race" was no usefully distinguishing factor in human relationships. During those same three centuries every academic discipline, including theology, history, and natural science, insisted "race" was the determining factor in human development. When blacks discovered that they had shaped or become a culturally formed race, and that it had specific and revered difference, suddenly they were told there is no such thing as "race," biological or cultural, that matters and that genuinely intellectual exchange cannot accommodate it . . . It always seemed to me that the people who invented the hierarchy of "race" when it was convenient for them ought not to be the ones to explain it away, now that it does not suit their purposes for it to exist. But there *is* culture and both gender and "race" inform and are informed by it.[3]

I do not want to move from a direct confrontation with race as quickly away as Morrison does above. However, I begin with these two extended quotations from Morrison to underscore the difficulty theoethical discourse has in addressing race and racism. We as ethicists have simply not done it adequately or thoroughly. Some see such analysis as veering into public policy, others cannot find an adequate philosophical construct from which to peer into the mysteries of race. But peer and veer we must. I propose a different tact: exploring what I call uninterrogated coloredness. The notion of race has been collapsed into this uninterrogated coloredness by academic, economic, ethical, social, theological, and political arguments.

Many of our discussions on race divorce it from the profound impact that color (un)consciousness plays in the deliberations. Further, we focus on darker-skinned peoples almost exclusively. This invites folks of European descent and others to ignore the social construction of whiteness. It allows darker-skinned racial ethnic groups to ignore their internal color caste system. It also often opens the door for weird bifurcations of class, race, gender, age and so on. Race is a social construction as well as a cultural production where there are both implicit and explicit costs and benefits to collapsing race into uninterrogated coloredness. This is usually, if not always, wrapped up in a whirlwind of personal choices and communal power dynamics.

Working with Sapphire

In order to navigate the rocky terrain of race and coloredness, it is necessary to find a tough conductor. The image of Sapphire will be our guide. Who, then, is Sapphire? Sapphire began as a joke in plays and minstrel music shows. She was smaller than Mammy and Aunt Jemima, but stout. She had medium to dark brown complexion, and she was headstrong and opinionated. She was loud-mouthed, strong-willed, sassy, and practical. The Sapphire stereotype made her husband look inferior, and in doing so, her image set detrimental standards for the Black family.

Such a negative stereotype may not seem to be a likely candidate for an incisive and progressive examination of race and racism. However, I argue that it is in this stereotype of the masculinzed Black female who must be subordinated so that the Black male can take his "rightful" place in society, that we find the necessary resources and methodological edginess to cut through much of the prattle and utter nonsense that often accompanies critiques of race and racism.

Sapphire is malicious, vicious, bitchy, loud, bawdy, domineering, and emasculating. I argue that it is these very characteristics that are necessary to disrupt our comfortable racisms. Sapphire is based on the oldest negative stereotype of woman: inherently and inescapably evil. Perhaps in the case of racism, only a stereotype or an image that is based on evil can help destabilize and deconstruct a structural evil such as racism.

Barbara Christian argues that the Sapphire image highlights the domineering characteristic of the Mammy image.[3] However, she is not maternal to Whites and she is unfeminine to Black men. Sapphire usurps the traditional (patriarchal, sexist) role of Black men. She is as tough, efficient, and tireless as Mammy. However, where Mammy operated within the prescribed boundaries for women, Sapphire is firmly anchored in a man's world.[4] Based on the character Sapphire Stevens in the "Amos 'n Andy" television show of the 1950s, the contemporary Sapphire has the ability to make Black men and White folks look like fools, partly because she is unfeminine, strong, and independent.[5] She is cold, hard, evil. And she is usually correct in her assessments and on point with her critiques. She is a walking, talking, thinking dialectic.

Sapphire is an electronic media creation more than a literary one. Melvin Patrick Ely describes this Sapphire well.

> Sapphire was strong-willed and decisive . . . much of whose scolding of her husband was understandable in view of his laziness and dishonesty. Yet her assertiveness often took on the shrill tone of the shrew, and the couple's relationship conformed closely to the stereotype of the female-dominated black family—as children . . . "Sapphire," in fact had already become a generic folk term among Afro-Americans for a domineering wife.[6]

As Ely's description suggests, this media-generated image of Black women that emerged in the 1930s and 1940s always portrayed Sapphire as obstinate, domineering, and contemptuous of Black men. Black men were depicted as oppressed, but they also usually do not appear to take Sapphire seriously—much to their detriment.

Sapphire is an image rooted in antifemale ideology and imagination. Mary Young argues that when the numerous negative connotations of blackness is joined with women, "the most pernicious and demonic images" emerge.[7] Young further argues that the image of Sapphire not only denigrates Black women, but that this negative image of Black women has been used by other groups of women to also enhance their own image. Young points to White women who can claim greater purity and innocence in relation to Black women. In addition, Young suggests that Black men can use the alleged wickedness of Black women to justify abuse—emotional, physical, spiritual.

Barbara Smith notes that Sapphire appears quasi-masculine in comparison to the ultrafeminine White woman because Sapphire is strong and independent.[8] Sapphire is a dangerous woman because she is not devoted to Whites and cannot be controlled by men. She does not live in the White world as the trustworthy loyal Mammy. In fact, she does not relate to Whites at all if she so chooses. Her relationships are primarily Black and her concerns are found solely within the Black community in which she resides. Smith points out that some Black male writers such as Eldridge Cleaver accepted this White-created myth and added their own embellishments to it. Cleaver describes Black women as "full of steel, granite-hard and resisting, not soft and submissive like a white woman."[9]

This image of the bitter, hostile, cold, and domineering Black women who is in-charge is dangerous for the White imagination. Whites had no "safe" place to put a Black woman who cared for her family, who had ideas and could articulate them, who did not relate to White culture—by choice, and who was fiercely protective of her family—keeping everyone (men included) in line, fed, and cared for if that is what the situation demanded. This kind of Black woman was impossible for the White imagination to grasp or conjure. She is fully human, and as such, she had to be demonized to fit the worlds of blackness the White imagination sought to create. Ultimately, Sapphire is threatening to authority/hegemony.

One final thing about Sapphire—she is *always* in control of herself when her hands are on her hips and she is practicing the fine art of being loud-mouthed. Her rage is precise and her speech is like chicory coffee—strong, black, and with a bite. These are the characteristics that I contend are needed to untangle and demystify the intractability of racism. Being polite (dispassionate) about it has not worked.

Practical Sapphire

Geneticists calculate that there is an average genetic variation of 5 percent between racial groups. This leaves 95 percent of variation that occurs within racial groups—a stunning figure given how much of what we call race is really about color. The translation of this is that genetic variations *within* any racial group as we now define them can be nearly as great as the differences *between* specific racial groups. Every population is highly variable. Phenotypical signs such as skin color, genetic features do not absolutely define a population and distinguish it from another.

We tend to use race and talk about race, but we very rarely stop to think about what is it that we are talking about when we use the word "race." What images are being conjured up consciously and unconsciously? How do those images write themselves large across the academic, theoethical, economic, political, and social landscapes? How do these images situate themselves, if not simply plop themselves down, in the life of religious communities? So much of what we have come to understand as race was set before we had a clear understanding of genetics, and now that our knowledge has increased in this regard, we are caught with our old categories of skin color (the primary one), the texture and color of hair, the color of eyes, the shape of our noses, the size of our lips as the markers for race. We practice a highly selective process of ranking our biological differences in an enormously nuanced and decidedly unscientific system that ignores the fact that color is the least rigorous way to determine race.

Steven Fenton notes that race has been described as social science's phlogiston—a substance invented in the minds of scientists before a proven understanding of combustion.[10] The error of race is that it is designed to mark discrete divisions of human beings based on visible characteristics. Technically speaking, a race is a population that differs from others in the incidence of certain hereditary traits such as color of skin, texture of hair, facial features, stature, shape of head, on and on. This has driven much of what we perceive as race for the better part of the nineteenth century and all of the twentieth and twenty-first centuries. Somehow, race has come to be seen as the natural biological grouping of humans and has served as a key measure of "civilization."

Fenton also provides an intriguing distinction between ethnicity and racism. According to Fenton, ethnicity is the way in which social and cultural differences, language, and ancestry unite as a dimension of social action and social organization and form a system of classification that is socially replicated.[11] For him, the "cultural stuff" of ethnicity is grounded in social relationships that are features of daily practices. Racism is an array of ideas that classify different races and see them as fundamentally different and unequal. Ethnicity, then, refers to the mobilization of ethnic ties and the social significance of ancestry, language, and culture, whereas racism is the reproduction of a racialized system of equality.

Thus for Fenton, racialization is the social process that confers social significance on our biological differences that are social markers that are then enforced through oppressive measures.[12] Interestingly, Fenton argues that given the problems he identifies with the (mis)use and conceptualization of race, "ethnic" is a better generic term from which ideas about race can be taken as a subset. He goes on to state that an ideology of dominance that supports an ethnic elite can use language, genetically transmitted traits (racism), or culture.

Fenton submits that "black" as a category became a social marker of primary significance and the foundation for an entire social structure based on the Black-White binary divide.[13] This makes Sapphire put her hands on her hips and thrust out her jaw; we simply cannot ignore—however ill conceived the notion of race has been and still remains—the impact of the ways in which we use coloredness to mark it.

However, Fenton's argument fails to recognize that changing (or reducing) racial identities to ethnic ones does not reckon the intractability of color caste that is foundational to our understandings of and reactions to race.[14] I argue that racialization is more focused than this. In the United States, it confers social significance to coloredness to an inordinate degree. In our fascination/fixation on coloredness, we have developed a thoroughgoing yet often unconscious color caste system based on degrees of darkness and lightness.[15] Far too often our initial response to one another is built from these color cues we have inherited through history, ideology, and memory. This is part of the harrowing impact of the fantastic hegemonic imagination. I find the conceptual work of Michael Omi and Howard Winant more helpful and ultimately more precise in addressing race and racism in the United States.[16] In summary, they argue that race is not an essence, something to be fixed, or concrete and objective. Rather, race is unstable and decentered. It is a complicated and interstructured set of social meanings that are always being transformed by political struggle. They call this process racial formation. The functionality of this understanding of race is that it recognizes the world and our social structures as processes of historical and social transformation. It enables us to explore the dynamic of myth, memory, and history with the element of imagination added to this dynamic—often as the spark that fuels racialized fires.

When yoked with coloredness as a fulcrum, myth, memory, history, and imagination expose race as a phenomenon that, as Omni and Winant and others suggest, is always in formation.[17] This provides an excellent window into the way in which coloredness is a racial construction. More importantly, it does not allow coloredness to be a phenomenon restricted to darker skinned peoples but extends it to lighter skinned ones as well. In short, whiteness, blackness, brownness, redness, goldenness are *all* historically located, adaptive, and conditional.

Fenton is right, however—race is not a natural division. However, understanding race as racial formation (as a historical process of ongoing transformation) or as relational unpacks race by recognizing that it gets most of its power from appearing to be a natural or biological phenomenon or a coherent social category.[18] For example, Martha Mahoney points out that for Whites, residential segregation helps give race a natural appearance.[19] Good neighborhoods are equated with whiteness and Black neighborhoods are equated with joblessness. Mahoney further argues that the ways in which we understand and then live out blackness and whiteness is that whiteness is dominant and blackness is the Other. To underscore this, she notes that whiteness is most often associated with being employable and blackness with unemployable.

Mahoney is helpful, but I want to push this exploration beyond a simple (or not so simple) black-white binary divide. This antagonistic dualism does not help us address the intractability of racism because it tempts us to continue to use hackneyed moral and theoretical traps that allow culture to be the convenient escape hatch to avoid looking at the way in which *coloredness* cultivates the social construction of race. Turning on a black-white primary axis obscures the ways in which whiteness, as a racial construction, functions as privilege and power on national and global stages. Simply put, *whiteness is a concept and a reality that reveals and explains the racial interests of Whites and links them collectively to a position of racial dominance.*

Obstinate Sapphire

It is important to keep in mind that the contemporary understanding of race is not the historical one. Colette Guillaumin notes that early definitions were "family" or "family relationship."[20] Further, Guillaumin points out that race was never applied to important dynasties such as the Bourbons or the Kingdom of David, nor was it applied to large groups of people with no legal link of kinship between them. Eventually the notion of race shifted from legally circumscribed, noble families to wider social groups that used common physical traits to mark the differences in races. Guillaumin states that the shift from surname to skin color is significant as the contemporary understanding of race involved legal, anatomical, and linguistic classifications.[21]

Echoing Fenton, Mahoney, Omi and Winant, and others, Guillaumin points out that race is not a "spontaneously given product of perception and experience." She succinctly sums up the various arguments I have drawn from thus far:

> [Race] is an idea built up slowly from elements which might equally well be physical traits as social customs, linguistic peculiarities as legal institutions, lumped together and homogenized according to the precept that they must ultimately all be biological phenomena.[22]

She underscores a key point to reiterate: race is not natural, biological, or psychological—but it does exist. What Morrison points out so well is the bitter irony among those who have benefited in varying degrees by orchestrating the social construction of race, these are people who are now turning away from their own handiwork.

It is more than coincidental that this comes at the precise time when those in literary and cultural studies and critical race theory, those who are developing more sophisticated and rigorous analyses of race, have thrown back the covers to expose the ways in which *whiteness* is a social construction and it functions largely unaware of its power or privilege in racialized societies such as the United States. White power and privilege translates directly into forms of social organization that shape daily life. Residential, social, and educational segregation have moved from *de jure* (by law) to *de facto* (existing) segregation. Housing patterns, home loan lending policies, educational systems, affordability and accessibility to health care, policing policies, availability and accessibility to public transportation and decisions about how it will be plotted out on city grids, all point to the myriad ways in which we continue to be a compilation of segregated societies in the United States.

It is cabalistic to argue with any level of sophistication or accuracy that a category that is used to organize entire states such as the Third Reich or South Africa and that is a part of our legal structures does not exist. As a fixed immutable category—no, race does not exist. As a relational process of shifting boundaries and social meanings constantly engaged in political struggles—yes, race does exist.

When lodged within the U. S. cultural and sociopolitical milieu over time, a more nuanced and articulate consideration of race is much more advantageous in understanding racism as a structural evil. The fantastic hegemonic imagination functions in U.S. culture in such a way that we, as its agents and victims, respond to race as if it is about Black, White, and other ethnic groups without regard to the unique isness that marks us as sociocultural beings. Further, by considering the ways in which coloredness is largely uninterrogated in our theoethical musings, we allow more productive space for examining the social patternings of daily life that reinforce and sustain racism.

Overwhelmingly, Christian ethical theories have not addressed race and racism. Until the 2004 edited volume by Jennifer Harvey, Karin A. Case, and Robin Hawley Gorsline, *Disrupting White Supremacy From Within: White People on What We Need to Do*, little was written in the discipline of Christian ethics by White ethicists since Joseph C. Hough's *Black Power and White Protestants: A Christian Response to the New Negro Pluralism* in 1968.[23] Two important books that fill in this period are James N. Poling's *Deliver Us From Evil: Resisting Racial and Gender Oppression* (1996) and Mary Elizabeth Hobgood's *Dismantling Privilege: An Ethics of Accountability* (2000). The more recent date of both of these is telling in a period that had many books on environmental ethics, feminist ethics, and postmodern ethics—to name a few.

It is not surprising, then, that an underexamined dynamic found within racism—whiteness as a social construction—has received little attention. Ruth Frankenberg and Alastair Bonnett provide important insights at this juncture. Frankenberg notes that "white" is as much an economic and political category sustained over time by changing sets of exclusionary practices that are legislative and customary.[24] The term "White" arose as a designation for European explorers, traders and settlers as they came into contact with Africans and indigenous peoples.[25] However, Bonnett points out that the ubiquitous contemporary use of "white" to refer to Europeans and their descendants does not appear as a firmly established category until the twentieth century.[26] Once established, however, White and European are used interchangeably in the majority of race theories that appear in English.

For Frankenberg, racist discourse often manufactures a hypervisibility of Blacks and a relative invisibility of Asians, Native Americans, and Latino/as. Importantly, Frankenberg also points out that racial naming is a partial product of the collective struggle of communities to claim or rearticulate their identities. The reification of whiteness, however, has licensed a towering obfuscation by those of European descent—imagining one's identity as stable and immutable. This has enabled many White folks to remain unengaged with their own socialization process that is ongoing and has tempted many into ahistorical mindsets afloat in a sea of illusions springing from materially ungrounded imagination that has and can move swiftly from stereotype to structural oppression.

Frankenberg describes three intertwined shifts within the U.S. context concerning our understanding of racial formation.[27] The first and most pervasive shift is that of essentialist racism that emphasizes hierarchical biological inequalities. In this phase, race as we know it emerged in the late eighteenth to early nineteenth centuries. The notion that a group of people were "white" did not imply that they belonged to a discrete biological entity with a set of immutable attributes. The most common meaning referred to skin color. One example of this phase can be found in the 1989 *Oxford English Dictionary* (OED) that offers examples of the use of white: "whiteness or fairness of complexion." This harkens to the earlier thirteenth-century use of whiteness.

The first usage of "white" as an ethnicity cited by the OED that is not applied directly to a non-European group is by the English cleric C. Nesse in 1680 where he makes a distinction between "the White Line, (the Posterity of Seth)" and the "Black Line (the Cursed brood of Cain)."[28] This line of thinking that eventually associated whiteness with an amoral lineage was strengthened with the intellectual conflation of "white," "Europe," and "Christendom," a line of thought that developed from the late medieval period and has carried forward.[29]

The rise of the late eighteenth-century pseudosciences added fuel to the flame. Using head size and shape, positioning and size of the nose, angles, and "the gaze," these pseudosciences elevated Europeans over the rest of the world.[30] It was at this point, that any multiracial use of "white" was lost in the United States. Our broad understanding of who is White includes those who have pale or olive skin, straight or wavy hair, straight noses, thin lips, and eyes without the epicanthic folds. This list is problematic. In addition to stereotyping, it does not take into account the vast number of lighter-skinned people who have kinky hair (the Americas), dark-skinned people with straight hair (Indians), dark skinned people with wavy blond hair, flattish round noses, and full lips (Native Australians).

Another cadaverous aspect of essentialist racism is the rise of White supremacy in the United States. It served as a unifying theme for the defeated Confederacy and ultimately destroyed the legal transformation of the entire political system initiated in the Reconstruction era. Such terms as "miscegenation" were coined to raise the specter of race mixing and the mongrelization of the United States.[31] Once in power, deposed Southern politicians used legal and extralegal (such as the Ku Klux Klan) terrorism to brutally repress newly freed Blacks.

In essentialist racism, the impact of White supremacy whiteness extends beyond Black folk. Kathleen Neal Cleaver points to a classic appropriation of whiteness in the case of Irish immigration.[32] The Irish were viewed as an inferior race—often being called names reserved for Black people: bestial, simian, savage, wild. They were considered niggers turned inside out. Despite a centuries-long hatred of the British, the social and political forces within the United States forced many Irish immigrants to appropriate whiteness as a buffer to a society that held them in contempt.

The second shift springs from the assertion that we are all the same under the skin and that failures to live into this sameness and achieve it is the fault of colored peoples. Examples of this phase include much of the rhetoric justifying the gutting of the social welfare system discussed in greater detail in chapter 5. The name of the act alone, The Personal Responsibility and Work Opportunity Act of 1996, sends a clear message—if you are poor (read Black or Latina) it is *always* your fault and you must take responsibility for finding work to support your child. A second example of this phase are the declamations against affirmative action and multiculturalism discussed in chapter 2.

A third shift appeals to difference but, unlike essentialist racism, it marks the varying autonomy of cultures, values, and aesthetics. This is the most recent of shifts and is a methodological assumption of my appeal to uninterrogated coloredness. Within this phase, the inequities of the social structure are brought into the theoretical and sociopolitical mix. Rather than rest on autonomous individualism, the theorists and activists in this phase recognize the deep interplay between self, society, and culture in creating and maintaining our understandings of race and racism.

In this shift, whiteness as part of uninterrogated coloredness is a thoroughgoing evasion of color. It assumes that there is no richness within the worlds of White folks and proclaims a vanilla (as in color, not spice) neutral existence where whiteness, ultimately, is the norm. The enduring impact of essentialism racism is felt within this third shift each time race is used as the primer for racial inequality. Intentional, explicit racial discrimination becomes the only form of racism easily recognized by most Whites.[33] The structural dimensions of racism and the racially structured political and economic inequalities that shape our moral and social order elude their (our) grasp.

Uninterrogated coloredness, also functioning, in part, as the myth of whiteness in the world of the fantastic hegemonic imagination, views whiteness as an immutable condition that carries with it clear and distinct moral attributes: being racist, not experiencing racism, being an oppressor, not experiencing oppression, silencing, not being silenced.[34] Darker-skinned peoples are defined in relation to this myth as "non-whites" who are acted upon by Whites and have found their own identity through their resistance to White supremacy. Aside from it being problematic for any group to find its identity through "non-ness," uninterrogated whiteness ignores the plurality within Whiteness.

Like race, whiteness is not an eternal or immutable category—it is susceptible to the same kinds of transformation within political struggle over time as race itself is. Whiteness is not static or fixed, and acknowledging the ways in which we have treated whiteness as static, ahistorical, and objective helps to break open its uninterrogatedness. As Bonnett points out so well, racial terms have contested histories, however whiteness tends to be excluded from the list of acceptable and debatable racial nouns.[35]

Bonnett offers an important cautionary tale at this point: the slippery slope of White confession. Although the aim of White confession is to enable if not provoke White folks into realizing and admitting their own whiteness, it can quickly degenerate into a moralizing altruistic end game in which Whites are characterized, first, by their moral failings and, second, by a fixed site from which to exercise the "ultimate" resistance to racism. White resistance to White supremacy is weirdly elevated to a higher ethical and moral terrain. Yet another form of supremacy emerges—one that does not recognize the level playing field of coloredness when engaging racism—and in failing to recognize it, we slip into paternalistic patterns that always belie too-quick moves of confession.

The shifting and multiple boundaries of whiteness echo the changeability of race. Like White confession, attempts at colorblindness also fall far short of recognizing the dynamic nature of race itself. Frankenberg aptly notes that colorblindness exemplifies "the polite language of racism."[36] Avoiding the messiness and complexity of race in the quest for a color-blind stance only serves to make palatable a bootlicking selective engagement with our genuine differences—differences that are assumed to be divisive rather than enriching. In reality, much of the discourse on colorblindness actually brackets and ignores our coloredness. When taken to the extreme, it assumes a noncolored self who, when disrobed, is actually whiteness redux.

Tackling the hegemonic imagination means exploring key questions lodged within Morrison's "How?" How can the enormous power of uninterrogated coloredness be acknowledged and confronted? More importantly, once this process is set in motion, how can it be eradicated and destroyed? The obstinate nature of Sapphire will not let these questions drift into ethereal theories or be absorbed into liberal humanist essentialist constructs. Sapphire, with hands firmly on her hips and her mouth running full steam, will not settle for muted or mumbled theories or strategies that do little more than provide new layers of protective clothing for racism. Obscuring the reality of race that glides so easily from the interior world of the fantastic hegemonic imagination is one thing Miss Sapphire will not abide.

Strong-Willed Sapphire

Essentialist racism, White confession, colorblindness, and racially structured political and economic inequalities operate in conscious and unconscious modes. Only a Sapphire who stands up to the withering onslaught of real, feigned, or inadequate attempts to avoid racism and it roots can counter such an unrelenting juggernaut. Aida Hurtado, echoing Morrison, explains that silence and evasion have historically ruled literary discourse on race.[37] This has extended far beyond literary discourse into theoethical discourse among others. Exploring yet another track, Hurtado points out that ignoring race allows Whites to assume that they are *just* like other colored people— they share profession, gender, geographic residence, family structure, artistic difference. These may all be true and there may be other points of commonality as well. However, we must still reckon with the relational dynamics of race, the active transformation found in process-historicity-politics, and those attendant social interactions that maintain a racialized social order that includes other processes such as social class and gender to maintain and aid its sustenance.[38]

The recent rise of discourse on multiculturalism points to the difficulties we will have when addressing race and racism. Albert Spears notes the way in which multiracialism can conflate race and culture.[39] Spears calls the "propagandizing of multiracialism" as fitting neatly with the historical process of promoting darker-skinned colored peoples to whiteness. For Spears, this is a new divide-and-conquer strategy in which White ruling elites create smaller blocks of colored peoples while attempting to keep the White block as large as possible.

As compelling as Spears' argument may be, Farai Chideya points out that the U.S. culture is experiencing a massive generation gap when it comes to race and racism.[40] She notes that the United States (and by extension many theorists) is led by baby boomers and the people in the generations that came before them. These people (such as many noted ethicists and theologians) came of age before and during the Civil Rights era. Chideya's research with youth in their teens and twenties points to another reality within contemporary life: these folk see firsthand evidence in their schools and neighborhoods of the emerging multiracialism in U.S. society. The youth in Chideya's study do not understand or experience race on a black-white axis and she notes that the diversity that many youth represent is viewed as suspect by many in older generations.

The point-counterpoint provided by Spears and Chideya is instructive in illustrating the way in which the fantastic hegemonic imagination creates its own "truth." A simple reliance on race along a dualistic axis does not describe the reality of who we have become and where we are going as a nation regarding race. An unwillingness to address the relational character of race detracts from our ability to provide moral moorings for how to navigate and eradicate racism. One strategic option to combat the fantastic hegemonic at this turn is to tarry more with how we have constructed coloredness in this country and, more specifically, how whiteness has been constructed and how it is maintained as a largely uninterrogated phenomenon of alleged neutrality, or worse of being the norm.

Loud-Mouthed Sapphire

Adrienne Davis states that darker-skinned racial groups form their identity around shared cultural norms, common histories of immigration, mythologized homelands, or racial oppression.[41] She goes on to note that White American identity that does not have Latina/o roots appears to be formed solely around the experience of being not-Black, not-Asian, not-Latino/a, not-Native American. Further, for Davis, White Americans do not appear to have a sense of racial identity that is not linked to ethnicity or class unless they are juxtaposing themselves against darker-skinned races. Ultimately, the social and legal construction of darker-colored identities is critical to the maintenance of White identity.

If Davis is correct, then all of us are in trouble. As I have argued earlier, constructing an identity around what we are not is unhealthy and supremely deadly on economic, sociopolitical, and theological levels. Addressing racism as a structural evil means recognizing that we must be able to construct our identity, our selves, in such a way that we integrate the lives and histories of different peoples and cultures. Carl Anthony notes that we have an official story in this country that tells us and the world who we are and what we view as important. Anthony then notes that "this story is like refined sugar. It's not a real story about real people. It's been packaged and processed beyond recognition."[42]

For Anthony, the colonial expansion of Europe into the Americas brought with it a whiteness that unified Europeans who would not have been united if they had remained in Europe. Part of this process included a cultivated contempt for Blacks and indigenous peoples. Anthony states that whiteness is "an unmarked, unnamed status, a structured invisibility that lends itself to false, universalizing claims that reduce other people to marginality simply by naming them as different races."[43] Anthony argues for the creation of a multicultural self that is formed from the deconstruction of the idea of whiteness coupled with meeting one another as equals.

Anthony is a bit ahead of the process. Whiteness has not been adequately recognized or defined—this must be the first step. In many ways, whiteness has been made an abstraction—it has been distanced from our immediate concrete material experience. We see it, we experience it, but we cannot define it or codify it like we do so easily with darker-skinned peoples. As abstractions, whiteness and White supremacy are amorphously transcendent in the case of the former and intractable in the case of the latter. To fight either is to take on massive self-projections that are often unconscious and unacknowledged. These projections are abstractions—neatly if not completely disassociated from the history of strife, death, and annihilation that White supremacy and uninterrogated whiteness have left as their gruesome legacies.

The vexing reality of uninterrogated coloredness with a particular focus on whiteness within it is that Whites benefit from being White whether or not they, as individuals, hold supremacist notions or actions. This makes the individualists among us squirm, but attacking racism at its roots is not an exercise in comfort and ease for it is a direct encounter with the fantastic hegemonic imagination in one if its most entrenched homes.

Ultimately, there is no monolithic human identity. It does not exist and I doubt that it ever will or should. To ring ourselves around a deadly May pole of uninterrogated coloredness is to dance, literally, with the devil. We fool ourselves if we believe that continuing to obscure whiteness eradicates it or erases its history and deadly effects. Whiteness has been and continues to be strategically maintained through trumpeting its colorlessness. The values, belief systems, privileges, histories, experiences of White folks is marked as normal—all else is the exception to it. This gigantic superego is deadly for it either fails to see the work it does, obscures its domination through evocations of neutrality and objectivity, or remains sublimely indifferent to the devastation it inflicts as long as the status quo is maintained and we do not have to do the tough work of looking at ourselves and doing our first works over. In a weird and warped way, uninterrogated whiteness uses its own comfort level as the measuring stick for how other people should exist. If we were dealing with perfection or divinity this would not be problematic.

Cheryl Harris notes that not only is whiteness constructed as a race, but also as race privilege.[44] She argues that whiteness as racialized privilege is embraced in legal doctrine as objective fact and legitimated by science. For Harris, this rests on the false assumption that the racial categories used in previous generations were accurate and that their categories translate into the present without revision or nuance. In short, there is such a thing as racial purity—no ideologies need apply.

Unfortunately ideologies abound and I argue that whiteness is a concept that reveals and explains the racial interests of White folks. Whiteness links Whites to a position of racial dominance and it is a political color that binds disaffected or disempowered Whites to elite Whites in defending what is termed "the American way of life," a term that in reality represents White culture and privilege. When this alliance is achieved, whiteness is not a race but a unique thing. There is, then, no need to place it under the social studies and policy lens as we do "genuine" races—Asian, Black, Latina/o, Native American. The work of making whiteness is complete when it becomes a special ideological and social place apart from race, because we have crippled our ability to understand whiteness as part of the coloredness that is part of race in a highly racialized (as well as sexualized and classist and so forth) society.

Part of maintaining whiteness as an abstraction involves cluttering our common discourse with ostensibly race-neutral words, actions, or policies. When we begin to interrogate coloredness, the terms or subjects of the debate in political campaigns, the placement or funding of highway projects, the placement of waste sites, the criteria for determining access to home financing, the delivery of health care—all these and more are rescrutinized. Often times, they will be found wanting. Many of us across the color spectrum would like to engage in genuine movements of reconciliation and liberation, but we must also remember that good intentions do not necessarily breed good strategies. This is particularly true if we fail to cross-examine our histories and our experiences.

The slippery slope over which we are catapulting downward keeps us from coming to terms with the fact that whiteness, like all other forms of coloredness, is a complicated and interstructured set of social meanings that is always being transformed by political struggle—it is as intricate a part of racial formation as is blackness, redness, and goldenness. Whiteness is the invisible thing that *is* there. Perhaps bell hooks is on to something when she notes that since most Whites do not have to "see" Blacks (thus making them invisible), they can therefore imagine that they are invisible to Blacks as well.[45] This helps explain, in part, why whiteness functions as an abstraction on a conscious and unconscious level. As a creation of the hegemonic imagination, it also is and can be a strategy of subterfuge and suppression that continues feasting on a diet of domination, diminishment, and disavowal. This, quite frankly, sucks.

Emasculating Sapphire

Reminder: Sapphire is also a precious stone.

The collective experience of Black women, like the experience of any subjugated group, can inform and challenge the dominant worldview. For a Black woman to forget her blackness is to deny a rich heritage that crosses the continent of Africa, moves in the waters of the Caribbean, touches the shores of South America, and is vibrant in the rhythms of Alice Coltrane, Miriam Makeba, Marian Anderson, and Sweet Honey in the Rock. She loses part of her very soul if she turns away from Zora Neale Hurston, Alice Walker, or Phillis Wheatley. African American women must continue to draw from the deep well of the lives of Fannie Lou Hamer, Cora Lee Johnson, and Septima Clark.

However, because we exist in a living community, care must be taken to neither idealize nor romanticize Black women. An even greater danger is in following the lead of abstract whiteness and in confusing collective with monolithic. The crux of the matter is to increase our knowledge of our history and the myriad ways folk have done analysis, responded to circumstance, visioned a future, and also failed to do so. Miss Sapphire reminds us that we can do this when we recognize that all of us owe much of our being to a community of communities within the larger cultural landscape and its society.

Sapphire does not seek to assign blame, rather she calls us to a radical account with one another within community and with other communities in the U.S. cultural landscape as well as globally. It is hard work to listen to histories and traditions that have not been a part of dominant discourse. There are those (within and without the Black community) who respond to such revelations with guilt, shame, and anger. Rather than explore the emotion of the response, too often the rational impulse takes over, creating mincing yet deadly abstractions that result in refusing the invitation to justice and liberatory resistance.

The response may be one of feeling blamed or held responsible for the sins of the forbearers and/or to deny contemporary complicity with practices of injustice. Sapphire makes the appeal to history and tradition and asks, how can an authentic ethic of justice be separated from where we have been and who we have been to one another? The contemporary scene did not emerge from a vacuum; it evolved historically and is immanently contextual. That context has its moments of brilliance and its seasons of mourning. We cannot divorce ourselves from the totality of our history and expect even a glimmer of efficacious justice or a vital community that crafts wholeness for its members.

Therefore, Sapphire urges us to be relentless in our analysis and inclusive in our recovery of history and sociopolitical analysis when prying open and interrogating the previously uninterrogated. Sapphire cannot be content with a justice that addresses only a particular person or group's wholeness. A womanist social ethic that springs from Sapphire's steel-edged tongue must embrace all segments of society if it is to be thorough and rigorous and continue to push us into a critical dialogue that enlarges the boundaries of our humanness. Class, gender, and race analyses are crucial. But we need to challenge the ageism (of both the young and the seasoned), the homophobia and the heterosexism, the myriad issues around accessibility, the U.S. color caste system, and the

Pandora's box around issues of beauty. The work of womanist ethics that is guided by Sapphire is not only eradicating a White cultural, political, and theological hegemony that names darkness less than, it is also exposing, examining, and eradicating the ways that Black folks help that system find *new* ways to deem us children of a lesser God.

There are many challenges in addressing the uninterrogated coloredness that comes from the fantastic hegemonic imagination. However, Sapphire never left the situation hanging on the problems or resting with the challenges. Consider these following moral benchmarks as a template for a more rigorous theoethical analysis of race and racism.

First, take up the challenges that racism and uninterrogated coloredness present despite the fact that it will hurt. It might cause some guilt. However, you need to understand that guilt, in this case, is a strategy that reifies oppression. Guilt does not help you if you live your life in its meandering miasma. To counter this, a key goal is building a community in which you are willing to risk. This takes time, energy, and honesty. It also means learning to stop providing defense strategies and rationales before you have come to know and appreciate our collective stories. You often tend to think that this will always be gruesome work— perhaps you focus too much on the Fall. Rather, in facing the pain and the guilt, you will learn that our collective story is far richer than the pathetic master narratives you tend to cling to. Our richness is found in our commonalities *and* in our diversities—the Creation may be a more apt and profound theological resource.

Second, you must work together in the time that you have to put into place new patterns of understanding and analysis. These patterns will require a lifetime of practice beyond the classroom or our scholarly careers. One way to begin this new work is to find at least one thing you can commit to, one that will be a lifelong commitment to antiracist behavior, thought, and ideology and then to do it every day—perfectly and imperfectly. The point is not success. The objective is commitment and striving for consistency.

Third, you must stop collapsing race into coloredness that can beget an essentialist swamp that blinds us from seeing the ways in which race and racism are parts of the larger web of oppression. This is obvious from what I have argued thus far in this chapter. However, like those passages and ideas that appear in Christian scripture more than once, if it is important it bears repeating.

Fourth, you must take an uncompromising look at our social locations and the ways in which you are a socially constructed being. This is in response to the rampant individualism that marks contemporary

U.S. life where you often hear sentences that include "I am not personally . . . ." You or I may not be personally doing anything, but we are socially doing a great deal. None of us are in the world all by ourselves.

Fifth, you must realize and accept that none of us can do this work alone and none is an unsurpassable expert on race and racism. You are both victim and perpetrator—it is largely a matter of where you are standing and whom you are standing in relation to as you move into the varieties of social landscapes in the United States and in global cultures. This makes us all, ultimately, experts on race. The question is will you acknowledge how much you know and do not know about race—consciously and unconsciously—and then work from that place? This means recognizing that the unconscious levels of racial discourses in which we all participate are most deadly and signal the ways in which collapsing race into coloredness is one of the most incredibly inept, destructive and, seductive uses of power as a tool of domination and subordination that you have in ethical reflection.

Sixth, as individuals, you must be willing to be changed, grow, admit *your* participation and *your* resistance to race and racing in the communities of the classroom, the church, the society, the academy, the city. It is far too easy for you to project onto others that which you do not work on within yourself. The realities that shape an uninterrogated coloredness depend on such projections to help maintain the status quo. To broaden ourselves as people we must be willing to look within ourselves as we recognize that we are also social beings in communities of communities.

Finally, you must give yourself permission to be tired and weary, besides, you must also find ways of renewal so that you can be a creative and healthy participant in dismantling oppressions. Burned out, bitter people do not help bring in justice very often and they are of little help in any search for [T]ruth.

Given all the locust activity that womanists are often charged with committing, it is hard work doing the actual toil we do in fact do in facing down the fantastic hegemonic imagination. Nevertheless, even in the face of the gross intractability of willful oblivion in uninterrogated coloredness in high camp drag, I still hold on to a great hope that I will be old when I die. For dying of old age for a Black woman in my generation who spends a good deal of her life awash in not only uninterrogated coloredness, but also in uninterrogated gender, sexuality, aging, class, and more. . . For someone like me, living a long and good life is the ultimate act of defiance and resistance. It is, in fact, living Sapphire large.

Legends Are Memories Greater than Memories: Black Reparations in the United States as Subtext to Christian Triumphalism and Empire

I. The islands from Charleston, south, the abandoned rice fields along the rivers for thirty miles back from the sea, and the country bordering the St. Johns river, Florida, are reserved and set apart for the settlement of the negroes now made free by the acts of war and the proclamation of the President of the United States.

II. Whenever three respectable negroes, heads of families, shall desire to settle on land, and shall have selected for that purpose an island or a locality clearly defined, within the limits above designated, the Inspector of Settlements and Plantations will himself, or by such subordinate officer as he may appoint, give them a license to settle such island or district, and afford them such assistance as he can to enable them to establish a peaceable agricultural settlement. The three parties named will subdivide the land, under the supervision of the Inspector, among themselves and such others as may choose to settle near them, so that each family shall have a plot of not more than (40) forty acres of tillable ground, and when it borders on some water channel, with not more than 800 feet water front, in the possession of which land the military authorities will afford them protection, until such time as they can protect themselves, or until Congress shall regulate their title. The Quartermaster may, on the requisition of the Inspector of Settlements and Plantations, place at the disposal of the Inspector, one or more of the captured steamers, to ply between the settlements and one or more of the commercial points heretofore named in orders, to afford the settlers the opportunity to supply their necessary wants, and to sell the products of their land and labor.[1]

—Order by the commander of the military division of Mississippi on January 16, 1865. Special Field Orders, No. 15.

I begin with part of the actual text of the special field orders because I find many things about it noteworthy. First, the phrase "and a mule" is no where to be found—not in sections 1 and 3 above, not in sections 2, 4, 5, or 6 that are more concerned about loyalty to the Union and military service and defense. Second, this was a decidedly un-universal field order. The boundaries are clear: islands from Charleston, south, the abandoned rice fields along the rivers for thirty miles back from the sea, and the country bordering the St. Johns River, Florida, in other words, the sea islands on the coast of South Carolina and Georgia (These included Edisto, Hilton Head, Port Royal, St. Helena, and many other smaller islands that had been under Union control since 1861.)

The limits of the field order are surprising. Throughout my life I have heard and spoken versions of "Where is my 40 acres and a mule?" I thought—as, I suspect, many of us did—that these 40 acres could be anywhere in the United States. I had no idea that Beulah Land was such a small area of possibilities given the geographical vastness of this country. This new knowledge has caused me to rethink the context of a discussion of reparations for Black folks in the United States.

Part of this context begins in April 1861 when the Civil War began with the Confederate attack on Fort Sumter, South Carolina, and President Lincoln issuing the proclamation that led the troops to put down the rebellion. In May 1862, General David Hunter declared freedom for all slaves in South Carolina, Georgia, and Florida. However, President Lincoln issued a proclamation nullifying General Hunter's emancipation edict and urged Kentucky, Missouri, Maryland, and Delaware to embrace gradual, *compensated* emancipation.

In January 1863, Lincoln issued the Emancipation Proclamation that declared freedom for all slaves in the Confederate states *except*Tennessee, southern Louisiana, and parts of Virginia. In 1864, the Senate approved a constitutional amendment to abolish slavery in April, however in June, the House of Representatives failed to approve the constitutional amendment. In addition, in June, Congress made the salaries of black soldiers equal to that of white soldiers (from $10 a month to $13 a month). It also increased the salaries of all privates to $16 a month with corresponding increases for higher ranks. In November of that same year, Lincoln was reelected.

In January 1865, Sherman issued Field Order 15 and the House of Representatives approved the constitutional amendment to abolish slavery and sent it to the states for ratification. As Inspector of Settlements and Plantations, General Rufus Saxton was required to make the proper allotments and issue promissory titles as well as to defend them until Congress could confirm Sherman's Field Order. The army of Confederate General Robert E. Lee surrendered at the Appomattox Court House in Virginia in April, and later that month, Lincoln was assassinated and Vice President Andrew Johnson succeeded to the presidency. In December, the Thirteenth Amendment of the United States Constitution was ratified, an amendment that abolished slavery throughout the United States "[e]xcept as a punishment for crime whereof the party shall have been duly convicted."[2]

These events are only parts of the whole context, to be sure, but they signal that historically any conversation about reparations for Black folks in the United States stands on some terribly troubling ground—actually shifting sand. This causes me to seek a tangential course to set this discussion in a broader context and explore a theme ranging around as an abysmal sylph inhabiting the air around us but largely unseen: empire. Although many discussions about reparations do not include financial solutions as the sole answers, this does not remove us—as people drawing our breath in the largest imperial power in the world—from what holds this country in its place on the global scale. Versions of "can't we all just get along and move on" only speak to the ways in which we are suspect historians in this country. We only teach and learn, in most cases, what is pleasing to the myth of the city on the hill. There is measly attention given to who and what may be at the foot of that hill (or clinging to its side) or to the cost we pay to keep our houses on top of the mountain. If we do not factor these things into reparations talk, then any notions of fairness, justice, reconciliation, or any of their kin will stumble and fall before the massive juggernaut of turbo capitalism twined with a studied, oblivious amnesia.

A little reported fact in reparations demands our attention: General Sherman and Secretary of War Major-General Stanton met with twenty Black leaders just three days before issuing the Field Order. What is often unreported is that these twenty Black leaders were Black male ministers and church officers. Their ages ranged from twenty-six to seventy-two. Some were freeborn, some were freed by their masters and mistresses, some had bought their own freedom, and some were freed by the Union army. Yet, even here the mutterings of empire begin to manifest themselves. The minutes of the meeting contain some interesting details for those who were pastors: the size of the congregation, the race of the trustees, the value of the property, and whether or not the congregation owned the property. For those who had bought their freedom: the amount they paid for themselves was included.

After the first question to the men, one that asked if they understood Lincoln's 1863 proclamation to the rebellious states, was the question that asked if they understood what slavery and freedom meant in the proclamation. Their chosen representative, Brother Frazier, was clear.

> "Slavery is, receiving by *irresistible power* the work of another man, and not by his *consent*. The freedom, as I understand it, promised by the proclamation, is taking us from under the yoke of bondage, and placing us where we could reap the fruit of our own labor, take care of ourselves and assist the Government in maintaining our freedom."[3]

The next question asked if they thought they could take care of themselves and how they believed they could best assist the government in maintaining their freedom. Again, Brother Frazier was clear.

> "The way we can best take care of ourselves is to have land, and turn it and till it by our own labor—that is, by the labor of the women and children and old men; and we can soon maintain ourselves and have something to spare. And to assist the Government, the young men should enlist in the service of the Government, and serve in such manner as they may be wanted. (The Rebels told us that they piled them up and made batteries of them, and sold them to Cuba; but we don't believe that.) We want to be placed on land until we are able to buy it and make it our own."[4]

The fourth question asked them to "state in what manner you would rather live—whether scattered among the whites or in colonies by yourselves."[5] Again, Brother Frazier responds,

> "I would prefer to live by ourselves, for there is a prejudice against us in the South that will take years to get over; but I do not know that I can answer for my brethren."[6]

In a notation, it states "Mr. Lynch says he thinks they should not be separated, but live together. All the other persons present, being questioned one by one, answer that they agree with Brother Frazier."[7]

The fifth question asked, "Do you think that there is intelligence enough among the slaves of the South to maintain themselves under the Government of the United States and the equal protection of its laws, and maintain good and peaceable relations among yourselves and with your neighbors?"[8]

Answer: "I think there is sufficient intelligence among us to do so."[9]

None of the men disagreed with this assessment.

The effect of Field Order 15 was that an estimated 40,000 Black folk received land and regarded themselves the permanent residents and owners of over 549,000 acres of abandoned land if residing there for more than six months. W. E. B. Du Bois noted that the seizure of the land and its redistribution by government mandate, "further strengthened these ignorant people in the conviction that they were to have the lands of their late masters; and with the other reasons before stated, caused a great unwillingness on the part of the freemen to make any contracts whatever."[10] Taxes on the freedmen furnished most of the funds to the administration of the program. Saxton settled nearly 30,000 Blacks on the Sea Island and adjacent plantations. Of these, 17,000 were self-supporting within a year, and 12,000 to 13,000 were still receiving rations but understood that they were responsible for paying for them.[11]

The 1866 Freedman's Bureau Bill, including the provision that the president set aside lands for freedmen and loyal refugees in unoccupied land in the South in no more than forty-acre allotments, passed the Senate in January by a vote of 37–10. The House passed the bill in February. The details are important because it extended the power of the Freedmen's Bureau across the entire United States.

> [It] provided food and clothing for the destitute, a distribution of public lands among freedmen and white refugees in parcels not exceeding forty acres each at a nominal rent and with an eventual chance of purchasing. The land assigned by Sherman was to be held for three years and then, if restored, other lands secured by rent or purchase.[12]

On February 9, the Senate accepted the bill with minor changes, making this the first great measure that Reconstruction took to signal that southern slavery was definitely abolished by constitutional amendment. Additionally, a permanent Freedmen's Bureau assured government guardianship of Blacks with land and court protection.

Johnson vetoed the bill. Within one year, the lands returned to the White planters who had abandoned them. Du Bois recounts that when a brigadier general was sent to the Sea Islands to inform them that they would lose their land, an old woman on the periphery of the crowd began to sing the spiritual "Nobody Knows the Trouble I've Seen." The crowd joined her in swaying lament as the soldier wept.[13]

Although Johnson's decision was both ideological and political, Du Bois notes that there was also a severe economic downturn that was also factored into the decision. Yet, the economic seeds of these actions were sown before Johnson. What is often not reported in Lincoln Abrahamic myth is the fact that the coalition that won the 1860 election for Abraham Lincoln, rather than advocating for the rights of Blacks, stressed protecting free White labor against the competition from slavery in the West.

The Tragic Mulatta Stereotype as Legend

In response to this narrative, consider these counternarratives.

> One day, probably in the season of his coming death, he whispered: Sophie, bamboo flower, crutch of my old age, raindrop on my thirsty tongue. Oh Marie, my sweet madou syrup, *one must not answer all questions*.[14]

Later,

> In what I tell you, there's the almost true, the sometimes true, and the half true. That's what telling a life is like, braiding all of that like one plaits the white Indies currant's hair to make a hut. And the true true comes out of that braid. And Sophie, you can't be scared of lying if you want to know everything . . . [15]

Again,

> But legends are memories greater than memories.[16]

In response,

> So Idomenee would say: But what is memory?
>   It's the glue, it's the spirit, it's the sap and it stays.
> Without memories, no City, no Quarters, no Big Hutch.
>   How many memories? she would ask.
>   All the memories, he would answer. Even those the wind and the silences carry at night. You have to talk, tell, tell the stories, live the legends. That's why.[17]

These lines are from the notebook kept by Marie-Sophie Laborieux, the protagonist in the Martiniqan writer Patrick Chamoiseau's novel *Texaco*. Chamoiseau forces the hand of the fantastic hegemonic imagination as he chronicles the path to freedom of Martinique from colonial rule through the eyes of Marie-Sophie and her ancestors—slaves and former slaves. As I have discussed the power of history, memory, imagination, and image throughout; Chamoiseau tantalizes with the notion of legend—memories greater than memories. Memories, for Chamoiseau, are the glue, the spirit, the sap—and it stays. Here, Chamoiseau responds to the pessimism of Nora in a Francophile parry and thrust. Memory has not faded for Chamoiseau—it cannot. In memory, one has the true true through the braided plaits of the almost true, the sometimes true, and the half true. Chamoiseau captures in novel form an important subtext that runs throughout this book—we have existed in and on the almost true, sometimes true, and half true without looking for the true true. The true true is in *all* the memories, and not only in those that are remembered selectively or are imposed as history. Chamoiseau provides an island guide for understanding how "40 acres and a mule" and the Tragic Mulatta stereotype legends function as a mediating ethic in understanding empire in American face. Telling all of her story demands a rigorous commitment to understanding how a legend can function as truth or as stereotype. The Tragic Mulatta is the unabashed creation of the White imagination. Abolitionist Lydia Maria Child first brought her into print as Rosalie in the 1842 short story "The Quadroons" and again a year later as Rosa in the short story "Slavery's Pleasant Homes," both published in *The Liberty Bell*. The character of Rosa is more radical than Rosalie. In a departure from the more common stereotype of the Tragic Mulatta, Rosa loves a Black slave and they openly rebel against their master. Rosa is whipped to death for her rebellion—despite the fact that she is pregnant.

Nineteenth-century stories, novels, and plays on biracialism featured the Mulatta as a tragedy *for Blacks*. Generally, abolitionist writers such as Child, Elizabeth Livermore, and Dion Boucicault portray a pitiful creature bound by race and sex to tragic, hegemonic death. The Tragic Mulatta appears as the heroine in many abolitionist tracts as the light-skinned woman of mixed race. She is beautiful, virtuous, and possesses all the graces of White middle-class true womanhood. Ignorant of her mother's race and status, she is usually the daughter of an enslaved mother and slave-owning father. She believes she is White and free until her father's death reveals her real status and race. She is

formally enslaved and then deserted by her lover who is usually a
White man and then dies, tragically, a victim of the racial and sexual
dynamics of the peculiar institution. As exotic other, the Mulatta
underscores the conflation of color and gender in a socioeconomic system designed to produce a cheap labor pool. Historian Gary B. Nash
underscores this point well.

> Though skin color came to assume importance through generations of
> association with slavery, white colonists developed few qualms about
> intimate contact with black women. But raising the social status of
> those who labored at the bottom of society and who were defined as
> abysmally inferior was a matter of serious concern. It was resolved by
> insuring that the mulatto would not occupy a position midway between
> white and black. Any black blood classified a person as black; and to be
> black was to be a slave . . . . By prohibiting racial intermarriage, wink-
> ing at interracial sex, and defining all mixed offspring as black, white
> society found the ideal answer to its labor needs, its extracurricular and
> inadmissible sexual desires, its compulsion to maintain its culture pure-
> bred, and the problem of maintaining, at least in theory, absolute social
> control.[18]

The nearly white skin of the Mulatta is the image of the systemic racial
and sexual violence. However, an interesting divergence occurs between
White abolitionist novelists and Black novelists in how they understand
and bring the Mulatta to life. The Mulatta portrayed by White writers
is usually a barrel drum of pathologies: self-hatred, depression, alco-
holism, sexual perversion, and suicidal. This is more complex given that
these authors, such as Child, sought to elicit sympathy and outrage
against slavery and were ardent advocates of its eradication. As Child
constructed her (and later White authors followed), the Tragic Mulatta
was the representation of White women's sympathetic perception of the
commonalities between their own status and that of the slaves. Yet, as
we will see later in the creation of Topsy by Harriett Beecher Stowe, this
figure reinforces prejudice. In this case, color is indeed the basis because
her light skin attracts White readers' identification with her while her
Black heritage condemns her to misery.

For these writers, she is light enough to "pass" as White but doing
so leads to self-loathing and self-denial. She is despised or pitied by
Blacks and feared or hated by the very Whites from whom she seeks
acceptance and approval. As sociologist David Pilgrim notes, "[i]n a
race-based society, the tragic mulatto found peace only in death. She
evoked pity or scorn, not sympathy."[19]

Many Whites in the United States believed that Mulattas and Mulattoes were a debased race. Their "White blood" made them ambitious and power hungry. Their "Black blood" made them animalistic and savage. White writers such as Charles Carroll, author of *The Negro a Beast* (1900), did not hesitate in describing Black folks as apelike. For Carroll, Mulattoes and Mulattas were the offspring of what he described as "unnatural relationships." Carroll was not alone in his belief that they did not have "the right to live" because most of them were rapists and killers.[20]

In the twentieth century, the White image of the Mulatta is that of a selfish woman who gives up absolutely everything to live as a White person. The Mulatta character Peola in the 1934 movie *Imitation of Life* captures this self-annihilation: "Don't come for me. If you see me in the street, don't speak to me. From this moment on I'm White. I am not colored. You have to give me up."

In contrast to White authors, nineteenth-century Black writers such as William Wells Brown, Charles Chestnutt, and Nella Larsen developed Mulatta heroines who used their "betweenness" as a means of empowerment.[21] Unlike the Tragic Mulattas from the imagination of whiteness, the Mulatta who emerged from blackness did not have her biracialism as a marker of inevitable tragic death. Black writers captured more aptly the complexity of Mulattoes and Mulattas. They were a symbol of the systemic nature of racial and sexual violence under slavocracy—and its contemporary manifestations.

Brown's *Clotel* (1853) constructs a paradoxical image of the Mulatta. After being forced into slavery, Clotel, whose "complexion [was as] white as most of those who were waiting to become her purchasers," escapes by passing as a White man and near the end of the novel, her daughter also passes as a man to liberate her imprisoned lover. The "superiority" of her light skin did not prevent her from the victimization of slavery. Yet Clotel is able to earn money of her own and is skilled at escaping prison and sexual condemnation. In the end, Clotel kills herself to save her daughter. However, Brown's emphasis is on her refusal to remain in slavery and the degree of agency and subversion she uses to try to achieve her goal of freedom for herself and her daughter.

Contemporary Black feminist critics such as Mary Helen Washington point to the complexity of the Tragic Mulatta figure. In postmodern terms, her decentered identity is not chosen but enforced by historical circumstances, politics, and the racial dynamics of their times.[22] Washington finds that nineteenth- and early twentieth-century

Black writers such as Frances Ellen Watkins Harper (*Iola LeRoy*, 1892) and Pauline Hopkins (*Contending Forces*, 1900; *Hagar's Daughter*, 1901–1902) turn the Tragic Mulatta into a political and social activist. In short, working within the traditional genres of White American fiction but, as literary critic Suzanne Bost notes, "hav[ing] a different investment in destabilizing that genre, encoding the difference of black women's experience and finding agency for the doubly oppressed black female character."[23]

These early Black writers took an antiessentialist stance against the fantastic hegemonic imaginative conventions of the sentimentalist literature of their time on one hand, and the racist ideologies of White demagogues on the other. Much like the figure of the Mammy, the Tragic Mulatta of the white imagination did not exist historically. She is a legend who is a memory greater than memories. More sylph than reality, the Mulatta emerging from the mind of whiteness is tragic because she is near White but not White. The "almostness" that her condition is ought to be both pitied and shunned in the world of the fantastic hegemonic imagination.

Let me hasten to acknowledge the presence of light-skinned Black men and women who were and are, historically and in our time, marginalized by our color-conscious society. However, the Tragic Mulatta stereotype from the White imagination sits on the margins of two worlds that do not accept her and in which she does not fit. Paradoxically, the Black community largely accepted mulattoes and Mulattas and they were often among its leaders and spokespersons. For every tragedy such as Dorothy Dandridge, there were many more "successes" such as Frederick Douglass, W. E. B. Du Bois, Booker T. Washington, Mary Church Terrell, Jean Toomer, Langston Hughes, Thurgood Marshall, Billie Holiday, Malcolm X, and Louis Farrakhan. In addition, Walter White and Adam Clayton Powell, Sr. and Jr., were light enough to pass for White.[24]

The difference between stereotype and complex reality is telling when placed within the context of empire building. As a commodity of the White imagination, the Tragic Mulatta represents the deceit of slavery and the sociopolitical and economic relations used to maintain it as a moral good in the face of massive dehumanization of all involved. In contemporary face, she becomes both the witness and critic of U.S. empire making and empire building—not of democracy or free-market capitalism. Her contemporary siblings in almostness are poor peoples, darker-skinned peoples, peoples who live outside of the West (which means most people), immigrants, and sexual minorities.

However, if we take seriously the challenge of the reality of the Tragic Mulatta, we find that she is the spy in the house of evil. Her ability to live and breathe in two worlds makes her agency potent when teasing through issues of reparations and empire. We can use her almostness as a mediating ethic—not to seek easy reconciliation, but, as womanist ethicist Marcia Y. Riggs suggests, as an ethic that is a "process of acknowledging seemingly diametrically opposing positions and creating a response that interposes and communicates between opposing sides. It is living with tension rather than aiming at integration, compromise, or reconciliation as ultimate ends. These may be outcomes, but mediating as process occurs whether or not mediation as an end does."[25]

Empire or empire?

Nearly 150 years later, Black folks are still answering the kind of questions Grant and Stanton asked about who we are, what we think, and are we able. It would be a flawed strategy to think about reparations without acknowledging that some of its roots are lodged in this field order that was not issued out of a sense of humanitarianism, strong support for the newly freed, or a universal notion of place and property. Sherman was trying to relieve his army of the thousands of freed men and women who had been following it since his invasion of Georgia. As he marched, slaves had abandoned the plantations to follow the army. Feeding and clothing these folks had become a strain. Even more importantly, what often gets lost is Sherman's later claim that his order was a temporary solution and not one designed to grant permanent possession of the land to Black folks.

I rehearse the history of the Field Order and the Tragic Mulatta in cursory form to highlight the fact that "40 acres and a mule" has always been on tenuous ground because, like the Tragic Mulatta, it stands in that strange area of almostness. Sherman did not really mean it. Congress never fully supported it. President Johnson began dismantling it just one year later. As I read this part of the history, this has never been a *moral* argument. However, it has been, most decidedly, a parochial act of economic expedience. We should always be wary of "gifts" passed our way, gifts that have serious economic ramifications that are not discussed, acknowledged, or recognized at the time of the gift-giving. They have a way of being withdrawn, dismantled, and disavowed. Those who were the supposed beneficiaries of the "gift" are pathologized and subjected to all manner of moral condemnation and devaluation.

While I do not consider reparations as a gift or as something related to gift giving, I want to be incandescently clear[26] that a major part of the context of the reparations debate regarding Black folk is that it is taking place at a time when imperialism is being dwarfed by the twin engines of Christian triumphalism and empire in the United States. Alone, either phenomenon is problematic. Yoked as they are now, as tools of the fantastic hegemonic imagination, each is deadly and devastating.

Christian Triumphalism

"Do you accept Jesus Christ as your personal Lord and savior?" This question is one that many of us have encountered in various settings—church, the street, public parks, camp, bars, and on and on. When presented in an aggressive and domineering way, it suggests—if not demands—an acquiescence that assaults and maims deeper engagement with other faith traditions and probably negates any possibility of tapping into God's ongoing revelation. Because in the background of Christian triumphalism is an appeal to the victory over sin, evil, and death by Jesus Christ through our baptism, Christians share this victory with Christ and the triumph becomes ours as well. This extension then proceeds to go too far when it suggests that this triumph includes victory over non-Christians, who are deemed evil if not satanic. In short, an invitation to grace can quickly degenerate into persecution and a ruthless drive seeking to make converts—regardless.

Hence, we sing hymns such as "Standup for Jesus" often, I think, without hearing the mean edge to triumphalism.

> Stand up, stand up for Jesus,
> The trumpet call obey;
> Stand forth in mighty conflict,
> In this his glorious day:
> Let all his faithful serve him
> Against unnumbered foes;
> Let courage rise with danger,
> And strength to strength oppose.
> (George Duffield, Jr., 1818–1888)

Who are these "unnumbered foes"? Are they devils? Are they people? Are these people evil? By foes, do we mean anyone who is not Christian? Are we suggesting that non-Christians, by their very nature of being non-Christian are foes and thus evil? When I actually listen to many of the hymns I grew up singing with gusto, I am caught up short with the realization that I am singing what I believe is heresy. These hymns often signal a quest for a victory that I believe has already been accomplished in the death and resurrection.

Close on the heels of this, in many respects, is the theme that the United States is a Christian nation. This theme carries within it the potential and actual for the kinds of religious intolerance we see that shapes the political, ethical, cultural, theological, moral, religious, social landscapes we all inhabit. The comments of Randall Terry, founder of the antiabortion group Operation Rescue, is an example of this. Making no bones about wanting to build a Christian nation, Terry's arrogant absolutism sees a pagan nation as the only other option. Although Terry's push for a Christian nation is extreme, it carries the marks that some of the deadly ways in which the fantastic hegemonic imagination marks its territory: executing doctors who perform abortions, championing male patriarchal leadership in the United States, quoting the Bible and having it revered in political gatherings, and abolishing the welfare state—all in God's holy name.

This kind of hegemonic absolutism is made more powerful because we in the United States are a deeply ahistorical nation. We are historically illiterate and we are largely unaware that this is the case. We tend to want to have our history unambiguous, true, and without competing narratives. Too many students grow up with grade school history teachers that skip over sections in history books—sections that speak of slavery, suffrage, the holocaust, the civil rights movement, the Vietnam War, and more. Despite the conservative and neoconservative hue and cry that college campuses are overly liberal, professors in undergraduate education and graduate school tend to treat resources beyond the White European without rigor or sophistication—as though these resource were not part of the *real* canon of knowledge. Hence, adding to the problem of ahistoricism is the vexing reality that we cannot remember what we never knew.

History is messy, far from antiseptic, and often not kind. Although we sometimes remember that God acts in history, we often lapse into thinking that we are alone in this unfolding of creation and then we proceed to make God a partner to our wishes (rather than we being partner to God's wishes) and believe that God then chooses to be on *our* side. In short, we hold God hostage if not prisoner as we, the faithful followers, assume God's will.

President G. W. Bush is not the first president who ends his speeches with the prayer, "God bless America." Until of late, it had become a sort of platitude of political oratory. But now, there is a different edge to this invocation for the United States is being invoked as the heart of God's heart and our actions as being representative of God's will—unilaterally and unequivocally and with our own weapons of mass destruction.

The problem with Christian triumphalism is that it gets away from being Christian so quickly. The goal is to win, dominate, conquer, convert—at all costs—even if that cost means lying, stealing, killing, and subverting justice. Winning becomes more important than helping bring in the Kingdom, the Realm of God. Winning—doing it my way or no way—becomes the doctrinal creed that fuels the piety of annihilation that is often the refuse of triumphalism.

Our ahistoricism may allow us to miss the fact that this triumphalist spirit was planted by the early seventeenth century Puritans who believed that their Calvinist-based colonization experiment in the New World was a divine charge and mission to build the shining city on a hill for all the world to see. In its contemporary face, President Ronald Reagan was one of the best at invoking this metaphor. Indeed, at Reagan's funeral, Justice Sandra Day O'Connor read some of the words from the final section of governor John Winthrop's 1630 sermon, "A Model of Christian Charity," that he preached during the voyage to the Americas.

> We shall find that the God of Israel is among us, when ten of us shall be able to resist a thousand of our enemies; when He shall make us a praise and glory that men shall say of succeeding plantations, "may the Lord make it like that of New England." For we must consider that we shall be as a city upon a hill. The eyes of all people are upon us. So that if we shall deal falsely with our God in this work we have undertaken, and so cause Him to withdraw His present help from us, we shall be made a story and a by-word through the world. We shall open the mouths of enemies to speak evil of the ways of God, and all professors for God's sake. We shall shame the faces of many of God's worthy servants, and cause their prayers to be turned into curses upon us till we be consumed out of the good land whither we are going.[27]

This Promised Land theology of the book of Joshua with its model of military conquest was used to justify the wars against indigenous peoples, the "Canaanites" of the New World. The Puritans saw themselves as God's elect, called to establish the New Israel. Frontier individualism and the optimism of progress through expansion and wealth yoked with Christian triumphalism led to the political slogan

"Manifest Destiny"—a biblical interpretation that encouraged an attitude of moral and economic superiority on the part of White Christians over all others and justified taking the of land of others, in the name of the Lord (and the nation).

We cannot dismiss the drive to dominate that rings through to us from 1630 for it has remained with us through the centuries—sometimes with deeply held notes, sometimes in staccato. What endures is the self-image of being God's chosen people who are called to establish the new Israel. In 1776, both Benjamin Franklin and Thomas Jefferson wanted Promised Land images for the new nation's Great Seal. Franklin wanted Moses parting the Red Sea and Pharaoh's army being overwhelmed by the waters. Jefferson wanted the Israelites being led in the wilderness by the pillar of fire by night and cloud by day. George Washington was depicted as the "American Joshua" in Ezra Stiles's 1783 sermon. Samuel Langdon's 1788 sermon declares, "We cannot but acknowledge that God hath graciously patronized our cause and taken us under his special care, as he did his ancient covenant people." Jefferson's second inaugural address in 1805 recalls the Promised Land:

> I shall need . . . the favor of that Being in whose hands we are, who led our fathers, as Israel of old, from their native land and planted them in a country flowing with all the necessities and comforts of life.[28]

This Promised Land theology of Christian triumphalism has cost indigenous peoples millions of acres of land through theft, murder and warfare, forced removal, deception, and official government land programs. As Roy May, Jr., notes, the land rights of Native Americans were never taken seriously as they were seen as obstacles to the colonists' need for land. The Puritans did not respect the farms of Native Americans and they sought "legal" ways to get their land.[29] For example, when a Native American broke one of the rigid Puritan religious laws, the fine collected was a piece of his/her land. Strange to say that some Puritans were able to amass large landholdings through the Massachusetts courts in this manner, and John Winthrop alone obtained some 1,260 acres along the Concord River by this method. The Indian Removal Act of 1830 led to the forced march of the Eastern tribes of Choctaw, Chickasaw, Cherokee, and Creek along the "Trail of Tears" to the Oklahoma territory. Eventually most Indian nations were forcibly relocated as the United States government broke virtually every treaty it made with native peoples. Millions died from disease and genocidal war. Survivors were confined to "reservations" on the worst lands, and Christians often used the Bible to defend and justify these realities—just as slavery was rationalized on the basis that since Africans were not Christians they were therefore "heathens" and subhuman.

Near the turn of the twentieth century, the nation as a whole increasingly saw itself as "the Protestant empire"—something born straight out of the Christian triumphalism that suffused the air of United States culture at that time. The chosen people/Christian triumphalist spirit soon embodied itself after the Spanish-American War of 1898. Much like what we see today, the United States pursued an expansionist strategy of global influence, engagement, and expansion in terms of both economic interests and territory. As a nation, we grew more involved overseas as a result of business, missionary, and military ventures fueled by a sense of U.S. exceptionalism—another offspring of Christian triumphalism.[30] In sum, United States expansionism involved nationalism, religion, profit, and a sense of mission.

Social Darwinism was then added to this quadrilateral.[31] Social Darwinism mixed with exceptionalism and grounded in Christian triumphalism led folks to believe that the peoples of the Caribbean, the Pacific, Asia, Africa, the Middle East, and Eastern and Southern Europe were racially inferior. They feared that both immigration to the United States and annexation would undermine *our* culture. This has incredible echoes in much of the public and private talk we hear today when it comes to immigration and the liberation of the people of Iraq—it is just that we have become more sophisticated in our language to mask our intent.

In 1901 a diplomat in Washington remarked, "I have seen two Americas, the America before the Spanish War and the America since." The noted Rev. Josiah Strong proclaimed that we needed a new, more encompassing foreign policy expressive of a new world life—a new world order—epitomized by the opening up of the Pacific and the Far East. The United States had become rapidly industrialized, poised for a major penetration of global markets and fully prepared to invoke the use of its expanded military forces to protect corporate aggrandizement abroad.

There was little public discussion after World War II about imperialism. We had defeated fascism in Europe and in the Far East, but we had done so with our allies and this left our international reputation clean and largely unquestioned. Imperialism was something practiced by "Old Europe." Although we became a different nation, almost overnight, after the terrorist attacks in this country on September 11, 2001, this was no less true of an openly imperialistic nation that had suddenly arisen by the end of the nineteenth century that replaced a more provincial country largely dominated by "the New England idea," signifying chiefly the intellectual culture of Boston and Concord.

However, it was not without internal debate and ideological tensions that the United States assumed a role on the world stage at the turn of the last century. In 1899, Felix Adler argued that the then popular notion of the "White Man's Burden" cribbed from Rudyard Kipling's 1899 poem was little more than "sentimentalism."[32] Kipling's poem mixed exhortation to empire with sober warnings of the costs involved. But the imperialists within the United States latched onto the phrase "White Man's Burden" as a euphemism that justified imperialism as a noble enterprise

In the previous year, in 1898, noted sociologist William Graham Sumner gave a lecture before Yale's Phi Beta Kappa Society in which he prophetically summarized the likely outcome of all this unprecedented burst of nationalistic enthusiasm to take over half the world if need be.

> The great foe of democracy now and in the future is plutocracy. Every year that passes brings out this antagonism more distinctly. It is to be the social war of the twentieth century. In that war militarism, expansion, and imperialism will all favor plutocracy. In the first place, war and expansion will favor jobbery, both in the dependencies [abroad] and at home. In the second place, they will take away the attention of the people from what the plutocrats are doing. In the third place, they will cause large expenditures of the people's money, the return for which will not go into the treasury but into the hands of a few schemers. In the fourth place they will call for a large public debt and taxes, and these things especially tend to make men unequal, because any social burdens bear more heavily on the weak than on the strong, and so make the weak weaker and the strong stronger. Therefore, expansion and imperialism are a grand onslaught on democracy.[33]

Sumner's observations served as a harbinger for today as we see these and some of the other worst-case scenarios of Christian triumphalism playing themselves out from 2003 to 2005 in Iraq—Operation Shock and Awe: a premature announcement of the end of hostilities that has served as a mere prelude to the extended, deadly street-to-street fighting against a continuing popular insurgency, and to the uncertain length of our occupation of Iraq. And then we saw the endorsing of a constitution in Iraq that does not grant women and minorities basic rights and that enshrines one religion as the fundamental source of law by pointing to the fact that it *mentions* democratic values (but does not define what they are) and that the U.S. Constitution allowed slavery, denied women the right to the vote, and granted property rights only to White men. (There is something wrong with thinking that the inadequacies and sexisms of 218 years ago should be the standards we use for justice 218 years later). Body bags from Iraq being covered with the shame of not being able to mourn our war dead publicly because it does not fit the script that says, we are winning, we are winning, we are winning, is poignant in itself. The roll back of individual rights and freedoms in the name of national security further exacerbate the situation—a war that was declared on knowingly flawed data skewed to fit the designs of few. Wars that are "resolved" through poorly timed and ill-prepared elections to bring democracy and stability that only increases political polarization and violence—see Angola 1992, Bosnia 1996, Liberia 1997, Iraq 2005.

Our actions in Iraq are yoked with domestic atrocities in triumphalist apparel. Massive voter disenfranchisement in the 2000 presidential election and serious questions about what happened in places such as Ohio and Florida in the 2004 election remain. Compassionate conservatism looked more and more like the jagged edges of broken glass running across the throat, as many of us watched in horror and most of us responded out of our faith and a sense of justice, when we saw the abject devastation and annihilation of the poor and darker-skinned people in New Orleans, Mississippi, and Alabama when the levees broke after Hurricane Katrina and laid bare the fact that we have no adequate disaster plans and our federal government is riddled with people who do not have a clue how to do the important jobs they have been appointed to do—cronyism is not a synonym for compassion. Then there are tax cuts that benefit the wealthy and wealthier. God bless America with cuts in welfare programs to give tax relief to those who need it the least.

These worst-case scenarios and more are the backdrop of the worlds that the fantastic hegemonic imagination creates as normal and just in triumphalism. Because as a nation and as communities of faith we are blinded by the rhetoric and the actions of Christian triumphalism, we often do not see that we cannot be a democracy and an empire at the same time. As a nation, we have made it a political, social, economic, and religious policy to dwell on the land of false conscious-ness.[34] We consistently and persistently refuse to come to terms with the "reality of the obvious,"[35] as we live off the bitter fruits of a fan-tastic hegemonic imagination that caricatures and pillages peoples', all peoples', lives—our thoughts, our culture, our religion, our isness. We have logoized versions of ourselves: Native Americans are reduced to spiritual, Blacks are reduced to hip-hop, Asians are reduced to intel-lect, Latinos/as are reduced to salsa, and Whites . . .well, Whites have no culture, no is-ness, they are simply . . . White. There is definitely something wrong with this equation and it is doubtful that we are truly engaging in a healthy version of democracy.

All this is heightened by the fact that President Bush's religious sup-porters do not act as spiritual guides, but more like faithful disciples. He is the leader of the America they think God has ordained. This is triumphalism, not Christianity—a zealous form of nationalism, bap-tized with Christian language. This pump-you-up Christianity is the abridged version of a gospel of sound bites filled with biblical allu-sions. Christian triumphalism is an ideology that is meant to defeat permanent vulnerability and put celebration in the place of fear. The real reason why we are who we are and how we do what we do is not so much informed by deep piety and pithy discernment. No, what we really are after is the power of the church triumphant through a gov-ernment headed steadily toward theocracy. So we capture domestic resources such as inflated military budgets and soldiers to continue a colonial war and paranoia to justify the concentration of dictatorial powers such as the Patriot Act to repress, silence, and cower the anti-war opposition. As the old Black women I grew up with used to say: ummph . . . ummph . . . ummph.[36]

Empire

Michael Hardt and Antonio Negri argue that unlike imperialism, Empire (with a capital "e"), with multinationals functioning as its chattering, chuckling cheerleaders, has no territorial center of power and it does not rely on fixed geographic, cultural, religious, or social boundaries or barriers because it incorporates the entire global realm in its ever-expanding frontiers.[37] For Hardt and Negri, nation-states, including even the United States, have less and less power to regulate economic and cultural exchanges around the flow of money, technol-ogy, people, and goods under Empire.

Hardt and Negri argue that the construction of Empire is still in process. This means that there remains much to be said about what is going on within the United States and how this shapes the reparations debate in this country. From the beginning of this country as a republic, the myth of universal uninhibited freedom has always had its evil twin—studied sadistic subordination and anal retentive annihilation. Our history is one that cast Native Americans outside of the constitution and included Blacks in the constitution—but not as 5/5ths human being. This has always been a great problematic in our self-understanding as a nation. We have not been the land of unfettered liberty, equal access, and open markets. But we have, domestically and globally, been a nation of imperialistic domestic and global outrages that carry kinder and gentler names such as the Personal Responsibility and Work Opportunity Act of 1996, USA Patriot Act 2001, Economic Growth and Tax Relief Reconciliation Act of 2001, Free Trade Area of the Americas.

Under Hardt and Negri's Empire, our reliance on foreign savings has pushed the value of the dollar up. This makes goods produced in the United States less competitive in world markets and it contributes to unemployment and low sales in those parts of our economy that are vulnerable to international competition. Things have changed. The United States no longer produces the cheapest, best, and most profitable goods. We no longer have a strong economy. In fact, we are recovering from a recession sparked by overinvestment and two ill-conceived tax cuts. The first spawned a $165 billion deficit for fiscal year 2002. The second, in May 2003, was passed in the face of a $465 billion deficit for fiscal year 2003. We are currently living with the strong likelihood that we will have $100 billion deficits each year for the rest of this decade.[38] We do not have low rates of unemployment and the federal solutions thus far continue to be tax breaks for the wealthy and upper middle class. This sadistic smiley-face, economic policy is being powered by going off to invade someone (Afghanistan and Iraq) so that we do not notice rising unemployment and nervous stocks because we have the flag being whipped in our faces and our grief and anger being molded into unrighteous vengeance and sprained patriotism.

No, we no longer have the United States of the late 1990s, when the country was among the best and the brightest economic performers in a world economy plagued by high unemployment in Europe and financial disaster in Asia. Simply put, the administrations in Washington can try as hard as they can to keep us at the center of imperialism, but Hardt and Negri respond that the best we can attain with the rise of Empire is a privileged position within it. For them, Empire invites everyone and no one to the feeding trough of global capitalism because it no longer recognizes nation-states (only commerce in its purist form) because we have reached the age of ultimate commodification. This is part of the reality in which reparations talk sits—in a competitive global economy where our country tries to shift the rules in its favor. However, if Hardt and Negri are correct, we cannot ultimately control all of the game as we once did.

Empire is not a work of pessimism. For Hardt and Negri, ours is a world of insurgent possibilities. They begin by arguing that globalization cannot be understood as a simple process of deregulating markets, while also noting that state-based systems of power are unraveling quickly. For them, regulations form an interlocking headless supranational order that they call Empire. This, then, is not a system but a network, a fantastic polity of peoples, information, and wealth that cannot be monitored from metropolitan control centers. As Gopal Balakrishnan notes, "The logic of this volatile totality evades and transgresses all the inherited divisions of political thought: state and society, war and peace, control and freedom, core and periphery; even the distinction between systemic and antisystemic agency is blurred beyond recognition."[39]

For Hardt and Negri, the new world order is comparable to past Empires such as the Roman Empire. Today, the nuclear supremacy of the United States represents the monarchical, the economic wealth of the G7 and transnational corporations represent the aristocratic, and the Internet represents democratic principles. Empire, to their minds, represents the depreciation of the nation state as a sovereign power. In its place is globalization that is not an exterior process working on peoples, institutions, markets, ideologies—but a reorganization of the centers of power. It represents the basis for a more progressive mode of social organization.

Where Hardt and Negri are optimistic and suggest a Polybiusian sense of ascendancy, one also wonders if Montesquieu's or Edward Gibbon's pessimism may be more apt for our current times. Teetering between these possibilities, Hardt and Negri see the potential revolutionaries of today as the Christians of the later Roman Empire—maintaining their position that Empire did not emerge from the defeat of systemic challenges to capitalism. Rather, it is clear and yet paradoxical evidence of what they see as the mass heroic struggles that shattered the Eurocentric old regime of nation states and colonialism.

They are convinced that contemporary capitalism is a vulnerable thing. Although it appears impervious to antisystematic challenge, they believe that it is vulnerable at all points to riot and rebellion because of the malleability of all social relationships and permeability of all borders.

Hardt and Negri argue that the global multitude (all those who work, or who are just poor) no longer imagines communities as integral nations. In short, the ideology of Empire deactivates the revolutionary possibilities of globalization. Taking on multiculturalists, community-based organizations, NGOs, and other assorted institutions from moderate to the Left, Hardt and Negri decry their effectiveness, they see the NGOs, for example, as the Dominicans of late medieval society and Jesuits of the dawn of modernity, communities that functioned as "charitable campaigns and mendicant orders of Empire. [They] conduct 'just wars' without arms, without violence, without borders . . . these groups strive to identify universal needs and defend human rights. Through their language and their action they first define the enemy as privation (in hope of preventing serious damage and then recognize the enemy as sin."[40] In short, they are "some of the most powerful pacific weapons of the new world order."

What emerges for Hardt and Negri is the reconstitution of the political on the level of the transnational where the political is the direct result of the activities and the productive and creative energies of the of the multitude. This notion of the multitude is key in Empire. With a nod to Spinoza and Gilles Deleuz, Hardt and Negri's concept of the multitude disrupts conventional conceptions of state sovereignty. This indeterminate category of the proletarianized and decentered majority has potential productive power, because, for Hardt and Negri, the capital demands of labor are in the intensification of the value of labor through the homogenization and differentiation of the concrete activity of work. Computerization, the service sector, sociobiological and cultural networks of production lose their distinctive separation from the field of work in Empire. Key in Empire is the fact that "cooperation is completely immanent to the laboring activity itself."[41]

In short, with Empire, there is no longer the centered imperialism of the past because production in the postmodern age forces society to the stage where immaterial labor creates the "potential for a spontaneous and elementary communism."[42] In sum, they argue that this world of the biopolitical is a place where value is produced even outside the regime of work—"the production of social life itself, in which the economic, the political, and the cultural increasingly overlap and invest in one another."[43] Yet, the global order works in and through a recognized criterion of human rights as a juridical category used for good or ill. Human rights has its origins in nongovernmental discourses and actions that seek to defend the language of human life itself in a world where this is continuously subverted.[44]

Hardt and Negri recognize that a politics based on high consumption will never effectively change capitalism because the presupposition of a market society such as ours remains based on what they see as unchallenged economic and social alienation. They point to the fact that spectacular images of societies that know themselves through consumption capture youth in particular (I submit that in the United States this is the majority of us). Yet, for them the multitude can subvert the pseudoreligious powers of capitalism because it (they, us) does not see the political as separate from the social. The real issue is the reclamation of our alienated social power.

For them, the end of biopower politics is the realization of the potential of people so that they reap the fruits of their own activity. This challenges the social power of capitalism and ethical discourses that seek to limit our desires and abilities. In their optimistic neo-Marxism, they locate the potential for politics in the real of the massive creative productive energy of the multitude. For them, anticapitalism need not degenerate into incantations of demands of reform dressed in utopian attire. Although they offer no concrete program, Hardt and Negri do clearly oppose the misery of poor with the "irrepressible lightness and joy of being a communist."[45]

Although *Empire* is a breath of fresh air within neo-Marxism, I am left with a sense of uneasiness about the myriad loose ends they leave. It is in these loose ends that I find the lives of people struggling to survive if not thrive in a troublesome economy where more and more state, county, and local governments face the three furies: budget shortfalls, the need to provide services, and shrinking resources. These folk are not abstract theoretical actors in an academic public policy debate. They have flesh and blood—they are real. It is in their lives that our commitment to justice and right relationships live and grow. This is where *we* answer God's call to faithfulness.

Along with Balakrishnan, I am unconvinced by a dualism they set up in which the world order is in a "permanent state of emergency and exception justified by the appeal to essential values of justice"[46] and their insistence that Empire is a juridical formation.[47] While order and chaos can (and certainly do) exist when the almostness that so many live in is factored into the analysis, there is more at stake by placing this, as they do, in the context of a constitutional system. For me, this legend that tempts being a memory larger than memory fails to account for who brought or brings Empire into being and who interprets the international law. The events of 2001 to the present bring this problematic into focus when the administration in the United States (and those in other countries) steadfastly refuse to be held accountable in the World Court if there is a possibility that it would be found guilty of wrongdoing.

In a puzzling slight of hand, Hardt and Negri reject a description of the United States as an imperial power while acknowledging our place at the top of the international power hierarchy. Gone are notions of state-based imperialism and sovereignty. In their place is the multitude—the dispossessed. These folk are the collective subject that are not always aware of their collectivity or their subjectivity. How these folk constitute Empire remains to be seen. Exchanging the industrial working class with the multitude because the former have proved to be inept at creating and maintaining social revolutions is not enough justification to broaden the pool of those who are the potential revolutionaries in the belief that they will be more apt, willing, and able to combat transnationals and nation states—some of whom are intransigent and unapologetic imperialists.

In a somewhat apolitical vein, Hardt and Negri argue that Empire is always vulnerable to the impact of destabilizing events caused by the multitude. This nouveau version of hegemony may be the most helpful insight of the work although I believe that it is much harder and takes more intentional and self-aware work than Hardt and Negri suggest. Not withstanding the insight that Empire is unable to control the global flow of workers seeking a better life in richer countries—therefore being immigrationist at heart—this tendency does not necessarily translate into revolutionary fervor or transformation. The opportunity to seek a better life for self and family does not in itself assure democratic or socialist citizens. What Hardt and Negri fail to factor in is self-interest and greed as possible personality flaws within some or significant numbers of those who constitute the multitude. For example, old-style liberal racial reform becomes nearly if not completely impossible in this kind of global economy and U.S. participation in it. What empires spend abroad, they cannot spend on hospitals, schools, roads, and health—amenities that are the hallmarks of good republican governance. Liberals are no longer able to undermine White supremacy by running budget deficits to finance education, housing, and health care for Blacks and other racial and social groups who exist between structural wickednesses that spawn oppression and the exclusion by free markets catering in response to the phobias of many middle- and upper-class Whites.[48] The Tragic Mulatta as mediating ethic and as representative of almostness points to the ways in which trying to link redistributive taxation and the high taxes that often come with this economic remedy with Black folks (and any person or groups not part of the near or real elite) is unpopular and probably unworkable today.

As helpful as Hardt and Negri are in stirring the pot, they do not convince me that the description of the contemporary world system as "Empire" is *not* because of the overwhelming concentration of financial, diplomatic, and military power in the hands of the United States. For me, it is a question of "empire"—that of the United States. Michael Ignatieff notes "the 21st century imperium is a new invention in the annals of political science, an empire light, a global hegemony whose grace notes are free markets, human rights and democracy, enforced by the most awesome military power the world has ever known."[49] Ignatieff continues with the observation that the U.S. revolutionary war against British tyranny has marked us with the patina of being the global freedom friend—we do not recognize ourselves as an empire and are brought up short when our policies and attitudes elicit resentment and hatred abroad. Benedict Anderson noted that this kind of forgetting is a key characteristic of modern nationalism. For him, the simultaneous forgetting and invention of the past and the projection of the nation into the future is a necessary construction of a myth of origins.[50]

Commiting ourselves, in our National Security Strategy in September 2002, to leading other nations toward "the single sustainable model for national success" (free markets and liberal democracy) has the unmistakable ring of empire to it. This, Ignatieff suggests, is not a new note for a president of the United States to sound. He points to Woodrow Wilson's 1919 rhetoric at Versailles when he told the world he wanted to make it safe for democracy. In 1960, Reinhold Niebuhr noted that presidents from Wilson and forward sound this redemptive note while "frantically avoiding recognition of the imperialism that we in fact exercise."[51]

Although empires are not omnipotent and omniscient, the emerging U.S. global policy pretends to be such. We should not be in the business of creating global order on our own—particularly through the use of force. Historically, this has been a dangerous and ultimately self-annihilatory stance. After the terrorist attacks of September 11, 2001, we have, as national and federal policy, reduced the role and input of nations that question the validity of war making to combat terrorism. Too often, I find myself shifting with discomfort in my seat as I hear the drumbeat of Christian triumphalism pounding the time out in the rhetoric and rationale for why we are doing what we are doing and for the rightness of our cause. As I think through the ways in which I see Christian triumphalism far too much alive and well in our nation's policies, the words image, power, and control keep bobbing up like those bobbin-head dolls of sports figures that sell so well when a team is winning.

I suspect my association is not coincidental given that ultimately, empire and empire building is about winning. The losers become a sad or pitied footnote to be considered by those who generations later mine the artifacts of their agony and defeat or their complete assimilation or ingestion or, perhaps, rebellion.

Winners also capture our attention, if not imagination. Empires hold a special fascination for us, be they Roman or Egyptian, Mongol or Songhai, British or American. Images of winning and the winners are captivating and sobering—dress, music, language, wealth, status, power—the *style* of these things shock and awe, as they demand obedience—if not submission. These images are meant to make sure that losers get that way and stay that way. Military might keeps people in check and with little ability or awareness of the fine features of hegemony that say that there are times when the losers become winners—if they believe they can.

These cultural productions as mechanisms of control blind many to the fact that hegemony, that ability to control reality and shape it into one's own image, itself can be a tool in the hands of those colonized because most of us feign modesty in these things and hate to admit that we like to win and that we like to control. Economic strangleholds block us from seeing that hegemony is crafted with the tools of power and control and a studied will to inflict manufactured realities that benefit a design spun from human insufficiencies that help compensate for our shortcomings much like the character Lord Farquaad, the four-foot-tall ruler of Duloc in the movie *Shrek*. It is Dulocs that we are creating with empires—manufactured perfections that ignore the realities of the messiness of living and the grubbiness of us humans being humans in creation.

Empire is on the eyeball when a simpleminded faith-based presidency plays on homophobia and heterosexism, sexism, gender control, and role routinization; jingoism and ethnocentrism, and specious loyalty to a patriotism that is built on the model: see no evil, here no evil, do no evil—at least not from American intentions; to advance its agendas and strategies. Empire and Christian triumphalism is found in the mindset of Hardy Billington, a 52-year old white man from Poplar Bluff, Missouri. Addressing a rally of 20,000 that he helped gather in support of President Bush when Massachusetts made same sex-marriage legal, Billington said that

> the United States is the greatest country in the world. President Bush is the greatest president I have ever known. I love my president. I love my country. And more important, I love Jesus Christ.[52]

The crowd went wild.

People of faith must begin to explore seriously and critically what might be found through a much more nuanced understanding of how much Christianity's very roots are situated in the Roman Empire.[53] We have an inherited tradition of ignoring the fact that the texts and history of the New Testament emerged from the political context of the Roman Empire and the imperial cult of the divine emperor. The emperor, through his armies and through military strongmen dictated life for the people of Galilee. Roman governors such as Pontius Pilate both appointed and deposed the high priests who ruled Judea. As Richard Horsley notes, "Roman military violence established the material, political, and cultural conditions in which the Christian movement originated. Particular acts of devastation and terrorization framed the period and disfigured the sites in which the movement took root."[54] For all the power of the gospel, we must not neglect the world from which it comes and the episodes of empire we inherit that have moved unconsciously into our Christian theological worldviews. We may not just be in the belly of the beast. We may be in its heart.

Christian triumphalism drives our unipolar and faith-based domestic and international policies in the American empire that we are sitting in as we breathe in and out. This is the meanspiritedness of Christian triumphalism dressed up as compassionate conservatism in which "faithfulness" seeks a position of power and dominance in the world through attitude and practice. Behind this, is the belief that the church is *the* locus of God's full and complete revelation. Forgotten or disremembered is that the church is not in possession of the truth, but on a pilgrimage toward it. This has always been an unwise tact and it turns deadly in the kind of political, sociocultural, and theoethical climate we have today that is often crafted from a fantastic hegemonic imagination that tempts us to gaze closer and closer at our navels rather than insist that we ask, as people of faith, tough questions about where we are headed as nations, as religious bodies, as local and global citizens, as seekers of the spirit, as doers of the word. We are tempted to do a religious version of turning down the main power generator to conserve energy and we can engage in some of the most internecine and inane turf battles while forgetting the flood, the locusts, the 500 prophets of Baal, the prophets, the disciples, the rainbow.

The "tragedy" of the Mulatta is evident here—one cannot have it both ways and maintain such a stance by blithely turning away one's head when the facts do not match the attempt at legend making. Like many, I have begun to wonder what kind of nation are we becoming. Domestically and globally, we are becoming, to some and already so to others, a boorish and dangerous bully that has an amazing ability to hide its federal narcissism under the dubious red, white, and blue flag of patriotism and peacekeeping. Rather than the democratic republic we were founded to be (which is already problematic given the enormous land grab and annihilation the founders of this country committed against the indigenous peoples of this land), we are steadily moving toward the status of an empire. We are the only nation that has five global military commands—we police the world. We maintain more than a million men and women in our armed forces on four continents—there are only seven continents! We have carrier battle groups on watch in every ocean. The analysis of Michael Hardt and Antonio Negri notwithstanding, we drive the wheels of global trade and commerce and have packaged our dreams and desires as commodities that are exported to other nations and peoples—whether or not they like it, want it, need it, or can benefit from it.

As Ignatieff points out,

> . . . being an imperial power . . . is more than being the most powerful nation or just the most hated one. It means enforcing such order as there is in the world and doing so in the American interest. It means laying down rules American wants (on everything from markets to weapons of mass destruction) which exempting itself from other rules (the Kyoto Protocol on climate change and the International Criminal Court) that goes against its interest. It also means carrying out imperial functions in places America has inherited from the failed empires of the 20th century— Ottoman, British and soviet. In the 21st century, America rules alone, struggling to manage the insurgent zones—Palestine and the northwest frontier of Pakistan, to name but two—that have proved to be the nemeses of empires past.[55]

Victory in Iraq will not end the world's distrust of the United States because the Bush administration has repeatedly abrogated international agreements. In just two years (2000–2002), the Bush administration told Europe it had no interest in dealing with global warming, told Russia that it had no interest in maintaining our mutual agreements on missile defense, told developing countries that it was not interested in dealing with onerous trade policies regarding lifesaving pharmaceuticals, told Mexico it would not honor the immigration agreements it has forged with it, mortally insulted the Turks and pulled out of the International Criminal Court. We act like an empire when then Under Secretary of State John Bolton tells Israeli officials that after defeating Iraq, the United States would deal with Iran, Syria, and North Korea.[56]

In the U.S. empire, any criticism of our latest land grab in Iraq is denounced as unpatriotic. Frankly, I find this neither patriotic nor democratic. Lies based on unchallenged and unsubstantiated claims are turned into strategic talking points. Moreover, the price paid for lying is the blood of men, women, and children who never spoke the deceptions. Leaders such as Vice President Dick Cheney who are leading us straight to hell in a handbasket collect $100,000 to $1,000,000 a year from Haliburton—a multibillion dollar company that was awarded noncompetitive bid major postwar contracts in Iraq. I find it highly suspect that the chicken hawks who were supporters of the Vietnam War but found all sorts of ways to avoid serving in it—George W. Bush, Dick Cheney, Paul Wolfowitz, Richard Perle, John Bolton, Tom DeLay, John Ashcroft, Lewis Libby, and a few others—are now sending others into and to create killing fields. To my mind, this is a gross display of hubris at best and of demonic self-interest at worst.[57] It should not be lost on any of us that this nation's military establishment has been critical of the Bush administration's war plans as early as the summer of 2002 and that the critique of Secretary of Defense Donald Rumsfeld's plan (a hawk who comes by his credentials honestly) continues.[58]

Reparations as Subtext

In 2003, 37.1 million people (13 percent) in the United States identified themselves as Black or African American.[59] Recent Census Bureau statistics reveal that Hispanics (which includes all those who are Mexican, Puerto Rican, Cuban, Central and South American, and of other Latino origins—a group rather than any particular race) have now passed Blacks as the second largest population group. Although the gap was found to be small—39.3 million to 36.2 million—the projections are that it will increase over the next ten years. These statistics are deceptive at face value. Because Hispanics could represent any of the above-mentioned races, their data overlaps with the Black and Asian and Pacific Islander populations. The 2002 Current Population Survey Annual Demographic Supplement noted that 3.7 percent of the Black population and 2.5 percent of Asians and Pacific Islanders were of Hispanic origin. These facts stare in the face of a rising poverty rate (from 11.3 percent in 2000 to 12.1 percent in 2002 to 12.5 percent in 2003 to 12.7 percent in 2004).[60] In terms of people, this means that in 2004, there were 37 million people below the poverty threshold— 5.4 million more than the 31.6 million poor in 2000.[61] The rate of poverty for children under 18 is the highest among all age groups. Their rate rose to 17.8 percent, up from 16.7 percent in 2002. Among the 18 to 64 year-olds, the poverty rate rose to 11.3 from 9.8 percent in 2000.

Among Asian American households, between 2003 to 2004, poverty fell from 11.8 percent to 9.8 percent; it remained unchanged at 21.9 percent for Latino/a families and at 24.7 percent for Black households, and rose from 8.2 percent to 8.6 percent for White households. In terms of median income, Black households had the lowest at $30,134, followed by $34,241 for Latino/a, $48,977 for Whites, and $57,518 for Asians.

The richest counties with population of 250,000 or more are Washington and New York suburbs. Fairfax County, Virginia, topped the list at $88,100 median income, followed by the New Jersey counties of Somerset ($84,900), and Morris ($83,600), and the Maryland counties of Montgomery ($83,000) and Howard ($82,100). Three of the poorest counties are on the Texas-Mexico border: Hidalgo at $24,800, Cameron at $26,300, and El Paso at $28,900.

Despite years of affirmative action, men earned most last year in management mining, technical and professional services, utilities and information jobs at $77,754 compared to women at $40,000. In each of the 20 categories men earned more than women, with the gap widest in management at 54 cents for women for every $1 a man earned.

These kinds of statistics that feature a rising poverty rates coupled with a rising federal deficit and a nation at war status do not make reparations a simple conversation in Pax Americana. This is even more so given the fact that no major group of Whites in the United States has taken responsibility for the past and lingering, nagging negative impact of slavery, segregation, and modern racism on all of us. Many decry the suggestion that an apology might be in order. The strong subtext within the reparations debate in the United States is forgotteness—the past is over and done with, let us move on to the future. This fails to acknowledge or address the unjust enrichment of Whites that is not only a past event it is also a current event. Rather than address the complex matrix of liberty, justice, and oppression that is a part of our legacy, many of us tend to cling to the legend of the city on the hill. For this becomes a memory greater than memory in the negative sense because it does not recognize that legal slavery ended less than 150 years ago, legal segregation did not end until the late 1960s, and racism endures to this moment.

Reparations talk is ultimately not about Black folk. It is about White power and privilege sashaying around with Christian triumphalism, empire, and imperialism. This kind of imperialism lets White supremacy off the hook and it feeds into empire building. It fails to address whiteness as a racial construction that functions as privilege and power over national and global stages. Attempts to talk about reparations for Black folk, domestically or globally, falter because of the ability or inability of elite Whites and their kin to recognize that they have attained their power and privilege on the backs of the poor, the darker skinned, the feminine. The elite White imagination creates a world complete with images built on stereotypes of utter otherness. It is time to have an honest conversation about this with Chamoiseau's observation that there are memories greater than memories as guide and prod. These legends, when spun at the service of hegemonic imagination, become evil sylphs with incredible destructive power. The Tragic Mulatta as a mediating ethic and a representative of the almostness that so many of us live in points to the fact that White liberal conceptions of race are often problematic and may not bring us any closer to reparations or a more balanced relationship between democracy and capitalism. All too often, the liberal and conservative White imagination is a servant to the fantastic hegemonic imagination. While opposing slavery, discrimination, and sometimes racism, it often makes Black folk a reduction of pathetic stereotypes. Yet, another area is important to include in this discussion. In the hands of White authors, an important subtext emerges—the inability, unwillingness, and/or incompetence of White fathers to protect and provide for wives and children. As Anna Shannon Elfenbeing notes, the father of "this near-white ingénue has not seen to things. His concern with attending to pleasure . . . betrays his daughter . . . to the auction block."[62] This betrayal runs hard, fast, and deep and is made even more disconcerting in the context of the call for reparations that is not a recent note in U.S. life.[63] Reparations talk enters into a loaded economic arena with a deep history of empire building, imperialism, and manifest stereotypes. Until we deal effectively and be honest about the images we carry around in our heads about one another, any talk about reparations in the United States is doomed to failure at worst and gradualism at best. The reality of empire makes this so.

Given the fiscal and ideological realities of contemporary society in the United States, there will continue to be much talk about reparations, but little will be done. The tenor of the current federal administration, though more obvious in its disinterest for the many, reflects the mood of previous administrations regarding reparations. Bankrupting our social services network moves us further away from actual reparations of any kind. It is hard to see the effectiveness of Hardt and Negri's Empire at work in this context. What does remain clear is that empire is at work—we export it once we perfect it domestically. Sadly, if not strategically, Stanton and Sherman's fifth question has never fully left the lips of many in this country

> "Do you think that there is intelligence enough among the slaves of the South to maintain themselves under the Government of the United States and the equal protection of its laws, and maintain good and peaceable relations among yourselves and with your neighbors?"

I have just enough of Aunt Jemima, Topsy, Black Matriarch, Sapphire, the Tragic Mulatta, not to mention Miss Nora and Momma Mary, in me that my answer has not changed and will not change. Not in the context of empire. Not in the context of imperialism. Not even in the context of the fantastic hegemonic imagination.

For there is sufficient intelligence among us to do so.

I worry more about the intelligence, intentions, and will of my neighbors. True true.

To Pick One's Own Cotton: Religious Values, Public Policy, and Women's Moral Autonomy

*if I had known then
what I know now, I would have
picked my own cotton.*[1]

Public policymaking is, regrettably, often seen as exclusively political or social.[2] The sometimes deeply religious and/or theological underpinnings of our basic attitudes concerning the nature of peoples and the kind of public policies we must respond with remains unacknowledged or unconscious. We are often unaware that moral landscapes are driving our public policy decisions and that this makes our public policy decision-making problematic at times. The other side of this coin is that there are times when we are *very* aware of the moral landscapes driving the creation of some of our public policies. It is equally regrettable that in these instances, a rather narrow and damning view of the individual, government, and society dominate.

I begin this discussion of the impact of religious values in and on public policy issues with an exploration of epistemology. Epistemologies involve an interplay of ethical issues.[3] This is particularly true when this exploration of knowledge and truth is grounded methodologically in Christian social ethics and an interdisciplinary framework that considers class, gender, and race such as womanist moral thought.[4] Teleologically, knowing is an act that has consequences for the individual and for the community. This ethics of knowing—the act of knowing—is always contextual. It is always fraught with our best and worst impulses. It is never objective. It is never disinterested—no matter how many rational proofs we come up with to argue to the contrary.

This dynamic dance of consequences and context create a peculiar playing field for a womanist exploration of whether or not any given knowledge claim is true.[5] For Patricia Hill Collins, this knowledge validation process has two influential political criteria. The first is that knowledge claims are evaluated by experts who represent the viewpoints of the groups they represent. The second is that these experts must maintain their credibility with the group they represent. This makes knowledge claims deeply contextual. However, our awareness of this rich contextuality is often muted by assumptions of a kind of austere objectivity in which truth is pristine. What often emerges, none too subtlely, is the assumption that there is only one truth, one correct answer to the puzzle of the diversities that form us culturally, socially, and theologically.

For Collins, when White men control the knowledge validation process, these two preceding political criteria can and often do work to suppress Black feminist thought.

> Since the general culture shaping the taken-for-granted knowledge of the community of experts is one permeated by widespread notions of black and female inferiority, new knowledge claims that seem to violate these fundamental assumptions are likely viewed as anomalies . . . . specialized thought challenging notions of black and female inferiority is unlikely to be generated from within a white-male-controlled academic community because both the kinds of questions that could be asked and the explanations that would be found satisfying would necessarily reflect a basic lack of familiarity with black women's reality[6]

Collins' insight illuminates an essential matter that we are liable to miss: context (and truth) shifts from one group to another. Additionally, empathy is not the same as lived experience. We experience the same thing and different things simultaneously and this can become somewhat chaotic. However, it is highly representative of the realities that shape us. Often, we are tempted to live our lives as if we live in a monolithic society and as if our responses to events and histories should reflect this. One example of this is the way people variously responded to the successful terrorist attacks on the Pentagon in Washington, DC and the World Trade Center in New York city and the foiled attempt that ended in a field outside Pittsburgh, PA on September 11, 2001. For many, these attacks evoked feelings of dread, fear, and the need to live one's life on constant alert. For many, these attacks did not elicit these reactions because this is how these folk already live their lives every day as members of a dispossessed community. Still others fell in between these two responses. The difficulty came at those points where anyone who did not express feelings of fear and anger were judged unpatriotic. Is there really only one way to respond to horrific destruction and death? Collins's point is that we are often trapped in our unexamined particularity. My point is that this makes us dangerous when from this stance we then try to shape public policies that affect the nation and the world.

Part of the problem is that we often rely on positivist approaches that seek to create scientific descriptions through objective generalizations.[7] This is accomplished by banishing (or attempting to banish) all other human characteristics except rationality and then decontextualizing (or attempting to decontextualize) ourselves to become detached observers. As Collins notes, this is paralleled by similar efforts to remove the objects of study from their contexts—a potentially deadly and inaccurate separation of information from its context and ultimately from that which provides it the very foundation of its meaning. Distance and the absence of emotion become desired values in methodology and research. Ethics and values are not considered appropriate, and adversarial debates are the ruling discourse for determining truth. Collins points out that this set of criteria asks Black women to objectify themselves, devalue their emotional life, displace their motivations for developing greater knowledge about Black women, and adopt an adversarial position with those who have more social, economic, and professional power.[8] It is vital that we realize that Black women are not the only ones asked to participate in this ghastly rending of self/community from context. This chilling spectacle of death is visited on millions more.

Theoethically, such a positivist stance is fundamentally unworkable for womanist epistemological explorations. The self-aware contextuality of womanist thought demands a passionate engagement with life where neutrality is impossible. From a womanist epistemological perch, we echo what Brasilian theologian Ivone Gebara points out so well: actions and relationships change depending on our style of knowing.[9] Rather than divorce ethics and values from our consideration, we must use such insights to force ourselves to acknowledge the limits we place on how much of the rich diversity of our is-ness we actually know and to recognize that we do not know enough about others and ourselves globally. It is, then, to recognize the troubling hierarchizing of knowledge that *all* of us participate in.

This hierarchizing of knowledge affects our perceptions and understandings of social order on a communal, national, and global scale. A womanist response to such evil potations is to resist any argument that suggests that every viewpoint has a more accurate view of our social realities than another. Structural evil is not so easily addressed. It is vapid methodology to suggest that oppressions can be quantified and compared in a system that ranks people from the most oppressed to the least oppressed. All this does is create a hierarchy of oppression to match a hierarchy of knowledge. Such pairings must be resisted and then eradicated.

My emphasis on context regarding epistemology is formed from my belief that experience is a priceless criterion and foundation. Though it presents profound challenges to our ability to see and analyze, experience deals with concrete material existence, not abstractions. This challenges us to move beyond ourselves to develop empathy *and* respect for others and, more importantly, for the creation of public policy, to *share* in the experience of others.

It is at this point that we confront some of our toughest challenges for we are dared to combine reason and experience as equal methodological tools. This is not something most of us do easily or naturally for we are often unconscious hostages to antagonistic dualistic epistemological frameworks. Experience pushes us to consider the radical messiness of life and opens the door to the realization that our theoretical viewpoints are often too constricted to accommodate the mélange of creation. Experience can also tempt us to fall into narcissistic navelgazing. Therefore, it is integral that reason enter our methodology as well as that it help to push for a broader expanse in our worldview as experience prods us into a deeper perception and appreciation of the worlds surrounding us.

In short, we need each other to help us understand the worlds we have created and are creating. This assumes a positive value for interdependence and dialogue. This invitation to growth, as it were, admits that we are a complex of historical interactions on a cosmic playing field. Further, dialogue signals this connectedness as we seek to hear and understand our lives within the profundity of creation. This helps us recognize that ideas (knowledge) cannot be detached from the individuals who create and share them. It is to return to the importance of context.

Gebara calls this "sacred interdependence" that is not mechanical but alive, vibrant, and visceral.[10] This kind of interdependence eschews the linear epistemology that drives so much of our common discourse and is often present in public policy deliberations. Interdependence helps us realize that progress rarely moves in a straight line and that despite our best efforts to make it so, progress is an unruly dynamic that delights in sidebars and dead end roads.

Gebara helpfully argues for a process epistemology in which new elements are always being added to human knowledge and in which we accept that knowledge, like revelation, does not follow a predictable causal path.[11] This means that ethics, emotions, and reason are interconnected components for assessing knowledge claims. As contextual, these components are often marked by class, gender, and race formations. When joined with religious values, these are powerful actors in public policy formation.

Within this context, Sonia Sanchez's haiku haunts. Knowing and when we know it and how we know it are crucial. Being aware that there are many sites of epistemological privilege and authority is emancipatory for others and for ourselves.

The Black Matriarch

One result of expanding the epistemological playing field is questioning the images of Black womanhood such as those stereotypes that are addressed in this book. In the worldviews created by the fantastic hegemonic imagination, Mammy and her morphed twin Aunt Jemima have historically represented the sexual and maternal embodiment of ideal Black womanhood—a perfect mother (to White children), a perfect slave to all. Sapphire is the castrating shrew whose mouth runs like a bell clapper. The Tragic Mulatta is the ultimate victim in whiteface and a revolutionary in blackface. Now I turn, in the midst of rethinking epistemology to better understand how unexamined religious values are a part of public policymaking, to the Black Matriarch. In doing so, I complete an arc from the older Mammy image in which Sapphire and the Tragic Mulatta have been touchstones. The Black Matriarch is the Mammy gone bad.

You know her. She is the domineering female head of the Black family in the United States. She is the single Black mother who was featured in the 1986 CBS special report, "The Vanishing Family: Crisis in Black America." Yes, she is the one who Bill Moyers told us represents the moral depravity of Black childbearing. She is the one who represents *the* cause for all social problems because of her singleness and her blackness and her children. At times, she is also called the Welfare Queen.

The Black Matriarch is an image largely shaped by powerful representatives of the White dominant group through the fantastic hegemonic imagination. Like all these images and stereotypes of Black womanhood, she serves to throttle Black life into narrow, haunting spaces. The damaging effect of such epistemological musings is that they take bits of Black reality and transform them into moral depravity as the norm for Black existence. This is structural evil working at its best (or worst). What this and the other stereotypes do is detract and deflect from examining the structures framing our existence and the assumptions we have made about the veracity of our knowledge about others and ourselves.

Before the 1960s, female-headed households *were* more common in Black communities. However, it is important to note that an ideology racializing female-headedness as a causal feature of Black poverty and moral depravity had not yet emerged.[12] The Mammy is the Black mother figure in White homes; the Matriarch is the Black mother figure in Black homes. As Collins and Robin Good note, she is the bad Black mother who spends too much time away from her home working to support her family. In a twisted bit of logic, the Black Matriarch can also be the Mammy at the same time—proving that context and perception *are* important. Because she is single and works, she cannot supervise her children and this contributes to their failure in school and in society. She is single because she is overly aggressive and unfeminine. She emasculates her lovers and husbands who either refuse to marry her or desert her.[13]

How expedient—the perceived moral failures of Black children and Black men are placed, literally, in the laps of Black women. The Matriarch opens the floodgates for social theorizing about the intergenerational character of Black poverty through the transmission of values in Black families. Good notes that from an elite White male epistemological view, Black children lack the attention and care allegedly showered on middle- and upper-class White children and this deficiency retards Black children's achievement. The Black Matriarch becomes the failed Mammy.[14]

This view, perched from the abyss of the fantastic hegemonic imagination, conveniently diverts our attention away from structural issues such as economic, political, and social structural inequalities that affect not only Black mothers and their children, but all of us. The solution becomes simple: teach good values in the home and anyone can rise from poverty. While I do not deny the importance of teaching good values and reinforcing those values throughout our lives, this is not the sole or even best response to structural inequalities that spawn poverty.

Blaming Blacks who are poor for their plight and using Black women's perceived performance as mothers to explain economic apartheid yokes classism, racism, and sexism into a tight, neat package that labels Black family structures as deviant because they challenge patriarchal assumptions about the ideal construction of the family. As Good notes, the absence of a Black patriarchy is used as evidence for Black cultural inferiority. This also extends to the political, social, and theological. Unchallenged is the assumption that patriarchal social arrangement should be the unassailable norm.

In short, the Matriarch does not model "good" gender behavior. Collins notes that this image is a powerful symbol for women of all colors for what can go wrong when White patriarchal power is challenged.[15] The not so subtle message is that aggressive, assertive women are penalized with abandonment, poverty, and stigmatization.

The Matriarch represents Black women who refuse to be passive. This refusal leads to the stigmatization of Black women who insist on controlling their sexuality and fertility. These women do not serve the interests of the classist, racist, and sexist social order of the fantastic hegemonic imagination. They break the mold of what is acceptable for women and therefore they must be banished into a demonic image that represents pathology and moral depravity. Left in place, as if pure and uncorrupted, is a nasty and vindictive social order that preys on people like mantises. This deceptive nonthreatening posture of the social order hides the rows of sharp spikes that consume whole peoples in its carnivorous lust.

The Black Matriarch and the thesis that grew up to rationalize the stereotype represent the social problems approach to the Black experience popularized in the 1960s by the work of Daniel Patrick Moynihan (*The Negro Family: The Case for National Action*, 1965).[16] However, the notion of the Black Matriarch has its origins in the early works of W .E. B. Du Bois (*The Negro American Family*, 1908) and E. Franklin Frazier (*The Negro Family in the United States*, 1939 and *Black Bourgeoisie: The Rise of a New Middle Class*, 1957).

A brief look at Frazier's work is instructive in informing us of how in sociological theory sexual hegemony functions as epistemological privilege that then moves to public policy formation when fueled by the fantastic hegemonic imagination. Sociologist Cheryl Townsend Gilkes argues that Frazier presumed that "failure to conform to the canons of patriarchy was a source of deviance in black families and communities that constituted 'disorganization.' "[17]

Frazier's description of Black women in *Black Bourgeoisie* runs counter to his work in *The Negro in the United States* (1949) where he uses such phrases as "considerable equality," "generally equalitarian," "tradition of independence," "spirit of democracy," and "considerable cooperation" to describe Black female-male relationships.[18] By 1957, the Frazier of *Black Bourgeoisie* presents husbands as slaves of their wives and, as Gilkes notes, accuses these men of not being real men.

> As one of the results of not being able to play the "masculine role," middle-class Negro males . . . use their "personalities" to compensate for their inferior status in relation to [white] men. This fact would seem to support the observation of an American sociologist that the Negro was "the lady among the races," if he had restricted his observation to middle-class males among American Negroes.[19]

Frazier equates lack of male dominance with male subordination rather than with the egalitarian tradition he describes in *The Negro Family in the United States* in 1939.

> The middle-class Negro male is not only prevented from playing a masculine role, but generally must let negro women assume the leadership role in any show of militancy. This reacts upon his status in the home where *the tradition of female dominance*, which is widely established among Negroes, has tended to assign a subordinate role to the male.[20]

Gilkes argues that Frazier finishes his analysis by showing "extreme rhetorical disrespect for these families." He states that upwardly mobile husbands who married women from old families as playing "a pitiful role" in their homes and that "the greatest compliment that can be paid such a husband is that he 'worships his wife,' in other words that he cherishes her to the point that the wife's friends talk about this wonderful man."[21] Frazier saw these men as "pathetic" and labeled these families as quasi-pathological and delusional.

A different Frazier emerges from 1930 to 1957—a puzzling transformation given that Frazier spent his entire professional career attacking racial essentialism. He becomes a sexual essentialist whose theories were used to wreak havoc on Black women's lives in the public policy arena. Gilkes notes that although Frazier supported women's suffrage, he did not consider women working outside the home as ennobling and prided himself in the fact that his wife did not have to work.[22] Further, Gilkes notes, Frazier refused to concede Melville Herskovitz's observation that "the important position of the woman in the Negro family" was a continuation of African traditions. Instead, Frazier argued that "the Negro family has developed as a patriarchal organization or similar to the American family as the male has acquired property and an interest in his family and as the assimilation of American attitudes and patterns of behavior has been accelerated by the breaking down of social isolation, sometimes through physical amalgamation."[23]

Like W .E. B. Du Bois before her, Gilkes concludes, "Frazier's analysis was exaggerated and grounded too heavily in the anecdotal." Gilkes quotes Du Bois's description of Frazier's work in *Black Bourgeoisie* in his essay "The Present Leadership Among American Negro": "he lashes Negro society with bitter and sarcastic invective." Du Bois reminds his reader that one must consider the world Frazier describes in the context of violence and monopoly capitalism, although Frazier failed to do so.[24]

As problematic as Frazier's work is, Gilkes notes that he did separate the issues of organization and disorganization from actual structure. "A father-headed family could be disorganized and a mother-headed family disorganized. These were empirical questions."[25] However, in a highly selective reading of Frazier, Moynihan selected mother-headed families as disorganized and did not deal with any of the complexity that Frazier did show in his work regarding Black families. Drawing on what Gilkes notes as the "rhetorical context of extreme disrespect for middle class Black women," Moynihan portrayed Black men as deviant, effeminate, and passive. Black women were labeled doubly deviant, masculine, and unnaturally superior.[26] Moynihan did not believe that Black women would play a positive and crucial role in Black families without dominating men and male-female sexual activities. However, Frazier, the premier Black sociologist of his time provided potent ammunition for Moynihan's invective. For Moynihan, "the fundamental fact of Negro American life is the often reversed roles of husband and wife . . . [calling for a] dramatic and desperately needed change."[27] As I have argued elsewhere, this damning view of Black womanhood and the proper place of Black women is not confined to elite White males.[28]

These kinds of images of Black manhood and womanhood transmit clear messages about the "proper" connections among femaleness, fertility, sexuality and Black women's roles in the political economy. The Black Matriarch/Welfare Queen is a sexual being whose sexuality is linked with her fertility. She dominates and emasculates while birthing babies ad infinitum. She represents the easy meshing of oppressions that serve as both epistemological and ideological justifications for economic exploitation, gender subordination, and racial oppression. In the hands of a fantastic hegemonic imagination, when yoked with the certain religious values, she and other stereotypes engender public policies that assume the worst about Black women (and all Black folk). These policies rarely, if ever, question the structures in which we all exist and the economic, moral, political, and social impact that these structures have on our lives.

The Protestant Work Ethic

Mary Jo Bane asserts that though religious viewpoints are present, these are implicit and unexamined in public policy debates.[29] In light of Bane's assertion, I want to trouble the waters a bit more in exploring our assumptions about the nature of the individual, the state, the church, and the poor. These assumptions are *very* contested terrains within religious disciplines in general and within Christian ethics in particular. This, yoked with my concerns about epistemology, sparks a very basic question: Just who are we as religious folk when we enter discussions of public policy?

Human beings are prone to radicalizing certain behaviors: we can turn initially positive knowledge into negative values; we can make good things emerge from disastrous quagmires. However, just as epistemologies are contextual, so are all our other reference points for living. We become dangerous when we fail to recognize this about ourselves and then suffer the temptation of absolutizing our knowledge.

One instance of this is found in Max Weber's Protestant work ethic that values hardwork, thrift, and honesty. It is ironic that the modern day Protestant work ethic has moved so far from the sixteenth-century theologian and church reformer John Calvin's ideal. This becomes striking when paired with notions of the poor and poverty. The late social worker Alan Keith-Lucas argued that every Western society has had people who are dependent on others for help.[30] Historically, theologians such as Ambrose and Chrysostom have offered theological explanations for why the poor are poor. For Ambrose, such inequalities are the result of the Fall. Chrysostom believed that God permitted poverty so that those who were better off would have someone to give to and therefore earn their reward for such charity in heaven. Indeed, some Puritans believed that the poor were the nonelect and an insult to God.

Martin Luther and John Calvin gave Christianity and Western thought the first positive interpretation of work that was applicable to everyone. Luther believed that Christians were called to serve their neighbor in the world and one way this was made manifest is through our work. Calvin joined Luther in seeing work as a positive human activity. Calvin emphasized calling and vocation as demands of the Christian life that also necessitated obedience to God.[31]

Although Calvin viewed the world as sinful, his ethic is one of grateful obedience that leads to self-denial. He held together love of God and love of neighbor—we must extend charity to our neighbor and share with that person our blessings. For Calvin, neighbors include those whom we do not know and those whom we consider to be enemies. As Christian ethicist Joan Martin points out, this bond defines us as the human race created by God and we are made in God's own image.[32] Calvin saw work as the glorification of God and the building up of the Christian community.

Both Luther and Calvin maintained a rigid view of hereditary social status. Although Calvin allowed for a bit more room for changing one's occupation, both he and Luther believed that it was sinful to try to alter one's social position because to do so would be to alter one's calling. Joan Martin notes that the rigid social class structure in both theologians became problematic for the later development of a notion of the work ethic.[33]

Generally, there are myriad explanations for why the poor are poor. What remains constant throughout history and into the contemporary scene, however, is the accusation that the poor are lazy and intemperate.[34] John Locke, writing in 1696, believed that the increase of those in poverty was due to the "relaxation of discipline and the corruption of manners."[35] Poverty has been seen as a result of vice, a lack of thrift, and/or the failure to do the will of God. Weber notes that Thomas Adams believed that "God probably allows so many people to remain poor because he knows that they would not be able to withstand the temptations that go with wealth. For wealth all too often draws men away from religion."[36] The "deserving" poor are excused from these judgments, occasionally, with the moral burden shifted and placed on those who are wealthier and who exploit the poor. Such early twentieth-century social hymns such as Frank North's "Where Cross the Crowded Ways of Life" are an example of this.[37]

Western governments have used several strategies in their attempts to move the poor to independence or to correct their perceived moral flaws.[38] One strategy is to make the life of the pauper as uncomfortable as possible. A second technique is to make relief lower than what could be earned by a laborer in the lowest class. A third assigns diminished legal status to the pauper. Finally, some governments use supervision and control in which the poor must endure whatever conditions and demands for behavior that are imposed on them by the wealthier members of society who use government regulations to impose their worldviews on the poor.

At the same time that these methods were and are employed, the basic features of the work ethic as we know it today also emerged. They include a strong sense of duty to one's work, the perception that work gives meaning to life, valuing the necessity of hardwork and giving work the best of one's time, understanding that work contributes to the moral worth of the individual and to the health of the social order, viewing wealth as a major goal in life, viewing leisure as that which is earned by work and also through preparation for work, that success in work results primarily from personal effort, and that the wealth that one amasses from work is a sign of God's favor. Some see these features as too rigid; others advocate a more flexible understanding of work and our understanding of calling in relation to it.

As Keith-Lucas notes, there is a fine line between believing that God has chosen those who are successful and believing that if one can manage to be successful, then God will choose one. It is not surprising, then, to find a tension in Calvin's moral command to pursue one's vocation in the world with vigor because it is a sign of being chosen by God *and* his moral injunction against ostentation and spending. In a revival of the Hebrew Bible's concept of divine blessings and looking to God in all that we do, Calvin placed severe limitations on usury and considered divine blessings as a trust that should benefit our neighbors. Clearly, Calvin's views do not represent the contemporary spirit of global capitalism.

Calvin's ethic does not necessarily justify Weber's thesis, but it is important to note that Weber's point is that a religious ethic can legitimize a socioeconomic form that was not a part of its original intent. R. H. Tawney built a modified version of Weber's thesis in which he argues that the work ethic is not a purely Protestant phenomenon. Tawney notes that the understanding of calling and pockets of capitalism emerged before the Reformation. Combining Weber and Tawney's insights gives us much to consider when dealing with how this might affect public policymaking.

In part, this had led to public policies that are often unaware of the kind of religious values that form their roots, and the makers of these policies are ill equipped to critique their assumptions because they cannot remember what they never knew.[39] We are inheritors of a work ethic that has shifted from its early roots, *and* for many, if not for most Protestants, a major part of who we are religiously in the United States stems from an Enlightenment conception of the self. This self is formed from the basic understanding that there are natural inherent rights for all people and each person is an independent unit that is an autonomous, self-determining ego. Key, here, is the notion of autonomy. In Protestant religious face, such autonomy represents a concern for principles of authentic belief and practice. It is validated by an appeal to human experience and reason. In short, we *are* the world.

This has loosed an unrestrained or rampant individualism in many of our private and public beliefs and practices that stress personal responsibility and despise any hint of or the reality of dependency. This, to my mind, meanspirited duo oozing from the fantastic hegemonic imagination encourages envisioning society as a necessary evil to monitor so that it does not inhibit personal freedom. Society should not get in the way of our individuality or our ability—often seen as God-given if not God-ordained—to use reason and personal experience to justify all manner of private behavior and public policy. These included those that enhance life and respect the dignity and worth of all persons *and* those that see attention to difference and context as anathema. Stressing personal responsibility while detesting dependency often wedges the diversity of human isness into a stultifying and in some cases death-dealing homogeneity that is healthy only for a precious (and elite) few. At times, Christianity has defended with great poignancy the autonomy of the individual in order to stress the value of every human being, of our freedom, and the great respect owed to each and every one of us. Regrettably, we have also radicalized these notions into a grasping individualism such that we are now reaping a bitter harvest from the unrestrained exercise of our passion for possessing, for self-assertion, for power—as individuals, as social institutions, and as a nation.

As this Enlightenment autonomous self emerged, it is ironic that the work ethic has also helped to build large segments of our culture and society. It has aided in carving out enormous national wealth based on a capitalist economy. It has often been one of the engines fueling some movements for social change such as the Civil Rights movement; recent movements in public housing complexes, often led by women, to take back and define their living spaces; and economic empowerment in which churches set up independent corporations to address community problems and issues. These rest, to varying degrees, on the values of hardwork and thrift *and* the dignity and worth of the individual.

The difference in these movements and in their understanding of society as a necessary evil is based in their very *understanding* of society itself. These movements yearn for a robust and vitally inclusive and interdependent society. In many, if not most segments of dispossessed communities, the notion of uninhibited personal freedom remains a utopian folly or a reality carved out of violence. Advancing public policies that see society as a necessary evil has truncated the lives of the poor, and many Black folk see current public policies as forms of genocide. This is even more deadly when we consider the public policies that have a direct impact on the lives of the Black Matriarch and her children: welfare, health care, reproductive health, childcare, domestic and sexual violence, and the U.S. prison industrial complex. This often means that the Black Matriarch and her children are at the mercy of public policies that stress equality and personal liberty as if our societal playing field is equitable and fair in its construction.

However, the religious values that are at the core of these policies—an appeal to the person as an independent unit; the autonomous, self-determining ego; stress on personal responsibility; and the abhorrence of dependency—belie a basic inability or unwillingness to recognize structural evil and/or inequities that require public policies that move *beyond* the notion that government must work through individuals who care about themselves first and foremost, if not exclusively.

We need public policies that are more complex than those that lead to the incremental conversion of individual souls. Far too much of our current public policy debates concentrate on individual morality and focus our attention on pieces of the social structure rather than the structure in its entirety. As Bane notes, it is *rare* that the specific moral and civil religious implications of such judgments are made explicit. Some religious values emphasize personal or private moral norms; other religious values emphasize public morality, such as social justice, poverty, corporate responsibility, working conditions, health care, and war. This epistemological minefield is deadly. There is much more at stake in public policy formation than abstractions and dazzling rhetoric. This becomes very clear if we look at one of the public policy issues that have had a direct impact on the Black Matriarch and her children—the 1996 welfare reform that ended welfare as we knew it.

The Theoethics of Public Policymaking

Elected on a populist platform in 1992, President Bill Clinton believed that the federal government should play a major role in improving the competitive position of the United States in the global economy. However, counter to his populist claims, Clinton turned to enterprise economic theory in which he embraced a neoliberal approach that stressed the responsibility of government to stimulate economic growth. He rejected the conservative supply emphasis on stimulating private investment capital on one hand and the liberal Keynesian emphasis on stimulated demand on the other hand. Clinton called for government investment/spending in human capital (education and skill training for workers), in technology (especially communications and transportation), and in infrastructure (roads, bridges, ports, airports, and so on). The Clinton administration backed away from developing an industrial policy because of the danger that government subsidies to specific industries would make interest group politics the driving force in the economy.

The renewed drive for tax cuts and spending reductions in 1993 was partially due to Bill Clinton's attempt to shift the balance slightly in 1992. The wealthy paid 16 percent more in taxes the following year as a result and the antiwelfare rhetoric began in earnest once again. As the dust continues to settle on the Personal Responsibility and Work Opportunity Act of 1996 and as President Bush continues to call for tax cuts and for reduced federal social programs, it is becoming increasingly clear that low-income and poor people are the ones who must bear the weight of balancing the budget. The only deep and/or multiyear budget cuts that were a part of the tax reform of 1996 that were actually enacted affected only the poor and low-income folks.

Public policies reflect the working out of our national value judgments. The moralization of poverty in the age of empire is a gruesome and death-dealing pageant for low-income and poor women, men, and children. The poor in U.S. culture and society are often ignored, rendered faceless, labeled undeserving, considered an eyesore, their own worst enemy, or simply down on their luck. The Black Matriarch was joined with the Welfare Queen of all colors as the 1996 welfare reforms were crafted with these negative images playing a tremendous (sub)conscious role. These degrading images tell us that poverty is an aberration of the grand narrative of progress and success that fuels much of our culture or that it is an end produced by the poor themselves—they have simply brought this on themselves. In a rather curious circular logic, media portrayals of poverty point out the ways in which the poor suffer from forms of deprivation and define the very reactions of the poor to their deprivation as the cause of poverty.

The results are all too predictable—there is something fundamentally wrong with the victims. Pundits point to biology, psychology, family environment, community, race—or more often combinations of these—to map out the reasons for poverty and to plot strategies to deal with the gross assumption that turns into conviction that the poor are failures because they have not lifted themselves out of poverty. This cesspool of ideologies ignores the fact that poverty in the United States is also systemic and that most often it is the direct result of political and economic policies that deprive people of jobs, subsistence wages, and access to health care.

To speak of "the poor" in U.S. society is to attempt to synthesize a variety of highly diverse people who need different kinds of help. It is easier to formulate policies about a "person" such as the Black Matriarch rather than to wade into the troubling waters of systemic evil. The failure to engage structurally in the age of empire has been and will continue to be disastrous as governmental policies continually seek to formulate a single policy to deal with the poor through welfare reforms. Welfare is a complex and interlocking set of dynamics that combine—at bare minimum—education, jobs, housing and homelessness, crime, addictions, race, gender, class, health care, and geography.

The latest assault on welfare recipients is, I believe, a strategy being employed by political leaders, Democrat and Republican, to shift attention away from the government's redistribution of wealth among the wealthy. We have become an intensely stratified industrial nation economically. The top 10 percent of U.S. households owns 70.9 percent of this nations wealth, 90 percent of the households owns 29.1 percent.[40]

What does it mean when more than 93 percent of the budget reductions in entitlements have come from programs for low-income people?[41] When the 104th Congress finished its work in 1996, it reduced entitlement programs by $65.6 billion in the period from 1996 to 2002. Within this amount, almost $61 billion came from low-income entitlement programs such as food stamps and the Supplemental Security Income program (SSI) for the elderly and disabled poor, and assistance to legal immigrants. One frustrating reality in this is that although entitlement programs for low-income folks accounted for 93 percent of the reduction in entitlement programs, these same programs accounted for only 37 percent of the total expenditures for entitlement programs other than Social Security and only 23 percent of all entitlement spending.

Even those programs for low-income folks that are not entitlements experienced a disproportionate reduction in funding as a result of the 1996 budget cuts that ushered in welfare reforms. Although these programs represented 21 percent of overall funding for nondefense discretionary programs, they bore more than one and one-half times their share of the nondefense discretionary cuts. From 1994 to 1996 alone, funding for discretionary programs for low-income households were reduced more than 10 percent while funding for other nondefense discretionary programs shrank by 5 percent.

Almost lost in the midst of all the cuts is the important fact that the United States has one of the most individualized welfare systems in the Western world. Despite the welfare reforms of 1996, there remain hundreds of variables in our public assistance laws that can affect the amount of an individual's or family's grant. Keith-Lucas notes two problems with this.[42] First, is the fact that we have two contradictory desires—we want to be treated the same as others *and* we want our own individual circumstances to be taken into account. The second is that individualization compares people or compares people to a norm. This ignores the fact that we are more than our differences and obscures the fact that we are unique individuals.

The budget cuts proposed by Congress in December 2005 continue this unholy trend. Using the devastation of hurricanes Katrina and Rita as the rationale, the House Republicans chose to embrace what they termed "painful cuts" rather than add $100 billion or more to the deficit—a deficit that is fueled by tax cuts for the wealthy. The cuts would cost nearly $50 billion over five years—less than half of 1 percent of the $14.3 trillion in federal spending planned for the same period. The mandatory programs included are food stamps ($7 billion), Medicare ($8 billion), Medicaid ($5 billion), and student loans ($13 billion). These devastating cuts are made more monstrous by the fact that the Republican leadership, at the time of this writing, is planning to go ahead with seeking to make permanent previously approved tax cuts that would cost the federal treasury another $70 to $100 billion. The rationale is that this will keep the economy growing. While the economy *is* growing, the poverty rate is increasing as well.[43] Who is really benefiting from these cuts in real time and life?

Regrettably, the individualism of our welfare system is joined by the rampant individualism of our culture. It seems irrelevant to most people that viewing the self as an unproblematic center of the universe actually turns the Christian gospel on its head. It does not appear to create much cause for concern that one is hard pressed to find biblical warrant for the notion that one must first earn merit (meet an obligation) before being accepted (receiving an entitlement). No, the Christian faith is built on God's grace. For Protestants, this grace is not rare and does not have to be earned, it is constant and it is free. One is first accepted (the entitlement) and then one follows it with a life of joyous (but sometimes cranky) response (obligation).

Calvin's work ethic seems lost. True enough, as the Reformation faded, many gradually moved away from full dependence on the sufficiency of Christ's work for their salvation and sanctification. However, our current work ethic preserves some of Calvin's values to varying degrees—the virtue and dignity of work, the sanctity of all legitimate types of work, the importance of responsible work rather than sloppy work or idleness, and viewing the outcome of work as proceeding from service to God and society.

However, when it comes to work, the work ethic, and public policymaking, we would do well to incorporate other elements of Calvin's ethic: work as a calling or vocation rather than simply a career or job; recognizing that work should be in service to others and not only for our own self-fulfillment. We should acknowledge that work does not give us our basic identity or meaning—this comes from our relationships with God and the world around us and the people in it. Finally, work should be communal rather than individual in character.

Building on Calvin, three basic public policy questions emerge. The first two, What kind of society do we want? and What sort of people do we need to be to achieve this society? are asked frequently and seem to dominate current public policy debates and policies. They are, interestingly enough, based on the individual as an autonomous and independent being. These two questions are vital for our lives together, but they do not go far enough. It is the third question that helps to balance and enrich public policy formation: What kinds of social structures do we need to help form people to achieve the society we want? This last question pushes beyond the focus on the individual and character to include structures and structural change.

A closer look at the ways in which Enlightenment religious values fueled the presidential candidacy of George W. Bush illustrates the ways in which a focus on the first two questions that I mention above can play themselves out. Bush, an evangelical Protestant Christian, is the inheritor of a conservative evangelical tradition that dates back to the early to mid-1800s in which Protestant Christians founded benevolent societies to fund evangelism, distribute Christian materials, and reform the morals of the populace. The stress was on individual conversions that would eventually lead to a Christian moral order. Churches were to pronounce on issues of personal faith and morality but not on broad social policy—particularly if it had political ramifications.

Liberal evangelicals, who date back to the late-1800s, recognized the interconnections between social problems such as slavery, women's rights, and the exploitation of industrial laborers and began to develop a broad-based approach to social issues. Today there remains a sharp polarization: conservatives believe that stressing social action takes away the primary evangelistic mission of the church from it; liberals believe that stressing individual salvation and piety takes away the primary transformative mission of the church from it.

Bush's current public policy pronouncements concerning initiatives such as Charitable Choice grow out of his conservative Protestant evangelical values. He stands within a religious tradition that focuses on the individual and a nineteenth-century philanthropic tradition in which the wealthy not only distributed handouts, they also imposed demands and discipline on the poor. For them, the point was to provide the spiritual and material sustenance that shapes character. The latter day version of this is compassionate conservatism, a concept made popular by Marvin Olasky in his *The Tragedy of American Compassion*. Although the few scholars who reviewed it dismissed this 1992 book, some Washington Beltway conservatives such as William Bennett and Newt Gingerich and policy wonks picked it up.

These disciples argued that slashing the welfare state would unleash an outpouring of charitable works through Federal grants, tax credits, and partnerships between church and state. *Olasky's* ultimate goal is to turn the government's responsibility to the poor over to private charities, but the *socioeconomic and political realities* produced a set of public policies that paid lip service to compassionate conservatism. This response to the call for compassionate conservatism in public policy matters by politicians and policy wonks was a theological and political rationale that sanctioned guilt-free gutting of the welfare state.

Once again, the inordinate concentration on individual morality is evident. The political conservatism ushered in with the election of Ronald Reagan and the policies of that administration has now turned into a religious moralizing conservatism that focuses on infidelity and honesty, antiabortion, family cohesion, and homosexual illegitimacy that has spawned hate crimes ranging from bombing women's clinics to the brutal slaying of Matthew Shepard, a White gay twenty-two-year-old University of Wyoming student, in Laramie by two chronically unemployed young White men who had histories of violence and criminality.

The current welfare policy of the United States often lifts up the Black Matriarch as the poster child for its demonization of poor women, children, and men. Poverty is the problem of those who endure it, rather than a socioeconomic system structured to insure inequality while touting its openness to all—we must simply work harder to reap the benefits that are there for the taking. Seeking to do a womanist analysis of the transformation needed to deliver us from the fears and hatreds and absolute ignorance that often fuels our understanding of welfare policy, the lives of those who need welfare assistance and the policies that we then shape, is much like searching for a very small needle in an immense haystack. This can be a maddening search through the maze of socioeconomic inequalities that are spawning theoethical debates that are not anchored in the realities of poverty in the United States. Rather than factor in the cost of dead-end jobs and disposable workers in the social order, welfare reform ignored the fact that real wages for average workers are plummeting to levels below those of 1967—16 percent between 1973 and 1993 alone. This is happening in the midst of rising productivity—irony and obscenity combined. Since 1968, worker productivity has gone up, but wages have gone down. Productivity grew 74.2 percent between 1968 and 2000, but hourly wages for average workers fell by 3 percent, adjusting for inflation. Real wages for minimum wage workers—two-thirds of whom are adults—dropped from $315.37 in 1968 to $277.67 in 2000. Meanwhile, in 2004, the average CEO of a major corporation earned $9.84 million (including salary, bonus, and other compensation such as exercised stock options); average workers were still recovering from several years of falling real wages.[44]

In this age of empire, our postmodern culture suffers from the enormous impact of market forces on everyday life. Neoliberal economics is now the order of the day. It places the interest of those who own or manage corporations and wealth at the center of all major public policy considerations. As Manning Marable notes, neoliberal economic policy adopts market techniques and mechanisms to carry out the routine functions of government. According to Marable, market forces are viewed as that entity that should determine the accessibility of services and resources including health care, employment, housing, and public transportation.[45]

Everyday life has become commodified as corporate profits shoot through the roof in an ironic but deadly gambol—in 1994 alone, the profits of the Fortune 500 companies shot up 54 percent while the gain of sales was only 8 percent. This disjuncture was made possible by slashing payrolls, investing in technology, overhauling assembly lines, and reducing fringe benefits. Although 2001 and 2002 were lean years for the Fortune 500, they came roaring back to life after the U.S. invasion of Iraq in 2003. Wal-Mart led the pack with sales of more than $288,189 billion in 2004. This was an increase of 11 percent from 2003. Second on the list was ExxonMobil Corporation at $270,722 billion in sales—up 27 percent from the previous year. ExxonMobil also topped the profits chart with a record $25.3 billion in earnings.[46] Companies reduced their workforce and became more efficient in creating greater profits. Union jobs, which have better wages and benefits, continue to disappear. The downsizing of corporate America has meant the downsizing of the poor.

And then came Enron. Harkening back to the savings and loan scandal of 2001–2002, the same nonpartisan lawmakers and regulators who expressed moral outrage at the $60 billion-plus loss to investors (many of whom were Enron's own employees tied into their pension plan through stock options) were the very same people who, as part of New Gingerich's Contract with America through the Private Securities Litigation Reform Act, in 1995, successfully passed legislation that shielded companies and their accountants from investor lawsuits. In 2000, many of these same folks were able to force regulators to weaken proposed restrictions on accountants.[47] As more corporations admit that they practice the "aggressive accounting" (in the old days, this was called fraud) that Enron did, Enron's $644 billion meltdown increasingly appears to be just the tip of the corporate greed iceberg.

This tumbledown economic reality, with the fantastic hegemonic imagination churning in the background, has also ushered in the age of racist, sexist, and classist ideologies that mask the realities of an increasingly morally bankrupt economic climate in the United States. *These deadly ideologies function to mask the fact that majority of the poor and those on welfare are White.* Inner city neighborhoods are viewed as sites of pathology and hopelessness. Rural areas are ignored or painted with the pastoral gloss of rugged individualism and portrayed as the last vestige of true Americana.

With the fantastic hegemonic imagination running unchecked, our views of welfare and welfare reform are rimmed with these inadequate and specious views of life in America. We have created (and are now maintaining) a society that simply refuses to care beyond our narrow self-interests. The 1996 welfare reforms are testimony to the further institutionalization of this callousness. And worse, we have tied these reforms to the hope that our economy will remain strong and provide the jobs needed to give the enacted reforms a chance to work. This is dangerous and may prove to be a deadly assumption. The bottom line is whether these reforms, built on mean-spiritedness, self interest, stereotypes, and political expediency work to enhance the lives of those who are living in whirlpools of catastrophe in postmodern America? I think not.

The old welfare law needed reform because it did not adequately require or provide opportunities for work and parental responsibility to help families to get off the roles. Indeed, it often locked families into dependency that could, but not necessarily, become generational. However, the crafting of the recent reforms was built on an epistemology of the commodification of lives through spectacle and extravaganza and political, rhetorical absolutes that polarized and obscured lives. For conservatives, federal entitlements were equivalent to irresponsibility and lifelong dependency. For liberals, the replacement of entitlements with block grants was equivalent to work requirements. Left in the middle, as political fodder, are the Black Matriarch, her children, and many of her friends.

Picking Our Own Cotton: Searching for the Common Good

Public policy and public policymaking should give us institutions that guarantee that the mechanisms of a pluralist democracy such as the United States operate with a great deal of fairness for all citizens. Instead, too many of our public policies, as public policy researchers Anne Schneider and Helen Ingram point out, "deceive, confuse, and in other ways discourage active citizenship, minimize the possibility of self-corrections, and perpetuate or exacerbate the very tendencies that produced dysfunctional public policies in the first place."[48] This harsh judgment by Schneider and Ingram is justified when we look at the various ways in which public policies have been articulated of late. The general citizenry is often given half-truths, intentionally conflicting information, and less than full disclosure in many policy debates of our day.

Economist Paul Krugman provides a helpful example of how this happens when he describes the machinations around the first set of tax cuts the Bush-Cheney administration pushed through in 2001.[49] The fiscal policies of the Clinton administration left the country with projected federal budget deficits. However, the tax law did not mandate any future cuts or changes without legislation. This was an acceptable fiscal outlook because of the promise of surpluses later in the decade. The Bush-Cheney administration then proposed and won tax cuts that were not temporary measures to boost the economy but were permanent ones. Some of these cuts did not or will not take effect until 2005, 2006, and 2010. Krugman suspects that the rhetoric of the Bush-Cheney administration about these tax cuts will "be designed to maximize public confusion" about the real nature and probable fiscal effects of the cuts.

As Krugman states,

> First, administration officials will claim that people who want to cancel future tax cuts want to raise taxes. This is like George W. Bush's claim that the Enron chairman, Kenneth Lay, supported Ann Richards in the Texas governor's race (he did give Ms. Richards some money—but he gave Mr. Bush much more). That is, you can try to rationalize it with fancy word play—not cutting taxes is raising them from what they would otherwise have been, right? But it sure feels like a lie.
>
> Second, they will throw up a smokescreen of confusing figures to hide the agreed fact that tax cuts are a major reason for the abrupt collapse of the projected surplus. Let me repeat the words "agreed fact." Recently four independent projections were made of the budget surplus over the next decade: one each from the Democratic and Republican staff of the House and Senate. All four projections marked down previous surplus estimates by two-thirds; all four attributed about 45 percent, or $1.7 trillion, of the decline to the tax cut. Everyone expects the estimates that the nonpartisan Congressional Budget Office will release tomorrow to look very similar.
>
> Third, they will claim that the future tax cuts are just what the doctor ordered to deal with the current recession. The C.B.O. disagrees; it declared, in a recent report, that accelerating those tax cuts would be ineffective as a stimulus measure. And if tax cuts now are ineffective, tax cuts later are even less effective.
>
> Finally, the administration will try to convince you that the return of deficits won't hurt you personally. But for millions of Americans deficits will soon begin to pinch, hard.[50]

Krugman ends by noting that the impact of the cuts was already being felt when a bipartisan panel recommended increases in Medicare payments for 2002 but the Congressional response expressed skepticism

about doing so given "the current budgetary environment." This is
Washington Beltway speak for "we don't have the money."

The two cuts for 2006 stun.[51] They allow people earning upward of
$200,000 a year to claim larger write-offs for a spouse and their chil-
dren, and expenses such as mortgage interest on a vacation home.
Congressional estimates peg these cuts to cost $27 billion over the
short term and $146 billion from 2010 through 2019. In the last nine
years of these cuts, taxpayers making more than $1 million a year will
be the chief beneficiaries. President George W. Bush set off this tax cut
mania in his first year in office in 2000. His rationale then was that
this was the way to give back the Clinton-era budget surplus. The cuts
of 2001–2003 predictably busted the budget because they were predi-
cated on bad math. The surplus that provided the rationale for these
cuts has vanished and has been replaced with a deficit projected to
reach $530 billion by 2015 if the cuts are made permanent. There is
something very wrong here when this is contrasted to the gutting of
social programs.

Schneider and Ingram note that public policymaking is produced
through "a dynamic historical process" that involves the "social constructions of knowledge and identities of target populations, power
relationships, and institutions." They advocate public policy designs
that allow citizens to create, learn, and participate in shaping new or
different institutions that provide the framework for a more genuine
democratic society. For them, these designs, like all designs, reflect the
"social constructions of knowledge, target populations, power relationships, and institutions in the context from with they emerge."[52]

This highly subjective process can and does fall victim to political
manipulation by elected officials and others. This is evident when public policies reflect a deserving/undeserving mentality. One example is
the contrast between Medicare (deserving) and Medicaid (undeserving). The eligibility requirements and accessibility restrictions on those
who seek help from Medicaid can make the same process for those
seeking Medicare look like child's play.[53] The spirit of punishment and
punitive moralization dominates with stigmatization and disenfranchisement as (un)natural dance partners. These kinds of policies fall
far short of addressing structural injustice.

Schneider and Ingram observe that political leaders are quick to
rely on and follow the wisdom of scientific and professional networks
when issues are not treated simply as political cannon fodder.[54] The
epistemological worldview of these kinds of undemocratic public policymaking practices relies on a simplistic Cartesian duality that fails to

appreciate complexity, honesty, and inclusivity. A more democratic and perhaps more difficult epistemology such as one that stresses an interstructured autonomy, dependency, and interdependency dynamic calls for a more truth-filled and more open process of making public policy decisions. In short, a more inclusive epistemological stance in public policymaking appreciates the diversity of our experiences rather than see them as nuisances or representative of special interest groups.

It is apt, then, to add another set of religious values that shape public policies as we answer the third question: What kinds of social structures do we need to help form people to achieve the society we want? I do so, not out of any false notion of objectivity. Objectivity rarely works when it comes to theoethical reflection that also seeks to maintain an active and vital embodied, practical edge. I doubt whether objectivity actually works on a practical or actual level when it comes to public policymaking. The religious values that help us hold the personal and the structural together include accountability, justice, and interdependence. If, to return to Calvin for a brief moment, we value and respect our neighbors, then we take seriously a sense of accountability to and for one another—not only as individuals, but also as a society.

One of the earliest words I learned in church is love: Jesus loved me, Jesus loved all the little children of the world, that love could lift me, I should love to tell the story. Yet I also learned that love without justice is asking for trouble. Justice is the notion that each one of us has worth, and that each one of us has the right to have that worth recognized and respected. In short, justice lets us know that we owe one another respect and the right to our dignity.

Justice leads to public policies that claim rights as a part of the assertion of our dignity and well-being. It is relational, not autonomous, and leads to a sense of caring that is actualized in accessible and affordable health care and childcare, and to the development of a federal and rural development policy that is systemic rather than episodic. It recognizes the interdependence in which we all actually live.

Justice, then, is more than giving to each what is due or treating all cases equally. It requires attention to our diversities, particularly to those most marginalized. Simply put, justice involves uncovering, understanding, and rejecting oppression—which is but another way of saying that it involves structural evil. This means recognizing the privileges and benefits that often come a-waltzing[55] with oppression and the fantastic hegemonic imagination. A linear epistemology cannot engage this because it requires an appreciation for contradictions and struggle as natural—the struggle comes from conflict, not harmony. Within a framework of justice, conflict becomes a creative force and a methodological and strategic tool. The point is fundamental structural transformation. We cannot achieve this by simple reform—only through transformation.

The religious values of justice and love question public policies such as the Personal Responsibility and Work Opportunity Reconciliation Act of 1996 and The Balanced Budget Act of 1997 that require low-income and poor people to bear the weight of balancing the budget. These values shine a spotlight on the redistribution of wealth to the wealthy in which the richest 2.7 million Americans (the top 1%) will have as many after-tax dollars to spend as the bottom 100 million.[56] These values ask, what, then, do politicians mean when they argue for tax cuts, Charitable Choice, the Defense of Marriage Act, the Contract with the American Family and its predecessor the Contract with America, charter schools, and empowerment zones in public policy?

We have a maddening tendency to be troubled by poverty and constrained opportunity but we rarely do more than listen to those who must endure and survive inequities. Perhaps one reason we remain skeptical about the government's ability to do much about poverty is that our theological worldviews do not offer us much of an alternative either. If we keep the unrestrained autonomous self on our collective eyeball and if we refuse to yoke our individual selves and concerns with the matrix of life with others, we will never be able to truly engage in democratic politics with a spirit of justice or peace. Our traditional religious discourses will take us away from our daily needs. We will be even more complicit with the dominant political powers of religious folk and religious discourse, and religion itself will be *only* the sigh of the oppressed, the heart of the world without a heart, the soul of the soulless conditions—an opiate and not a source of transformation.[57]

We cannot be these things and offer any genuine alternative to the way public policy has been formed because we have become absorbed by the consumer market; we have and will continue to legitimize political deals. We have and will continue to lose our essence, our salvific power. Sadly, we, as people of faith, will end up with no vital or invigorating heart that beats for justice.

As we engage in notions of democracy and public policy within *conscious* religious frameworks, it is crucial that we make explicit our conception of the common good—not in terms of how the state sees it but in terms of how we understand it from our various religious worldviews and realize that we will not always agree. What is more important, for those of us who are middle-class Christians, is that we need to bring the poor to the center or our questions and our options and our decision-making—not theoretically, but concretely.

Discussions of the common good stretch back to the writings of Plato, Aristotle, and Cicero. More recently, John Rawls has defined it as "certain general conditions that are . . . equally to everyone's advantage." The Catholic religious tradition defines it as "the sum of those conditions of social life which allow social groups and their individual members relatively thorough and ready access to their own fulfillment."[58] Perhaps the simplest way to think about the common good is in terms of having the social structures on which all depend work so that they benefit all people as we strive to create a genuinely inclusive and democratic social and moral order.

Obvious examples of such would be health care that is accessible and affordable, a just and legal political system, equitable educational systems, effective and nondiscriminatory public safety, a clean environment, and an effective and humane social welfare system. Clearly, the common good cannot rest on public policymaking that exhibits a morbid fascination with the autonomous self. The common good calls us to think more deeply and strategically about our conceptions of community. Rather than see community as shaped solely by competition and domination, community can be a concrete site of strength and meaning making for engaged citizens. This understanding embraces individualism in the sense of encouraging self-definition and self-determination—but always in the context of the larger community as it joins other communities in defining and shaping the common good.

Such an epistemological and conceptual shift requires that we recognize the ways in which each of us shifts from dominant to subordinate groups depending on time and circumstance. In doing so, we may then possibly see that from where we stand we have only a partial perspective on the world. As such, it is not for us to garner absolute truth, but to be in a process of radical engagement with each other as we participate, together, in constructing the common good. This requires epistemological courage and theoethical fortitude.

Establishing and maintaining the common good requires all of our cooperation but the steps we take to engage in this demanding task is, I believe, part of what genuine democracy is about. To settle for a weak democratic system that runs roughshod over people is to reconcile with structural evil. An aid in our quest for a rich and vital common good rather than a barrier to it is our very diversity—but a diversity that understands its partial knowledges and the need for the opinions of others and to "see" the world around us and how we are shaping it. This is a very different stance than the one that rests on the autonomous self. Rather than negative competition that seeks to dominate and win at all costs, we practice a competition that pushes all of us toward excellence and growth. We shift our perspective just enough to realize that we are members of the same community, the same society, and that we *can* respect and value individual freedom *and* pursue those goals we have in common.

Will we find the wisdom and the will to craft public policies that hold the individual and the social in one breath? Will we rest on religious values that celebrate the experience and worth of each and every one of us? That sharpen our caring? That enhance our ability to probe and question? That encourage a rigorous and practical mutuality and challenge the kind of autonomy that spawns rampant individualism? Traditionally, we are left with a choice: either to submit to religious values weighted on issues of private character or ones that tilt in favor of public morality. There is at least one other option: find a healthier ground that crafts a creative, progressive, and inclusive space for *everyone*. This space would demand the best from us as individuals; this space would expect nothing less than corporate attempts to create a just society.

As we enter analysis, policy formation, and articulation in more conscious ways as people of faith and faithlessness, we must wrestle with the common good. We must wrestle with this, even if with twisted hips sometimes, but wrestle we must. It is my hunch that in teasing through a conception of the good that is not bounded by our individual skin but is within a collective ethos of individuals, groups, cultures and the like that we can discover what faithful citizenship truly means. We can know *now* what it will take to pick Sanchez's cotton. Finally, we can end the mad drive of creating stereotypes to justify a social order that is structurally evil. Perhaps it is best, then, to give the Black Matriarch and all her kin the last and most hope-filled laugh on behalf of us all.

Growing like Topsy: Solidarity in the Work of Dismantling Evil

She was one of the blackest of her race; and her round shining eyes, glittering as glass beads, moved with quick and restless glances over everything in the room. Her mouth, half open with astonishment at the wonders of the new Mas'r's parlor, displayed a white and brilliant set of teeth. Her woolly hair was braided in sundry little tails, which stuck out in every direction. The expression of her face was an odd mixture of shrewdness and cunning, over which was oddly drawn, like a kind of veil, an expression of the most doleful gravity and solemnity. She was dressed in a single filthy, ragged garment, made of bagging; and stood with her hands demurely folded before her. Altogether, there was something odd and goblin-like about her appearance,—something, as Miss. Ophelia afterwards said, "so heathenish," as to inspire that good lady with utter dismay; and turning to St. Clare, she said, "Augustine, what in the world have you brought that thing here for?"[1]

Solidarity amidst our differences in the face of structural evil may seem to be an exercise in tempting the agony of the absurd. Stowe's introduction of the character Topsy in her abolitionist novel, *Uncle Tom's Cabin*, is a case in point. In this acutely troubling introduction we have of Topsy, Stowe exposes us to the traditional stereotypes of Black women slaves (regardless of age). Topsy is black, her eyes are round and they shine—they actually glitter. Her eyes, not her body, move quickly and restlessly over the contents and the people in the room. Her blackness is contrasted with the brilliant whiteness of her teeth. Her hair is woolly and braided in such a way that her plaits stick out in every direction. Her face is a mixture of shrewdness and cunning, gravity and solemnity. She has a single, ragged dress made of bagging. She appears odd and goblin-like, heathenish.

This description of Topsy, which goes on to note her "black, glassy eyes [that] glittered with a kind of wicked drollery," puts in print a character who is lazy, mischievous, wild-looking, and prone to thievery. She needs constant guidance and beatings to keep her working and out of trouble. However, Stowe's point is that Topsy is all these things because of the dehumanizing system of slavery, not because of her blackness. Yet, Stowe's description of Topsy remains troubling. It is a swill pot of caricature—Topsy is a slave girl who perfectly fits the black stereotype of the time. Stowe's description of Topsy contains imagery of a barely human young girl. In all that Stowe attempts to do in speaking out against the institution of slavery, she clings to an imagery that never allows Topsy to be seen as fully human or humane. The reader never comes to know Topsy (or any of the Black females in the novel) as a person, for her character (both in print and as a person) is never developed. Stowe, regrettably, repeats the very dehumanizing process she seeks to critique.

Despite her best intentions, there is no indication that Stowe talked with Black folks—free or slave—to capture their view of slavery and its direct effect on their lives. Topsy's story is a semihumorous and semitragic subplot in Stowe's novel. As such, it is not unlike the story of other dispossessed groups in the United States. Stowe immersed herself in slave narratives, abolitionist tracts, and also interviewed Whites who had first-hand knowledge of slavery to pen an accurate depiction of Southern life. During her research, Stowe discovered the neglect many slave children experienced. Topsy is her literary and polemical response to the enslavement of Black children. Stowe's aim was to demonstrate that children born into brutalizing and dehumanizing slavocracy were destined to be wild and untamable—regardless of the most profound and sincere ministrations of the most stalwart and religious personas. In this case, these are Miss. Ophelia and Topsy's tragic mistress and playmate, Little Eva.

Stowe's intent was to evoke sympathy if not horror from her audience for Topsy's abysmal plight. Unfortunately, the caricature worked just as effectively in the opposite direction—a danger always possible with caricatures. Although many questioned the morality of slavery after reading *Uncle Tom's Cabin*, others used the book to mount a magnificent trivialization of slavery's brutality. It was the preconversion Topsy who captured the public imagination.

Topsy's kinky hair, filthy clothes, mischievousness, barely recognizable patois became the focus of countless stage shows based on the novel. This stage version of Topsy was the antithesis of Stowe's caricature. Stage Topsy was happy and lighthearted and basked in her enslavement. Patricia Turner notes that awkward speech, ragamuffin appearance, devilish habits and butchered English were sources of humor in minstrel and Tom shows.[2] Topsy, intended as an object to evoke moral disgust for slavery, was reinvented as carefree. She was transformed from a caricature spawned by abject evil to one that suggested that children did and could *thrive* within slavery.

Topsy as Pickaninny[3]

It did not stop with Topsy. The dynamics of structural evil rarely stop with one character or one caricature. Topsy-like images abound in what we now call Black memorabilia. One, the Topsy/Eva or Topsy/Turvy doll, featured two dolls who shared the same body. A pretty, well-dressed, blond-haired White doll whose opposite was a "grotesque, thick-lipped, wide-eyed, sloppily dressed Black doll."[4] These dolls were later modified in physical appearance and marketed as "integration babies."[5] The early 1930s Sears catalogues had ads for the once popular nineteenth-century Topsy and Eva babies. The 1930 Montgomery Ward *General Catalogue*, displayed Topsy (a "mischievous pickanniny") beside a "dear little white baby."[6] The 1945 Sears catalogue featured a Black doll whose outfit was held together by a safety pin. One doll collectors' encyclopedia displays a version of Topsy from the 1950s. This doll was described as a replica of the earlier topsy-turvey dolls that could be changed from black to white by a simple flip of its long skirt.[7] Although the original manufacturers are unknown, the dolls were most prominent in the South

From the nineteenth century until well into the twentieth century, Black baby dolls consistently symbolized negative images. If a boy is shown in overalls, they are either too short or one of his shoulder straps is drooping. The girls' dresses were either torn or too short or both. When a Black child is shown wearing a complete, clean outfit, some part of it is out of place. These dolls were often marketed with such langauge as " mischievous," "pickaninny," or "nigger." They were often described as "Negro doll in a melon," "darkey head," and "nigger baby." Eventually, pickaninny became a standard label for most Black baby dolls. As late as the 1960s, pickaninny was being used to describe a Black child.[8]

The probable roots of pickaninny in Portuguese (*pequeninho*) and Spanish (pequeño) do not have any pejorative social or racial significance. In Guyana and the West Indies it is still used as a term of affection for Black children.[9] It is a cultural and sociopolitical puzzle how pickaninny came to mean "Negro child" in English. It is also less clear whether Blacks or Whites generated the name and in what context Black folk started to perceive it as denigrating and racist.[10]

Generally, pickaninnies had medium brown to dark black skin, bulging eyes, unkept hair, red lips, and wide mouths.[11] Most appear to be between 8 to 9 years old. They were often depicted eating huge pieces of watermelon and/or as tasty morsels for alligators. On postcards, greeting cards, posters, sheet music, and other print media, the public saw little Black children out of doors either being chased or eaten. Sometimes they were adjacent to crops associated with the South. The public was treated to a sea of plump Black babies sitting on baskets of cotton or tobacco; older children crawling on the ground, climbing trees, straddling logs—in animal-like postures, barely recognizable Black children side by side with animals.

Examples include the trademark for Two Coons Axle Grease, which is an image of a semiclad Black child holding a raccoon. The cover of a washable fabric children's book *Pussies and Puppies* has one pussycat, one puppy, and one poorly dressed black child.[12] A 1907 postcard shows a Black child on his knees looking at a pig with the caption: "Whose Baby is OO?" A 1930s bisque match holder shows a black baby emerging from an egg while a rooster looks on. A 1930s pinback has a bird with the head of a Black girl.[13] A cigar company titled its 1890s card "Little African" at the top and "A Dainty Morsel" at the bottom. In between were a snapping alligator coming ashore and a naked Black baby crawling away. Marilyn Kern-Foxworth notes that "in addition to playing on the African theme, it also gave in to the notion viciously promulgated by Southerners that black children were only suited for 'gator bait.' "[14]

Black children depicted as pickaninnies were small and almost sub-human if not animal-like. They were often mistaken for animals and were often shown being pursed by hunters and other animals—dogs, chickens, pigs. Jennifer Craig details a cartoon in which a small Black girl with a head full of wild braids is picking fruit near a swamp as she dangles from a tree. A large alligator appears and leaps for the child and a chase ensues. The child then takes on animalistic qualities and begins to run on all fours, looking more like a creature of prey for the alligator than a person. Craig closes with the observation that "an alligator surely wouldn't pursue a human, so it must think this child is some type of beast."[15] Stories such as *Ten Little Niggers* show Black children being rolled over by boulders, chased by alligators, and set on fire. It is chilling, but necessary to note that these images of Black children were promoted at the same time as the numerous nineteenth- and twentieth-century pseudoscientific theories predicted confidently the coming extinction of the Black race.[16] Although no direct line of correlation can be drawn, it should make us uncomfortable that the pickaninny sits side by side with theories of Black extinction on the same historical shelf.

Black children were nameless, shiftless clowns who were constantly running from alligators and toward fried chicken and watermelon.[17] Postcards, souvenir pencil letter/opener sets, pipes, and cigar box labels flaunt these obnoxious and ultimately deadly images. Turner suggests that the presence of watermelons conveys two messages. The first is that Blacks prefer foods that they can eat with their hands. The second more lethal one is that the image of a small Black child's head peering over an oversized chunk of watermelon suggests that the nutritional needs of Black children can be met by accessible crops that grow profusely. Turner then makes a trenchant point: "during slavery, many black children have been underclothed, overworked, underfed, and safer in the company of animals than with some human being."[18] This racist memorabilia crafted by the fantastic hegemonic imagination is the remnant of the process that makes structural evils such as slavery and racism benign through comforting artifacts that suggest that Black children prospered under the abuses of slavery. In fact, slavery was a good and benevolent institution for them, for us—all of us.

Another troubling aspect of this depiction of Black children is that pickaninnies are often shown nude or seminude. This not-so-subtle child pornography sexualizes Black children as their genitalia and buttocks are often exposed. However, these were not the buttocks or genitalia (small for her or his age and most likely malnourished) of an emaciated nineteenth-century Black slave child, who often did not have enough to eat. Pickaninny buttocks are often the size of adults or those that the fantastic hegemonic imagination conjured in its objectification of Black bodies. This kind of nudity as spectacle and commodity could and did normalize the sexual objectification of Black children—boys and girls.

Pickaninnies allowed many White folks to rest easier in the (mis)belief that Black parents were inherently indifferent to their children's welfare. It also made racism palatable and economic apartheid (poverty) the standard fare. The existence and maintenance of these caricatures prevented or made difficult any acknowledgement or examination of how elite White-controlled economic factors might have contributed to the slovenly appearance and substandard education of Black children. Oddly enough, if pickaninnies were not eating watermelon or fried chicken, or running from or hanging out with animals, they were shown working. They were acknowledged as a valuable part of the workforce in society. All in all, it is difficult, though not impossible, to find public images of Black children other than the pickaninny until the mid-1960s. However, for at least 100 years, U.S. society suffered platoons of plucky little pickaninnies as the dominant image of Black children.

Being Women all the Time

Topsy became the first famous pickaninny.

What happens when Topsy speaks? That is a womanist question from this horrid history. What happens when Topsy moves from a literary character functioning as metaphor to the material history and lives of African American children, men, and women? What does it mean when the crude burlesque of the pickaninny who has been described and categorized by others starts to carve out and speak out of an identity in which she is an active agent? What does it mean to say that the dismantling of evil signals a commitment to *conscious* reflection on the interplay between culture, identity, community, theory, practice, myth, memory, history, life, death?

How might we lean into, walk into, run into, crawl into, shimmy into a truly liberatory space—a space in which Topsy and all her kin and friends can speak? A place that invites listening and hearing. A space that invites us to dare faithfulness, to drop our defenses, to accept responsibility to live in genuine accountability because we know that if *we* do not right the wrongs of the past (or at least attempt to do so), we leave it to future generations. And this is a gruesome legacy to pass on as a gift.

The best place for me to begin to synthesize this turn to solidarity and differences when facing the fantastic hegemonic imagination is in some of the spaces of what it means to be a Black woman in the United States. To look at the spectrum of coloredness we bring as womanists; and still on the way womanists; and those wondering just what is this womanism all about; and those who simply "cannot go there" but keep showing up. It is, then, to begin with pieces of what it means to being women all the time.

for being women all the time
    is like breathing in and out
    it is like the moments of smiles and whispers
    it is like warmth and passion
    it is like naming a voice through the song you sing
    it is like the roll of a dice weighed to come up doubles
        but to reach for your winnings
           and find nothing there
being women all the time
    is like breathing in and out
    it is like finding yourself in the midst of degradation
    and having the will to stake a claim for liberation
    it is like turning and turning and turning into a shimmering tomorrow
    it is like hearing a still, small voice
        that you craft into a roaring wind
        as you see and feel wholeness as no longer an abstract, sterile
        category
           but what we all yearn for
so black women can, if we must, begin with the wounds
    those scars, in Eula's word, that are our mothers', daughters', sisters'
    thick and hard so no one can ever pass through to hurt us again[19]
the folds of those old wounds, that in some cases maimed us
    with lies, secrets, and silences we are told about other women
        that are told about ourselves
these wounds mark us, but they do not need to define us
    for as wise women
    or women seeking wisdom
we must grasp a hermenuetic of suspicion
    that is, we must examine our first works over
        again and again
and consider how we are with each other
    and let our religious homes and the academy care of themselves for
    awhile
    and ponder
        what it means for each of us
        to be in this work of ornery hope
           this work of voicing Topsy
                knowing Topsy
                being Topsy
                growing Topsy
yes all of us gathered here in our global clearing are subject to the ravages of
structural racism, sexism, heterosexism, classism, agism, ableism
but what interests me is that african american women have and do join
others
    in holding these "isms"

these masters' and mistresses' tools
    in *our* hands
and we have used them
    sometimes relentlessly
we have used them
to avoid our depression and discontent
    by cheering ourselves and finding a woman who is worse off
    than we are
to avoid the questions we have about our beauty
    by failing to question who sets the standards
    and then dressing
        literally
                to kill
we have used these deadly tools to protect ourselves against charges that we
aren't feminine
    by pointing to someone who may
        or may not
    be tougher than we are
    to prove that we really *do* know the color pink
to cloak our fears that we may not be bright enough or talented enough
    by ridiculing other women and making them into postmodern
    pickaninnies
        by charging that they are sublimating their frustrations
            in their work
            in religious communities
            in the vision for a more whole black community
            within black communities across the landscape
to do this—amongst ourselves, at times
    means we bring fractured selves into all manner of relationships and that
    we often abide sexism and heterosexism
    rather than question their existence in the household of God
hear me now, we tolerate single issue politicians and pastors and academicians
    who spew venom into african american life
    and we think its milk and honey for soul salvation and we lap it
    up—greedily
        as we fail to recognize the death pangs that sear us
        with each dribbling drop down our throats
we turn away from injustice and run for the sanctuary of the alleged holy
    and fail to see the graves dug before us
    until we find ourselves
        our communities
        falling in
    as the dirt of judgment is mournfully
        if not gleefully

tossed over us
>> as it commemorates the remarkable assault all of us can
launch against ourselves
and then have the audacity and the stupidity to name it
righteousness
and black women are not the only ones in God's creation who do this
>> we have all manner and manifestations of this emanating from the vast
cultural communities that mark our common humanity
the rolling eyes and kinky hair of the pickaninny is no longer
confined to black children—they mark each and everyone one of us
in the american social order and beyond
as the women of my grandmother's generation used to say: hmph, hmph,
hmph

We Didn't Just Grow'd

To return again to Stowe's *Uncle Tom's Cabin,*

When arrayed at last in a suit of decent and whole clothing, her hair cropped short to her head, Miss Ophelia, with some satisfaction, said she looked more Christian-like than she did, and in her own mind began to mature some plans for her instruction.

Sitting down before her, she began to question her.

"How old are you, Topsy?"

"Dun no, Missis," said the image, with a grin that showed all her teeth.

"Don't know how old you are? Didn't anybody ever tell you? Who was your mother?"

"Never had none!" said the child, with another grin.

"Never had any mother? What do you mean? Where were you born?"

"Never was born!" persisted Topsy, with another grin, that looked so goblin-like, that, if Miss Ophelia had been at all nervous, she might have fancied that she had got hold of some sooty gnome from the land of Diablerie; but Miss Ophelia was not nervous, but plain and business-like, and she said, with some sternness,

"You mustn't answer me in that way, child; I'm not playing with you. Tell me where you were born, and who your father and mother were."

"Never was born," reiterated the creature, more emphatically; "never had no father nor mother, nor nothin'. I was raised by a specu-lator, with lots of others. Old Aunt Sue used to take care on us"

"How long have you lived with your master and mistress?"

"Dun no, Missis."

"Is it a year, or more, or less?"

"Dun no, Missis . . . ."

"Have you ever heard anything about God, Topsy?"

The child looked bewildered, but grinned as usual.

"Do you know who made you?"

"Nobody, as I knows on," said the child, with a short laugh.

The idea appeared to amuse her considerably; for her eyes twinkled, and she added,

"I spect I grow'd. Don't think nobody never made me."

"Do you know how to sew?" said Miss Ophelia, who thought she would turn her inquiries to something more tangible.

"No, Missis."

"What can you do? What did you do for your master and mistress?"

"Fetch water, and wash dishes, and rub knives, and wait on folks."

"Were they good to you?"

"S'pec they was," said the child, scanning Miss Ophelia cunningly.

Miss Ophelia rose from this encouraging colloquy . . . [20]

This conversation, between the Yankee Miss Ophelia and the young black girl slave Topsy, is instructive and subversive. Throughout the novel, Stowe's gross stereotyping of Topsy also contains a liberatory note. The reader is shown the ways in which Topsy is more than capable of doing her work and learning her lessons. She is revealed as smart and capable—but she is unwilling to do the tasks assigned to her because that is what is expected of her. Topsy chooses to wear the mask the White owners (and Stowe) had given to her.

Is the mask present in the conversation above? It is difficult to know and it is possible to build a case for both yes or no. This is not the most pressing point, however. In this conversation, Topsy, wittingly or not, subverts Miss Ophelia's ideological assumptions and outright ignorance of the fate of most slaves. It was not unusual for slaves to be unaware of their actual birth date, their parents, or their place of birth. It was also not a matter of rote that a slave would receive Christian religious instruction. Topsy's response speaks to the power of hegemony when it operates with such pervasiveness that it erases memories and/or that it never allows the subject(s) to know or learn their history. This is a more profound process than historical or social amnesia because the person or the community cannot remember what they never knew.[21]

Memory and remembrance, identity shaping and making, tradition and traditioning are pivotal functions in an ethical framework that emerges from an oppressed community. The struggle to move beyond double and triple consciousness that are endemic in oppressed communities is a confrontation with histories and peoples who have been and continue to be systematically and methodologically ignored. To recover the record of Black women, children, and men as *communities* rather than as autonomous experiences is a part of the work of womanist ethics.

These crucial functions of community are held in tension in womanist theoethical reflections. The task of religion-based womanism is to move within the tradition descriptively, and jump for the sun to climb beyond the tradition prescriptively. As such, womanist reflections *must* be based on the communities from which they emerge. If not thus grounded, womanist religious reflections can degenerate into flaccid ideologies that fail to espouse a future vision that calls the community beyond itself into a wider and more inclusive circle. This circle is neither tight nor fixed.

All too often, Black women must answer several questions—some well-intentioned, some not—Is this not just another form of separating us? How are the lives of Black women relevant to my world? Why am I blamed for something that I am not responsible for?

Womanist theoethical reflections respond from their own well of history and sociopolitical methodology: we cannot bring together that which we do not know. A unity forged on imperfection, romance, poor vision, limited knowledge, and fissured reconciliation will always benefit those who have the power and leisure to enforce and ignore differences. Unity as a teleological goal can be dangerous and life-defeating, for it can overwhelm and neglect equality. Unity is only vigorous in an atmosphere that is unafraid of difference and diversity. An atmosphere that does not view difference as a barrier but, like the proverbial stew, makes the aroma richer and provides greater sustenance for the work of justice and of forging communities of resistance and hope.

Cast in a more contemporary light, this attempt by Miss Ophelia to forge a bond with Topsy reminds me, all too often, of those instances when those of us who have some measure of power—either by position in our sociopolitical hierarchy or by the dent of our own will—decide to attempt solidarity with groups or individuals who are among the dispossessed. It is usually dismal business that erupts. The expected answers are never given, the hoped for common vision does not emerge, a recalcitrant commitment to justice remains deferred because the genuine differences among us are either glossed over,

ignored, treated as impassable barriers, or viewed with an impreg-
nable ignorance that veers into solipsitic ruminations about "why
can't they be like us, act like us, talk like us, feel like us, be us."

Growing Topsy means that naive and ill-designed attempts at solidarity are questioned and debunked. As Topsy and her kinfolk
and friends pull up their *own* chairs to the postmodern welcome table
and begin to speculate on what it takes to grow, notions of solidarity and difference must be met face-to-face. The womanist dancing
mind stares down the fantastic hegemonic imagination to stop it *and*
to defeat it in these strategy sessions. The challenges of forging a tough
solidarity demand all of our creativity and intellect as we step toward
a more just and whole society.

> We do not sweat and summon our best in order to rescue the killers; it
> is to comfort and to empower the possible victims of evil that we do tin-
> ker and daydream and revise and memorize, and then impart all that we
> can of our inspired, our inherited humanity.[22]

these words are from the black feminist theorist and writer June
Jordan

i have been pondering them of late as i feel and think about the major transi-
tions i am going through
        that all of us are going through in some measure
        with all the comings and leavings that are part of life and
        death
but i also think about them in relation to what they may have to say in
reminding me why i do what i do
        and how
        and in what ways
for me, to talk about standing with one another
        to conjure solidarity across differences
        to spark womanist wisdom on solidarity and differences
is, at first glance
        (and i must admit on several glances
           looks
               mullings later)
        to tempt the agony of the absurd
i feel as though i have been cast back in time
        to that 60s cocktail party in which Ralph Ellison
           the author of *Invisible Man*
        spoke in "clipped, deliberate syllables" to his peers

"Show me the poem, tell me the names of the opera/the
symphony that will stop one man from killing another
man and then maybe" he gestured toward the elegant
bejeweled assembly with his hand that held a cut-crystal
glass of scotch—"just maybe some of this can be justified."[23]

i am relieved to say that tempting the agony of the absurd
        does not leave me in Ellison's condemnatory despair
but it does leave me with a frustrated hope
      a hope that is imbued with Jordan's words
      as they echo
           "we do not sweat and summon our best in order to rescue
           the killers"
there are days, in fact,
      that i'll be damned if i rescue any killer
      or someone even approaching such a grotesque status
to work in solidarity with those who are like me
      unlike me
      or resemble me
does not demand or require that i save those who would see others dead or
annihilated
      either through neglect
        indifference
        calculation
        or theoethical musings
i will not rescue the killers
      of dreams and visions of a world better than this
      of hopes that continue to pulse, however faintly, in the midst
        of disaster and ruin
i will not rescue the killers
      who create optional reading lists
      that signal to me
        that some actual or alleged scholars really believe
        that there are optional peoples, cultures, lives, ideas,
        hopes, realities
      and secondary lists are little better
        when they traffic peoples' yearnings and expectations as
        ideologies and abstractions
i will not rescue the killer
      who remains silent when the innocent are murdered
        and it is called patriotism or cleansing or white male rage
        or horizontal violence
      when people starve on our streets
        while there is more than enough food for everyone to eat
        three squares a day and at least one snack

when children die unloved and unwanted and thrown away
and we shake our collective pious heads and shut the
doors of homes and our hearts
when money determines right and wrong
good and evil
unity and dissent
diversity and blandness
hope and despair
promise and lies
damnation and salvation
no, absolutely no, i will not rescue the killers
when the church functions like an efficient corporation
and numbers and spaces in parking lots and the joy of
multiple worship services
serve as the markers for spirit and love and
mercy and justice
hear me now, i will *not* rescue the killers
when the academy devolves into gigantic public holding pens
for creativity and intellect
in other words
for me and my house
growing Topsy while standing with others across differences
does not require that i be run over in a mad teleological drive toward a misbegotten notion of solidarity
that i accept a specious deontological notion of a disinterested love
that asks me to sacrifice my very soul
so that others may find comfort and ease in the macabre
spectacle of my self annihilation
or the obliteration of whole peoples
Topsy as a womanist does not find it acceptable that i acquiesce to a least
common denominator justice
that is really no justice at all
she does not require that i check my passions
my insights
my communities
at the door to enter the hall of kumbaya
and if there is any wisdom that can come
from *this* black woman
on notions of solidarities and differences that are strong
enough, wise enough, and ornery enough to go
toe-to-toe
with the fantastic hegemonic imagination
it is that
to engage in such work is absolutely dangerous
it may, in fact, not be good for one's health at all

it can lead to heart and soul-ache
it can make us old before our time
it can make us eat and drink too much or too little
     of all the unhealthy things
it can turn us bitter and sarcastic
it can make you ornery and mean as a snake
it can turn justice into vengeance
it can turn *us* into killers
but the danger does not stop here
     it is dangerous because it means that *we* refuse the emotional
     numbing panaceas
          of acquisition and status and competitive spirit that does
          not seek excellence, only winning
     we see through the straw figure of a free market
        and speak with increasing precision and accuracy about
        the impact of transnationals
             from agribusiness
             to munitions
             to clothing manufacturers
             to western tastes and cultures passing themselves
             off as neutral or the markers of progress
we become dangerous when
     we speak the truth that the king *is* naked
        when it comes to the U.S. prison industrial complex
        when we question declarations of war that are soon
        accompanied by massive bail outs for corporations that
        even that bastion of progressive monetary policies, *the*
        wall street journal, said "mainly padded corporate bottom
        lines"
        when we express confusion and dismay when terrorism is
        used as the reason for a sharp cut in the capital gains tax
            a tax in which 80 percent of the benefits would
             go to the wealthiest 2 percent of the taxpayers
        when folk hide behind conveniently literal interpretations
        of scripture that support their views
            on homosexuality, abortion, the roles of women
            and men, the place of clergy and laity, the
            pillaging of the environment, and just about
            anything else
              except individual and corporate sinning in the
              name of individualism and the alleged common
              good
yes, this is a naked butt king
        when it comes to public policy that is really the personal
        agenda of moralizing rhetoricians

who are dangerous because they now hold elected office
and someone believed that they should bring us back to
the good old days
>   that were, for many of us, deadly days
when almost every piece of legislation we are told is good for us
>   is sold to us with one price tag (like medicare drug bene-
>   fits for the elderly)
>   and then we are told—as many predicted on the left *and*
>   the right that the costs would be more and strain the fed-
>   eral budget more
>>   but we are told—just trust us, we know we are
>>   right
>>   and then we find that a $400 billion price tag
>>   over 10 years is now, weeks after the dust had
>>   settled from the debate, is really a $530 billion
>>   price tag[24]
when we are go to war based on claims about weapons of
mass destruction in Iraq based on "documentary evidence"
that was forged and doubted by CIA analysts from the
beginning
>   and each time any of us express doubt about this "evi-
>   dence," we were branded as weak or unpatriotic
>   and now, months and deaths later, we hear and see federal
>   officials recasting their words as if they never knew that
>   the "evidence" could possibly be cooked
>>   and that the president was not told the truth
>>   and we should be glad we invaded Iraq anyway
>>   because Saddam Hussein had to be removed
>>   from power
and it should not matter, ultimately, that we were lied to
>>   although most of us are taught that when you lie,
>>   you should be exposed and punished
>>   but the fact that these lies went largely
>>   unreported by U.S. domestic media that does a
>>   dangerous dance against free speech with the
>>   federal administration
>>>   is like the dead skunk in the middle of
>>>   the road
>>>   stinking to high heaven
>>>>   but we drive around it as if it
>>>>   were not there
no i am not here for the killers
>   when it comes to solidarity
>>   which i assume is another way to say justice

i am not interested in them
                    except for how to decrease their numbers
                    and their power
i have no wish to be objective about their behavior, methods, ideologies, or
strategies
when i do the work of justice
                    it is with and as an advocate for the victims
                              actual
                              possible
                              imagined
                                        of evil
it is subjective, it is emotional, it is passionate, it is *very* interested
and if i cannot find others who are interested and committed to this
                    then there is no solidarity
                    and our differences not only separate us
                              they make us adversaries
                                        or enemies
in other words, for me, i do not *assume* solidarity
                    when i join others in the work of justice
solidarity is something that is nurtured and grown
                    in the yearning for and living out of justice
solidarity comes from hard work
                              listening
                              hearing
                              analyzing
                              questioning
                              rethinking
                              accepting
                              rejecting
it comes from a place of respecting and being respected
                    and that, i think, does not come easily or naturally for most of us
if it were so natural, then we wouldn't be in the fix we are trying to get out of
                    for to respect others
                    means we must also respect ourselves
and centuries of inherited messages about the inherent evil of humanity (with
a large measure of this brutalizing swill aimed at women)
                    pose a wall of judgment and condemnation
                    that is hard for many of us to scale
so as we seek to work together, we must always be working on ourselves
and perhaps this is where the comforting begins
                    as each of us has that dawning and then awakening in us
                         that the point is in some religious version of perfection
                    but that we *live* our humanity with passion and vigor—
                    regardless

that we live our lives in justice and hope and even love—
relentlessly
that we recognize that none of us has the corner on righteousness
that we are the ones we have been waiting for
and ultimately, there is no one to do this work for us
this, then, is the first light of empowerment
when we realize that we cannot do the work of justice
to end structural injustice
by individual acts of valor and conviction alone
they may help, to be sure
but tackling structural evil takes a whole bunch of folks
with varieties of skills and insights
because structures of domination rarely come in such pristine
forms as
circles
triangles
rectangles
or rhomboids
no, structures of domination are like demonic ink blots
they have cores
but the splatter marks are far and wide and absolutely
dangerous
and they can cause so much collateral damage
that they disfigure and maim
to speak of solidarity
to conjure standing *anywhere* together
is, then, to tempt the agony of the absurd
but frankly, i simply don't know what else to do
and remain faithful
and although Jordan's description of tinkering, daydreaming, revising, and
memorizing
does not sit well for *this* womanist ethicist
i do believe in strategizing, envisioning, challenging, debunking, and
transforming
but always with an eye to sharing and receiving the dignity
and gift of humanity and creation
this means that a solidarity seeking the status quo is not one i can embrace a
solidarity that teaches a studied silence that rewards blind, thought-less, clue-
less obedience
and punishes vital curiosity
is not one that i can come near
a solidarity that only tolerates oppositional knowledge on playgrounds,
streets, homes, popular culture, youth groups
but never in board meetings, religious councils, strategy sessions
or in policy development or pulpits or curriculum revisions

is not a solidarity that is actually concerned about justice
and it does not deserve my time
but it does need to be watched, monitored, like a hawk
        and if need be, be destroyed
whatever wisdom i have on solidarity and differences
        has been crafted from the hard experiences
        of learning over and over again
                that just because folk espouse solidarity does not mean
                they either know it or mean it
                that there are *many* good works being done to bring in
                justice
                        but that there is only *one* of me
and that i must, as each of us must
                make some choices about who we stand in solidarity with
                and how we will or will not deal with the differences
                        that can enrich us
                                challenge us
                                deny us
                                destroy us
but to remember also that we must not take so long to choose
                that the choice gets made by our indecision or inaction
we may choose wisely or foolishly
                but the point is that we develop the ability to recognize where
                our actions are leading us
                        and where we have actually gone
                and reformulate and assess on a continual basis
                        if we are truly working for justice or if we have fallen into
                        cooptation
                                or complicity
                                or betrayal
there are *always* options
                i've learned this from the trickster tradition in my culture
                but they cut both ways and sometimes even slice and dice
to move beyond the tight circle that we often seem caught in that is hollowed
out by conservatism and liberalism
                means that we stop collapsing difference and diversity and
                plurality
                        and all those terms we use to signal humanity and creation
                        is large
                        into such neat and pristine buzz words
and instead realize that
                we will not always agree
                there will be times of reasoned (and unreasoned) dissent
                that we may *not* be able to work
                        together on everything or every issue

sometimes it is to recast
            from our worldviews
                  the things we've learned through the years
                        but even as small children:
                              the police are *not* always your friend
                              it is *not* always wise to wait to cross at
a corner
                              or even to cross only at corners
in other words, there are few absolutes in life
                  and solidarities and differences are just as caught up in this
reality as episodes or steady diets of disaster and ruin
no, as i continue being a part of growing Topsy, i do not sweat and summon
whatever best there is in me to rescue the killers
but i do try to give all of who i am to the work for justice
                  and hang in there with others who recognize that solidari-
ties and differences are messy
                        and ultimatly human
and in some small way this marks our humanity
                  and turns the absurdities
                        into living, breathing, active hope

8

Everydayness: Beginning Notes on Dismantling the Cultural Production of Evil

. . . and so we begin.

We begin with ourselves. Each of us must answer the question: What will we do with the fullness and incompleteness of who we are as we stare down the interior material life of the cultural production of evil? Rather than content ourselves with the belief that the fantastic hegemonic imagination, the motive force behind the cultural production of evil, is a force that sits outside of us, we must answer remembering that we are in a world that we have helped make. The fantastic hegemonic imagination is deep within us and none of us can escape its influence by simply wishing to do so or thinking that our ontological perch exempts us from its spuming oppressive hierarchies. These hierarchies of age, class, gender, sexual orientation, race, and on and on are held in place by violence, fear, ignorance, acquiescence. The endgame is to win and win it all—status, influence, place, creation.

Our world needs a new (or perhaps ancient) vision molded by justice and peace rather than winning and losing if we are to unhinge the cultural production of evil. Doing so is to respond to the call by the Black mystic and theologian Howard Thurman who joined others in encouraging us to blend head and heart.[1]-One source of sustenance for answering this challenge is in the speeches of the late former Congresswoman Barbara Jordan from Texas. She was a woman of firsts: first Black woman to serve as administrative assistant to the county judge of Harris County, Texas, first Black person elected to the Texas state senate since 1883, first Black woman to deliver the keynote address at the Democratic Party convention in 1976, first Black person to be buried in the State Cemetery in Austin, Texas, on January 20, 1996. Those of us who remember or have heard the recording of the crisp bell tones of her perfect diction and impeccable cadence will never forget her testimony before the house judiciary committee during Watergate in 1974 on prime-time television.

> Earlier today, we heard the beginning of the Preamble to the Constitution of the United States, "We, the people." It is a very eloquent beginning. But when the document was completed on the seventeenth of September 1787 I was not included in that "We, the people." I felt somehow for many years that George Washington and Alexander Hamilton just left me out by mistake. But through the process of amendment, interpretation and court decision I have finally been included in "We, the people."
>
> Today, I am an inquisitor; I believe hyperbole would not be fictional and would not overstate the solemnness that I feel right now. My faith in the Constitution is whole, it is complete, it is total. And I am not going to sit here and be an idle spectator to the diminution, the subversion, the destruction of the Constitution.[2]

I am struck by the profound trust she had in the notion "We the people." Jordan was the daughter of a Baptist preacher and a devout *practicing* Baptist her whole life. One of the bedrock principles she lived her life by was that human equality under God is categorical, absolute, unconditional, and universally applicable.[3] Therefore, when she said "We the people," she really did mean *all* of us. Because she was a public servant, Jordan did not do explicit God-talk in her public addresses. However, I think she provides a window into how we can think about the ways in which we can begin dismantling the cultural production of evil—it is to realize that this must be a group project. Our individual acts, while helpful, will not provide enough moral oomph to unhinge and dismantle the tremendously entrenched force of the fantastic hegemonic imagination.

One of the temptations we must avoid in this task is believing that engaging in this task with intellectual rigor means that we check our hearts at the door. I learned well from the older Black men and women who raised me in the church and outside of it that intellect with no heart is about as useful as a heart with no intellect. And missing both sides of that equation means you probably do not have much common sense to boot—in other words, you are not very useful.

Therefore, I recall a counternarrative to help address the expansion of moral hubris that we are experiencing of late in many of our religious and nonreligious homes that makes it difficult to address the cultural production of evil with both feet on the ground and a focused, relentless stare. This narrative springs from the kind of faith that Jordan placed in what it means to take our citizenship seriously as people of faith, something we must have in dismantling the cultural production of evil. It relies on the words in Marie-Sophie's notebook in Patrick Chamoiseau's *Texaco* that I drew on earlier in chapter 5:

> In what I tell you, there's the almost-true, the sometimes-true, and the half-true. That's what telling a life is like, braiding–all of that like one plaits the white Indies currant to make a hut. And the true-true comes out of that braid.[4]

I want to underscore that Chamoiseau captures in novel form the shorthand version of why I believe it is not only necessary but possible that we can begin to dismantle the systematic and decades-old work of the fantastic hegemonic imagination by holding on to justice and peace as relevant, vital, necessary, and indispensable values that we can craft into faithful action in our scholarship, in the lives of those in our religious communities, and in the worlds we live in. We have existed on the almost-true, sometimes-true, and half-true without looking for the true-true.

The true-true is our telos. Finding this takes seriously Marcia Y. Riggs' mediating ethic that does not seek easy reconciliation nor does it have reconciliation as a teleological lure. Rather, Riggs' ethic focuses on mediati*ng*-as a process rather than mediat*ion* as an end. As people of faith or people who hold deep values of respect for others and the rest of creation, we must live our lives not always comforted by the holy, but haunted by God's call to us to live a prophetic and spirit-filled life, and not just talk about it or wish for it or think about it— actions that mean that we remain in the tension. This is the process of uncovering and working through how we can build faith-filled responses to the thorny demand to dismantle the cultural production of evil in our lives in creation. In doing so, we may meet the needs of those who may be the least of these or they may be folks just like many of us—blessed with resources and abilities and a divine mandate to use them with a spirituality that will not let go of that relentless sense of justice that can only come from a rock-steady God.

We must be about these things because we are living in a time in which imperialism is being dwarfed by empire. For those of us who are citizens of the United States, we are drawing breath in a country, *our* country, that possesses an incredible concentration of financial, diplomatic and military power. It is disingenuous to refuse to admit the tremendous power and influence we have on a global scale and also to recognize the awesome responsibility that comes with this. We have the power to do incredible good—and we have done so—and must continue to grow this side of who we are as a nation larger and stronger on the global stage and here at home. We fail to do so at our own peril. We must resist and dismantle the hegemonic urge to care first and only for ourselves as a nation. Doing so leaks away whatever moral currency we have amassed domestically and globally as other nations and their peoples see the immoral acts we commit domestically translated into our foreign policy internationally.

This is part of the true-true Chamoiseau speaks of. The way that we respond is by telling the truth as we see it, know it, smell it, breathe it. Truth-telling is what the evil bred from the fantastic hegemonic imagination does *not* count on. If we can hold on to digging up the truth when it gets buried in geopolitical, sociocultural, and theoethical cat fights and mud-wrestling contests, then we will be able to bring together justice-making and peacekeeping to dismantle evil. However, this is true only if we take seriously the challenges of a mediating ethic that tells us that we are caught in H. Richard Niebuhr's web of creation.[5] As such, we are responsible for each other and ourselves. We may not always agree, nor should we expect to. We have to give an accounting of our actions and inactions. We may get tired and need a break, but we must always come back, because we do not get out of this life alone and we are responsible for what goes on in our names.

It is not an understatement, then, to say that we human folk are both challenge and hope. Living with ourselves is often a demanding or difficult task because many of us are called on to prove or justify our very lives in a court of law that may be structured so that some of us need not apply for justice or mercy or equality or harmony or peace. We see (when we do not sense) that there are false accusations lining the fabric of our lives, accusations that we are involved in an ill-designed and misbegotten contest that is deadly, oh so deadly. However, we have expectations of and for others and ourselves. We have dreams that can be more powerful than the nightmares, possibilities more radical than the realities, and a hope that does more than cling to a wish or wish on a star or sit by the side of the road, picking and sucking its teeth after dining on a meal of disaster and violence in our lives.

Facing down and dismantling the fantastic hegemonic is a call to respond to the challenge and hope found in each of us individually and collectively. Indeed, this is where challenge meets up with hope. This is not the hope of Pandora's box where hope is an evil that comes to confuse the human spirit. This is not the hope of Goethe who believed "Why roam in the distance? See, the good lies so near. Learn only to achieve happiness, then happiness is always there." This is not the hope of Camus's myth of Sisyphus to teach us that we should "Think clearly and [do not] hope." The challenge and hope we have before us comes from Miss Nora, Brother Hemphill, Ms. Montez, Mr. Press, Miss Rosie, and Mr. Waddell.[6] It comes from the generations before us who refused to acquiesce to demonic stereotypes. These folk placed a legacy within us of hope and the ability to strategize to resist the inaccurate and harrowing definitions of what is considered normal in the fantastic hegemonic imagination. It is a hope that is also grounded in the responsibilities we have toward future generations that *we* leave such a legacy to them. Hence, this hope is unequivocal and unambiguous. It does not detach the human spirit from the present through mad delusions and flights of fancy. This hope is one that pulls the promise of the future into the present and places the present into the dawn of a future that is on the rimbones of glory.

To combine challenge with hope is powerful. For together they enable us to press onward when we are at the verge of giving up; to draw strength from the future to live in a discouraging present. Challenge and hope make it possible for us to see the world, not only as it is, but also as it can be, so that it can move us to new places and turn us into a new people. This has the relentless and timeless force of water on the rock of the entrenched evils of the fantastic hegemonic imagination. Ultimately, the water wears the rock away through an unwillingness to alter its course.

Yes, there *is* something about challenge yoked with hope, when it is grounded in living for tomorrow as we live for today, that is solid enough to sustain our lives and overcome skepticism and doubt that the cultural production of evil encourages within us. But it *is* frightening because we know that loving and caring for others and ourselves interrupts the mundane and comfortable in us and calls to us to move beyond ourselves and accept a new agenda for living. Hope cannot simply be given a nod of recognition, for it demands not only a contract from us, but also a covenant and a commitment. When we truly live in this deep-walking hope, then we must order and shape our lives in ways that are not always predictable, not always safe, rarely conventional, and protests with prophetic fury the sins of a fantastic hegemonic imagination (and theological worldviews) that encourage us to separate our bodies from our spirits, our minds from our hearts, our beliefs from our action. Perhaps this is the most devastating impact of the cultural production of evil. It begins its work with the rending of the marvelously complex interlocking character of our humanity.

Therefore, we must yoke challenge and hope in our lives such that justice and peace mean something and are more than rhetorical ruffles and flourishes. To do so recognizes that none of us can hide from any of the "isms," war, the economy, confirmation processes, rising oil prices, calls by a conservative Christian leader to assassinate a duly elected president of an oil rich nation because it is cheaper than another 200-billion-dollar war,[7] HIV/AIDS, terrorism, and mixing jingoism with the death of innocents in our national mourning. We cannot hide from responsibility or accountability for we are never relieved of the responsibility that we have to our generation and future generations to keep justice, peace, and hope alive and vibrant.

Ultimately, somewhere deep inside each of us we know that perhaps the simplest, yet the most difficult, answer to the challenge of what will we do with the fullness and incompleteness of who we are as we stare down the interior life of the cultural production of evil is *live your faith deeply*. This is not a quest for perfection, but for what we call in Christian ethics the everydayness of moral acts. It is what we do every day that shapes us and where both the fantastic hegemonic imagination and the challenge and hope to dismantle it are found. It is in these acts that we do that say more about us than those grand moments of righteous indignation and action:

> the everydayness of listening closely when folks talk or don't talk to hear what they are saying;
> the everydayness of taking some time, however short or long, to refresh ourselves through prayer or meditation;
> the everydayness of speaking to folks and actually meaning whatever it is that is coming out of our mouths;
> the everydayness of being a presence in people's lives;
> the everydayness of designing a class session or lecture or reading or writing or thinking;
> the everydayness of sharing a meal;
> the everydayness of facing heartache and disappointment;
> the everydayness of joy and laughter;
> the everydayness of facing people who expect us to lead them somewhere or at least point them in the right direction and walk with them;
> the everydayness of blending head and heart;
> the everydayness of getting up and trying one more time to get our living right.

It is in this everydayness that "we the people" are formed. And we, the people of faith, must live and be witness to a justice wrapped in a love that will not let us go and a peace that is simply too ornery to give up on us—not even in the vice grip of the fantastic hegemonic imagination as it serves as handmaid and manservant to the cultural production of evil.

Won't you join me?

Notes

Chapter 1 The Womanist Dancing Mind: Cavorting with Culture and Evil

1. Toni Morrison, *The Dancing Mind* (New York: Alfred A. Knopf, 1996), 7–8.
2. H. Richard Niebuhr, *The Responsible Self: An Essay in Christian Moral Philosophy*, with an introduction by James M. Gustafson (New York: Harper and Row, 1963).
3. William Shakespeare, *Macbeth*, Act I, Scene I.

Chapter 2 Sites of Memory: Proceedings too Terrible to Relate

1. Toni Morrison, "The Site of Memory," in *Inventing the Truth: The Art and Craft of Memoir*, rev. and exp., ed. William Zinsser (Boston, MA: Houghton Mifflin Company, 1998), 186.
2. Ibid., 190.
3. Ibid., 191.
4. Ibid., 193.
5. Ibid., 193–194.
6. Ibid., 195.
7. Robert O'Meally and Geneviève Fabre, "Introduction," in *History and Memory in African-American Culture*, ed. Geneviève Fabre and Robert O'Meally (New York: Oxford University Press, 1994), 5.
8. Pierre Nora, "Between Memory and History: *Les Lieux de Mémoire*," *Representations* 26 (Spring 1989): 8.
9. I am referring to the Hegelian process of change in which a concept or its realization passes over into and is preserved and fulfilled by its opposite.
10. Nora, "Between Memory and History," 9.
11. *Les Lieux de Mémoire*, vol. 1, ed. Nora (Paris: Éditions Gallimard, 1984), xix.
12. Nora, "Between Memory and History," 24.
13. Ibid., 7.
14. An interesting amplification of Nora's work can be found in the work of James E. Young. Although Young's work is not a direct response to Nora, he

explores memory and countermemory in monument designs. See *Texture of Memory: Holocaust Memorials and Meaning* (New Haven: Yale University Press, 1993) and "Memory and Counter-memory: The End of the Monument in Germany" *Harvard Design Magazine* no. 9 (Fall 1999).

15. Nora, "Between Memory and History," 19.
16. O'Meally and Fabre, "Introduction," 7.
17. Ibid.
18. Georg Wilhelm Friedrich Hegel, *Lectures on the Philosophy of History: The Lectures of 1825–1826* (Berkeley: University of California Press, 1990), 98.
19. O'Meally and Fabre, "Introduction," 7–8.
20. Carolyn Walker Bynum, *Fragmentation and Redemption: Essays in Gender and the Human Body in Medieval Religion* (New York: Zone Books, 1991), 9–10.
21. Ibid., 24.
22. Ibid., 24–25.
23. Maurice Halbwachs, *On Collective Memory*, ed. and trans. with intro. Lewis A. Coser (Chicago: University of Chicago Press, 1992).
24. Ibid., 43.
25. Ibid., 49.
26. Ibid., 50.
27. Charles H. Long, *Significations: Signs, Symbols, and Images in the Interpretation of Religion* (Aurora, CO: The Davies Group Publishers, 1995; Fortress Press, 1986), 151.
28. The Quickstep is done to 4/4 music at 50 beats per minute. It features gliding and back-lock steps, plus rise and falls. Skilled dancers look as if they are "floating." Advanced Quickstep includes kicking and toe snapping.
29. Michel Foucault, "Afterword to *The Temptation of Saint Anthony*," in *Aesthetics, Method and Epistemology: The Essential Works of Michel Foucault 1954–1984*, vol. 2, ed. James D. Faubion, trans. Robert Hurley and others (Harmondsworth, Middlesex: Allen Lane, Penguin, 1998), 103–122. Antonio Gramsci, *Prison Notebooks*, ed. and intro. Joseph A. Buttigieg, trans. Joseph A. Buttigieg and Antonio Callari (New York: Columbia University Press, 1992), 245–276.
30. Foucault, "The Order of Discourse," in *Untying the Text: A Post-Structuralist Reader*, ed. Robert Young (New York: Routledge and Kegan Paul, 1981), 55.
31. Foucault, "Fantasia of the Library," in *Language, Counter-Memory, Practice: Selected Essays and Interviews*, ed. and intro. Donald F. Bouchard (Ithaca, NY: Cornell University Press, 1977), 90.
32. Ibid., 90–91.
33. Tzvetan Todorov, *The Fantastic: A Structural Approach to a Literary Genre* (Ithaca, NY: Cornell University Press, 1975, Press of Case Western Reserve, 1973), 25.
34. Antonio Gramsci, "Notes on Italian History," in *Selections from the Prison Notebooks*, ed. and trans. Quintin Hoare and Geoffrey Nowell Smith (New York: International Publishers, 1971), 57–58.
35. In this movement, which I detail in chapter 5, the earlier ill-conceived image of the Black Matriarch as the Black woman who runs the household (with or

without a man) and is responsible for the total moral upbringing of her children becomes the contemporary Welfare Queen. The debate that shaped the 1996 Welfare Reform legislation and the ongoing rhetoric of welfare reform vilified the Welfare Queen.

36. Susan Willis, "Memory and Mass Culture," in *History and Memory in African-American Culture*, 182–183.

37. Halbwachs, *On Collective Memory*, 51.

38. George Lipsitz, "History, Myth, and Counter-Memory: Narrative and Desire in Popular Novels," in *Time Passages: Collective Memory and the American Popular Culture* (Minneapolis: University of Minnesota Press, 1990), 213.

39. Foucault, "Nietzsche, Genealogy, History," in *Language, Counter-Memory, Practice: Selected Essays and Interviews*, ed. and intro. Donald F. Bouchard (Ithaca, NY: Cornell University Press, 1977), 139–140.

40. Ibid., 144.

41. Ibid., 150.

42. Lipsitz, "History, Myth, and Counter-Memory," 214.

43. Ibid.

44. Ibid., 223.

45. Barbara Christian, *From the Inside Out: Afro-American Women's Literary Tradition and the State* (Minneapolis: Center for Humanistic Studies, 1984), 4.

46. Lipsitz, "History, Myth, and Counter-Memory," 227.

47. Willis, "Memory and Mass Culture," 179.

48. See W.E.B. Du Bois, *Dusk of Dawn: An Essay Toward an Autobiography of a Race Concept* (New York: Schocken Books, 1968), *The Souls of Black Folk; Essays and Sketches* (Chicago: A.C. McClurg & Co., 1903), and *Black Reconstruction in America: An Essay toward a History of the Part Which Black Folk Played in the Attempt to Reconstruct Democracy in America, 1860–1880* (New York: Russell & Russell, [1935] 1966).

49. Herbert Aptheker, "The Historian," in *W.E.B. Du Bois: A Profile*, ed. Rayford W. Logan (New York: Hill and Wang, 1971), 254.

50. W.E.B. Du Bois, "The Propaganda of History," in *Black Reconstruction*, 711–712.

51. Ibid., 713.

52. Ibid., 722.

53. Ibid., 714.

54. Aptheker, "The Historian," 256.

55. For examples of this critique of multiculturalism, see Brian M. Barry, *Culture and Equality: An Egalitarian Critique of Multiculturalism* (Cambridge: Harvard University Press, 2001), William J. Bennett, *The De-Valuing of America: The Fight for Our Culture and Our Children* (New York: Simon and Schuster, 1994), Dinesh D'Souza, *Illiberal Education: The Politics of Race and Sex on Campus* (New York: The Free Press, 1991), and Alvin J. Schmidt, *The Menace of Multiculturalism: Trojan Horse in America* (New York: Praeger Publishers, 1997).

56. Du Bois, "The Propaganda of History," in *Black Reconstruction*, 725.

57. Morrison, "The Site of Memory," 191.

58. Ibid., 193–194.
59. Jitterbug is more formally known as Jive. This dance began in the United States but took root in wartime Europe. It is also the Lindy or swing. Jive music is usually the "big band" swing music with a lot of brass and wood-wind.

Chapter 3   Vanishing into Limbo: The Moral Dilemma of Identity as Property and Commodity

1. James Baldwin, "Too Many Thousands Gone" in *Notes of a Native Son* (Boston, MA: Beacon Press, 1955), 27.
2. Ibid., 25.
3. Ibid.
4. Jacques Derrida, *The Ear of the Other: Otobiography, Transference, Translation: Texts and Discussions with Jacques Derrida*, ed. Christie McDonald, trans. Peggy Kamuf (Lincoln: University of Nebraska Press, [1988], 1985), *The Other Heading* (Bloomington and Indianapolis: Indiana University Press, 1991) and "Structure and Play in the Discourse of the Human Sciences" in *Writing and Difference* (Chicago: University of Chicago Press, 1978), 278–293. Michel Foucault, *Power/Knowledge: Selected Interviews & Other Writings 1972–1977*, ed. Colin Gordon, trans. Colin Gordon, Leo Marshall, John Mephawn, and Kate Soper (New York: Pantheon Books, 1980) and *Discipline and Punish: The Birth of the Prison*, trans. Alan Sheridan (New York: Pantheon Books, 1977). Gayatri Chakravorty Spivak, *A Critique of Postcolonial Reason: Toward a History of the Vanishing Present* (Cambridge: Harvard University Press, 1999) and *In Other Worlds: Essays in Cultural Politics* (New York: Routledge, 1988).
5. Cheryl Thurber, "The Development of the Mammy Image and Mythology" in *Southern Women: Histories and Identities*, ed. Virginia Bernhard, Betty Brandon, Elizabeth Fox-Genovese, and Theda Purdue (Columbia: University of Missouri Press, 1992), 87, 91. Her image reached its greatest popularity with Progressivism, the New South movement, and the later phases of the Confederate Lost Cause movement. The Progressive era (1896–1920) focused on nationalism and the idea of the United States as a melting pot. This emphasis on "Americanization" did not extend to Black folk and focused n European immigrants as a means of forming a White national coalition to ward off the Black minority. The New South Movement (1895–1913) featured the goal of reconciliation between the New South and the North, agricultural diversity, and industrialization in the South. The New South movement was conservative in its racial ideology. It believed in the racial inferiority of Black folk while decrying the belief in equality and the radical belief that Blacks were savages and should be driven out of the United States. The Lost Cause Movement (1880–1930) was a celebration of the Confederate South by veterans of the Civil War. The next generation of Confederates,

represented by groups such as the United Daughters of the Confederacy and the Sons of Confederate Veterans, memorialized and celebrated their Confederate heritage. This second generation emphasized preserving now fading memories.

6. There were two overarching constructs used to describe Black women in the racist southern imagination of the antebellum and postbellum eras: Jezebel and Mammy. Jezebel was depicted as licentious and dangerous for White men. This stereotype fortified the perception that Black women were sexually loose and liked sex more than their White counterparts. In contemporary discourse, Jezebel has morphed into the Welfare Queen.

7. Thurber, "The Development of the Mammy Image," 88.

8. Catherine Clinton, *The Plantation Mistress: Woman's World in the Old South* (New York: Pantheon, 1982), 201–202.

9. Herbert G. Gutman, *The Black Family in Slavery and Freedom 1750–1925* (New York: Vintage Books, 1976).

10. Patricia A. Turner, *Ceramic Uncles and Celluloid Mammies: Black Images and Their Influence on Culture* (New York: Anchor Books, 1994), 44. Turner writes, "At no time during the pre–Civil War era did more than 25 percent of the white Southern population own slaves. . . . most slave owners possessed ten or fewer slaves, the majority of whom—men and women—were consigned to field labor."

11. Thurber, "The Development of the Mammy Image," 91.

12. Memoirs began touting the Mammy from the 1890s (the beginning of the lynching era) to the end of the 1920s.

13. Mrs. W.L. Hammond, "The Old Black Mammy," *Confederate Veteran* (January 26, 1918): 6.

14. Quoted in Thurber, "The Development of the Mammy Image," 99–100.

15. Jo Ann Gibson Robinson, *The Montgomery Bus Boycott and the Women Who Started It: The Memoir of Jo Ann Gibson Robinson* (Knoxville: University of Tennessee Press, 1987), 107.

16. Barbara Christian, *Black Women Novelists: The Development of a Tradition 1892–1976* (Westport, CT: Greenwood Press, 1980), 11–12.

17. The landmark film, *Birth of a Nation* (1915), was based on Thomas Dixon's racist novel, *The Clansman*. Both in print and on the screen, the Mammy defends her White master's home against Black and White Union soldiers. Later with *Gone With the Wind* (1930), the Mammy also fights Black soldiers whom she believes are threatening her White mistress. Hattie McDaniel won the 1950 Academy Award for best supporting artist for her portrayal of "Mammy." She was the first African American to win an Academy Award and this remained the case for the next 25 years. After a successful career as a singer in which she became the first Black person to sing on U.S. network radio, McDaniel went to Hollywood in 1931 in search of a film career. She began as an extra before capturing larger roles. When work was not available, she hired herself out as a domestic, a cook, or a washerwoman. When *Gone With the Wind* premiered in December of 1939, none of the African American performers had been invited to join the party in still-segregated Atlanta. When McDaniel's picture appeared on the back of a movie program, protests from

White Atlantans prompted the destruction of the programs and new ones were printed. Mammy's portrait was replaced eventually with Alicia Rhett as India Wilke.

As the twentieth century wore on, the Mammy stereotype was portrayed in the 1950–1953 television show "Beulah." The lead character, portrayed by McDaniel on the radio and Ethel Water and Estelle Beavers on television, was a domestic servant for the White Henderson family. This was the first nationally broadcast weekly television series starring an African American in the leading role. A White male actor, Marlin Hurt, originally created the role the Fibber McGee and Molly radio program. The character was spun off onto "her" own radio show in 1945. After Hurt's death in 1946, Hattie McDaniel played the role on radio until her death in 1953. The program was a half-hour situation comedy that revolved around the middle-aged black domestic, Beulah, the so-called queen of the kitchen, and the White family for whom she worked—Harry and Alice Henderson and their young son, Donnie. Beulah's boyfriend Bill Jackson ran a fix-it shop, but spent most of his time hanging around Beulah's kitchen. Beulah's other Black companion was Oriole, a featherbrained maid who worked for the White family next door. The shows storylines involved Beulah coming to the rescue of her employers, by providing a great spread of Southern cuisine to impress Mr. Henderson's business client, teaching the awkward Donnie how to dance jive and impress the girls, or saving the Henderson's stale marriage. Beulah's other major obsession was trying to get Bill to agree to marry her.

The Beulah role resurfaced in the 1980s when Nell Carter played a mammy-like role on the situation comedy "Gimme a Break." In this series, the lead character, Nellie Ruth Harper, was dark-skinned, overweight, sassy, White-identified and content to live in her White employer's home and nurture the family.

18. The movie dialogue betrays Black women:

> *Miss Bea:* "You'll have your own car. Your own house."
> *Aunt Delilah:* "My own house? You gonna send me away, Miss Bea? I can't live with you? Oh, Honey Chile, please don't send me away. How I gonna take care of you and Miss Jessie (Miss Bea's daughter) if I ain't here . . . I'se your cook. And I want to stay your cook."

Regarding the recipe,

> *Aunt Delilah:* "I gives it to you, honey. I makes it you a present of it."

Aunt Delilah worked to keep the White family together even though her own family disintegrated. Her self-hating daughter rejected her and ran away from home to pass for White and Aunt Delilah dies from a broken heart near the end of the movie.

19. Marilyn Kern-Foxworth, *Aunt Jemima, Uncle Ben, and Rastus: Blacks in Advertising Yesterday, Today, and Tomorrow* (Westport, CT: Praeger Publishers, 1994), 88.

20. This was reported in several newspapers and Black church denominational journals including the *Washington Tribune*, Washington, DC, February 2,

1923; the *National Baptist Union Review*, Nashville, TN, May 4, 1923; the *Christian Index*, Jackson, TN, February 22, 1923; *Birmingham Reporter*, Birmingham, AL, March 17, 1923; and the *New York Age*, New York, January 6, 1923.

21. A cakewalk is a rhythmic dance performed in a circle. Slaves performed cakewalks during harvest festivals in the U.S. South. Minstrel shows featured the cakewalk as the big finish of the show. In these shows, White men in blackface mimicked Black dances for the amusement of Whites. Members of the troupe danced in a circle, with couples taking turn promenading in the center. See M. M. Manring, *Slave in a Box: The Strange Career of Aunt Jemima* (Charlottesville, VA: University Press of Virginia, 1998), 61, 67.

22. James Grace, "Old Aunt Jemima," (Boston, MA: John F. Perry & Co., 538 Wash. St., Plate No. 245–2. Source: 0548@Brown/LoC.) The copyright claim on the cover page is for 1875, but on the title page it is 1876.

23. Manring, *Slave in a Box*, 67.

24. Ibid.

25. Kern-Foxworth, *Aunt Jemima, Uncle Ben, and Rastus*, 68. Green lived on the South Side of Chicago and was one of the founders of one of the largest Black churches in the world, Olivet Baptist Church. Green remained with the Davis Milling Company until she was killed when a car hit her on September 23, 1923.

26. The Aunt Jemima pancake mix and its marketing coincided with the ability to launch a national market food product. The story of Davis' success in doing this can be marked by the fact that until the emergence of Aunt Jemima pancake mix, the bulk of the flour sales occurred in the winter months. After the Nancy Green promotion, year-round flour sales became the norm and pancakes were no longer considered only a breakfast food.

27. See Philip A. Bruce, *The Plantation Negro as a Freeman: Observations on His Character, Condition, and Prospects in Virginia* (New York: G.P. Putnam's Sons, 1889), James Ford Rhodes, *History of the United States from the Compromise of 1850 to the McKinley-Bryan campaign of 1896*, vols. 1–8 (Port Washington, NY: Kennikat Press reprint 1967; 1892–1919), W.J. Cash, *The Mind of the South* (New York: A.A. Knopf, 1941).

28. Elliot M. Rudwick and August Meier, "Black Man in the 'White City': Negroes and the Columbian Exposition, 1893" in *Phylon* vol. 26, no. 4 (1965): 354.

The Columbian Exposition was an extremely contentious and sore spot for Blacks. The United States government invited the world to take part in celebrating the "discovery" of this country four hundred years before. Nations such as Haiti and Liberia participated, but U.S. Black participation in the Fair was blocked. The pain of this act for those members of this nation, just one generation from slavery, was acute. Blacks of the era hoped to use the Fair as a showcase for Black achievement. The 1893 Columbian Exposition galvanized Black protest. Blacks reacted in a similar fashion to the 1933–34 Fair, the New York Fair of 1939–40, and the New York World's Fair of 1964–65. Rather than a celebration of technological advance and prowess, Black folk viewed the Exposition as a symbol of moral failure. Meanwhile, Exposition officials awarded Nancy Green a medal and a certificate as they proclaimed her the Pancake Queen.

29. In 1926, the Quaker Oats Company of Chicago acquired the Aunt Jemima trademark and revived the Aunt Jemima portrayers in the 1930s. Also in the 1930, Quaker Oats chose Anna Robinson as the new model for the product. Her figure remained on the boxes until the late 1960s. From the 1930s to the 1960s, the various Aunt Jemimas were assigned to geographic regions although a few appeared in radio and print campaigns. Since 1968, the Aunt Jemima trademark is no longer based on a real person.

    Among the other women who played Aunt Jemima were Anna Robinson (1933–1951, best known for posing with Hollywood celebrities), Edith Wilson (1948–1966, who portrayed Aunt Jemima on radio and was the first Aunt Jemima featured on television commercials), Ethel Ernestine Harper (who was a college graduate and teacher before portraying Aunt Jemima), Aylene Lewis (who portrayed Aunt Jemima at the Aunt Jemima Restaurant at Disneyland). See Kern-Foxworth, *Aunt Jemima, Uncle Ben, and Rastus*, 68–69. One, Rosie Lee Moore portrayed Aunt Jemima until her death in 1967. She, like the other Aunt Jemimas, was treated well for a time in which Black women did not hold high profile positions. Quaker Oats, now the company that owned the Aunt Jemima trademark, covered her travel expenses and gave her an escort. This gave Moore some of the frills of celebrity although she was not paid like one. Sadly, Moore grave went unmarked for 21 years. See Ronnie Crocker, "Homage to Aunt Jemima Remains a Tricky Business," *Houston Chronicle*, www.cron.com/content/chronicle/metropolitan/96/04/07/aunt.jemima.html.

30. Manring, *Slave in a Box*, 75.

31. Kenneth W. Goings, *Mammy and Uncle Mose: Black Collectibles and American Stereotyping* (Bloomington: Indiana University Press, 1994), 28.

32. Kern-Foxworth, *Aunt Jemima, Uncle Ben, and Rastus*, 73.

33. Ibid., 76.

34. Manring, *Slave in the Box*, 140.

35. Ibid., 153, 155–157. Cyril V. Briggs, the editor and publisher of *Crusade* magazine first editorialized about the ads as the Young and Wyeth version of the Mammy began appearing on the pages of national magazines, billboards, and pancake boxes. Paul K. Edwards, an economics professor at Fisk University, conducted a study of Black consumers and the Aunt Jemima ads in the 1920s and 1930s. His research showed that Blacks resented the illusions to slavery, real and imagined, and servitude and ignorance the ads conveyed about Blacks.

36. The name "Jemima" has its roots in the Arabic and Hebrew languages. She was the oldest of Job's daughters and the name of a city in ancient Arabia that was named after its queen, Jemima. In the 1800s it was the name for a servant girl. In the 1800s and early 1900s, it was the designation for a chamber pot. From the 1880s to the 1930s, it was the name for a dressmaker's dummy. When it was Americanized, obesity was added.

37. Scripps Howard News Service, "Blacks' Image in Advertising Has Improved over the Years," *Bryan-College Station Eagle* (March 1, 1987): 1E.

In a telling observation in a chapter, "The Negro" that was omitted from Alex Haley's *The Autobiography of Malcolm X*, El-Shabazz (the name he took after his break with the Elijah Muhammad and the Nation of Islam) discusses Aunt Jemima.

> Aunt Jemima, beaming and black—used by the white man—has sold billions of pancakes. Her counterpart, Uncle Ben, has sold shiploads of rice—for the white man. Where is the black money pooled into an industry hiring blacks in the total processing of frozen black Southern cooking that could share in the frozen food millions?
>
> Where is this nation's black-owned chains of black-cooking restaurants? In the fall of 1963, Aunt Jemima moved from boxed pancake four to a nation-spanning restaurant franchise . . . .
>
> Guess who franchises the chain of Aunt Jemima restaurants?
>
> The activism of the civil rights movement, the resistance to police brutality coupled with the assertiveness of the Black Power movement thus made it almost impossible to portray African-Americans as loyal, service, but happy Aunt Jemimas and Uncle Mose [Aunt Jemima's husband].

See Kern-Foxworth, *Aunt Jemima, Uncle Ben, and Rastus*, 85.

38. Spike Lee, director, *Bamboozled*. New Line Cinema, 2000. Lee's film is a relentless satire on racism in U.S. network television that uses the blackface minstrel tradition with Blacks as the performers on the hit show, "Mantan: The New Millennium Minstrel Show," written by a struggling and frustrated Black writer.

39. Eminem is the handle for Marshall Mathers, a young White man from Detroit. He is following in the line of other White hip hop artists and groups such as the Beastie Boys who have co-opted Black and Latino hip hop for their financial benefit. This pattern of co-optation in music is not new, as various musical forms such as jazz, blues, and rock have been stolen from their southern Black cultural roots. This reveals a continued pattern of the commodification of Black identity.

40. "Hybridity" has its roots in biology. There it refers to the selective breeding of plants to produce new varieties with specific qualities—usually improvements over the original plants. The use of hybridity in wider discourse first signaled the colonial stigmatization of racial impurity and the dangers/horrors of miscegenation. With the rise of postcolonial studies, hybridity represents the intermingling of people and media from different cultures. For a more detailed discussion of hybridity in its postcolonial guise, see Gayatri Spivak, "Can the Subaltern Speak?" in *Marxism and the Interpretation of Culture*, ed. Cary Nelson and Lawrence Grossberg (Champaign: University of Illinois Press, 1988), and Homi Bhabha, *The Location of Culture* (New York: Routledge, 1994), and "Cultural Diversity and Cultural Differences" in *The Post-Colonial Studies Reader*, ed. Bill Ashcroft, Gareth Griffiths, and Helen Tiffin (New York: Routledge, 1995).

41. Manthia Diawara, "The Blackface Stereotype," www.tiac.net/users/thaslert/m_diawara/blackface.html.

42. Ibid.

43. Tom Zeller, "Recasting Racism, One Icon at a Time" *The New York Times*, September 9, 2001, Section 2:6.

44. "Property" in *The Oxford Dictionary of Current English*, ed. Della Thompson (New York: Oxford University Press, 1993).

45. "Proper" in *The Concise Oxford Dictionary of English Etymology*, ed. T. F. Hoad (New York: Oxford University Press, 1986).

46. Alan Ryan, *Property* (Minneapolis: University of Minnesota Press, 1987), 35.

47. Cheryl I. Harris, "Whiteness as Property" in *Critical Race Theory: Key Writings That Formed the Movement*, ed. Kimberlé Crenshaw, Neil Gotanda, Gary Peller, and Kendall Thomas (New York: New Press, 1996), 279.

48. Frederic L. Pryor, *Property and Industrial Organization in Communist and Capitalist Nations* (Bloomington, IN: Indiana University Press, 1973), 2.

49. The Clause increased the South's proportional representation in Congress assured that the political power of slave owners (but not the vote of slaves) would be factored in the representation and taxation. Article 1, Section 2, Paragraph 3 of the U.S. Constitution reads, in part, "Representatives and direct Taxes shall be apportioned among the several States which may be included within this Union, according to their respective Numbers, which shall be determined by adding to the whole Number of free Persons, including those bound to Service for a Term of Years, and excluding Indians not taxed, three fifths of all other Persons."

50. The Law of 1793 was not strictly enforced and helped lead to the creation of the Underground Railroad. The 1850 Law was more strictly enforced and stated if a federal marshal who did not arrest an alleged runaway slave could be fined $1,000. Anyone suspected of being a runaway slave could be arrested without warrant and turned over to a claimant on nothing more than his sworn testimony of ownership. A suspected black slave could not ask for a jury trial nor testify on his or her behalf. Further, anyone aiding a runaway slave by providing shelter, food or any other form of assistance was liable to six months' imprisonment and a $1,000 fine. Those officers capturing a fugitive slave were entitled to a fee and this encouraged some officers to kidnap free Blacks and sell them to slave-owners.

51. Slavery existed for 246 years from 1619, when the first Africans were brought to Virginia until 1865, with the Emancipation Proclamation.

52. "Property" in *The Westminster Dictionary of Christian Ethics*, ed. James F. Childress and John Macquarrie (Philadelphia: Westminster Press, 1967).

53. The sociolegal view refers to the factual legal arrangements of ownership. Positive human laws regulate, tolerate, or forbid transactions and relations among individual persons. The moral-philosophical view of ownership looks for the meaning of the concept of ownership-as-it-ought-to-be. Here, ownership is a relation between the owning person and all others to whom the owner excludes from or to whom the owner concedes possession. See Charles Avila, *Ownership: Early Christian Teaching* (Maryknoll, NY: Orbis Books, 1983).

From the perspective of Christian ethics, autonomy, at its most basic level means self law or self rule. It also refers to persons and their actions. Hence the autonomous person is one who has the mental capacities to reflect on and chose her or his moral framework. A key ingredient in this understanding is the notion of choice. I contend, following the line of argument presented by Katie Geneva Cannon in *Black Womanist Ethics* (Atlanta, GA: Scholars Press, 1988), that for peoples who live in situations of oppression, choice is often severely circumscribed, hence altering and challenging the traditional moral landscape of most normative ethical reflection. For a clear definition of autonomy presented from a normative perspective, see "Autonomy" in *The Westminster Dictionary of Christian Ethics*, ed. James F. Childress and John Macquarrie (Philadelphia: Westminster Press, 1986), 51–53.

54. Manring, *Slave in a Box*, 30–31. Carter G. Woodson and Jessie W. Parkhurst fall into the former camp. For Woodson, she is the "Negro washerwoman" who is the "towering personage in the life of the Negro." For Parkhurst, she was the "prime ministers" in the Big House. Charles Chestnutt fell into the latter camp in which the Mammy was more a liability than a savior.

55. Aunt Jemima's family was first created in 1895 with a cut out paper doll collection that consisted of Aunt Jemima and Rastus (her husband) and their children Abraham Lincoln, Delsie, Zeb, and Little Dinah. In 1905, a different rag doll family was offered in which Uncle Mose replaced Rastus as Aunt Jemima's husband and she only had two children—the twins Diana and Wade. See Jean Williams Turner, *Collectable Aunt Jemima: Handbook and Value Guide* (Atglen, PA: Schiffer Publishing, 1994), 7.

56. The Electric Slide is performed:

1. Step to right with right, slide left together
2. Step to right with right, slide left together
3. Step to right with right, slide left together
4. Clap
5. Step to left with left, slide right together
6. Step to left with left, slide right together
7. Step to left with left, slide right together
8. Clap
9. Step back on right foot
10. Step back on left foot
11. Step back on right foot
12. Touch back on left toe (don't put weight on this foot)
13. Step forward on left foot
14. Swing kick right foot
15. Step back on right foot
16. Touch back on left toe (don't put weight on this foot)
17. Step forward on left foot
18. Swing kick with right foot turning 1/4 turn to left

Dance begins again.

57. Lipsitz, "History, Myth, and Counter-Memory," 227.

58. Examples of these writers' works include: James Baldwin, *The Price of the Ticket: Collected Nonfiction, 1948–1985* (New York: St. Martin's/Marek, 1985), *Just Above My Head* (New York: Dial Press, 1979), and *The Fire Next*

Time (New York: Dial Press, 1963). Du Bois, *Black Reconstruction*, intro. David Levering Lewis (South Bend, IN: University of Notre Dame Press, 2001), *Color and Democracy: Colonies and Peace*, intro. Herbert Aptheker (Millwood, NY: Kraus-Thomson Organization, 1975), *Dusk of Dawn*, intro. Herbert Aptheker (Millwood, NY: Kraus-Thomson Organization, 1975), *Darkwater: Voices From Within the Veil*, intro. Herbert Aptheker (Millwood, NY: Kraus-Thomson Organization, 1975; 1920) and *The Souls of Black Folk*, ed. Henry Louis Gates, Jr. and Terri Hume Oliver (New York: W.W. Norton, 1998). Toni Morrison, *Playing in the Dark: Whiteness and the Literary Imagination* (Cambridge: Harvard University Press, 1992), *Sula* (New York: Knopf, 1974; 1973), and *Beloved: A Novel* (New York: Knopf, 1987). Katie Geneva Cannon, *Katie's Canon: Womanism and the Soul of the Black Community* (New York: Continuum, 1995) and *Black Womanist Ethics* (Atlanta, GA: Scholars Press, 1988). James H. Cone, *Risks of Faith: The Emergence of a Black Theology of Liberation, 1968–1998* (Boston, MA: Beacon Press, 1999), *Martin & Malcolm & America: A Dream or A Nightmare?* (Maryknoll, NY: Orbis Books, 1991), *For My People: Black Theology and the Black Church* (Maryknoll, NY: Orbis Books, 1984), *God of the Oppressed*, rev. edition (Maryknoll, NY: Orbis Books, 1997), *Black Theology and Black Power* (Maryknoll, NY: Orbis Books, 1997), and *A Black Theology of Liberation*, 20th anniversary edition (Maryknoll, NY: Orbis Books, 1990). Alexander Crummell, *Destiny and Race: Selected Writings, 1840–1898*, ed. and intro. Wilson Jeremiah Moses (Amherst: University of Massachusetts Press, 1992) and *Africa and America: Addresses and Discourses* (New York: Negro Universities Press, 1969). Delores W. Williams, *Black Theology in a New Key / Feminist Theology in a Different Voice* (Maryknoll, NY: Orbis Books, 2002) and *Sisters in the Wilderness: The Challenge of Womanist God-talk* (Maryknoll, NY: Orbis Books, 1993).

59. Robert C. Toll, *Blacking Up: The Minstrel Show in Nineteenth-Century America* (New York: Oxford University Press, 1974), 254 and Manring, *Slave in a Box*, 68.

60. Toll, *Blacking Up*, 259. Two versions appeared in Black minstrel songbooks in 1875. Another appeared in 1880.

61. Some minstrel performers such as Bert Williams responded to Black criticism by pointing out that Black entertainers were caught between Whites who only wanted to see them portray the antebellum darky and Blacks who only wanted to see "such characters as remind [them] of 'white folks.' " Williams sought to create Black characters drawn "from the mass and not the few." Quoted in Toll, *Blacking Up*, 257.

62. Manring, *Slave in a Box*, 61, 65, 67.

63. Toll, *Blacking Up*, 261.

64. Manring, *Slave in a Box*, 69.

65. Toll, *Blacking Up*, 260.

66. Manring, *Slave in a Box*, 69.

67. Toni Morrison, *Beloved* (New York: Plume, 1998). Gloria Naylor, *Mama Day* (New York: Vintage Books, 1989). Alice Walker, *The Color Purple* (New York: Washington Square Press, 1998). Sonia Sanchez, *Does Your House*

Have Lions? (Boston, MA: Beacon Press, 1998). Tina McElroy Ansa, *Baby of the Family* (New York: Harvest Books, 1991). Edwidge Danticat, *Krik? Krak!* (New York: Random House, 1996).

68. bell hooks, *Teaching to Transgress: Education as the Practice of Freedom* (New York: Routledge, 1994), 81.

Chapter 4   Invisible Things Spoken: Uninterrogated Coloredness

1. Toni Morrison, "Unspeakable Things Unspoken: The Afro-American Presence in American Literature" in *The Black Feminist Reader*, ed. Joy James and T. Denean Sharpley-Whiting (Malden, MA: Blackwell Publishers Inc., 2000), 34–35.
2. See Joel 1–2, especially 1:4 and 2:3–10 NRSV (New Revised Standard Version).
3. Morrison, "Unspeakable Things," 26. Barbara Christian, *Black Women Novelists: The Development of a Tradition, 1892–1976* (Westport, CT: Greenwood Press, 1980), 77.
4. Deborah Gray White, *Ar'n't I a Woman?: Female Slaves in the Plantation South* (New York: W.W. Norton and Co., 1985), 165.
5. Sapphire Stevens' husband was The Kingfish. The Amos'n Andy Show began as a black face radio, Sam and Henry, show created by two White actors, Freeman Gosden and Charles Correll in 1928. When it moved to television in the summer of 1951, the show was recast with Black actors. Only Ernestine Wade (Sapphire) and Amanda Randolph (Mama) were brought over from the radio cast. The show centered on the activities of George Stevens (Tim Moore), a conniving character who was always looking for a way to make a fast buck. He was the head (Kingfish) of the Mystic Knights of the Sea Lodge and often involved his lodge brothers with his schemes. This put him at odds with them and his wife Sapphire, and her mother. Mama, in particular, didn't trust him at all. Andy Brown (Spencer Williams, Jr.) was the most gullible of the lodge members—husky, well-meaning, but rather simple. Amos (Alvin Childress) was a minor character and the philosophical cabdriver who narrated most of the episodes. Madame Queen (Lillian Randolph) was Andy's girlfriend and Lightnin' (Horace Stewart) was the slow-moving janitor at the lodge.

The NAACP and other Civil rights groups protested the series from its inception as fostering racial stereotypes. The show had a large following during its two-year run on CBS run. It was widely rerun on local stations for the next decade. In 1963 CBS Films, which was still calling Amos 'n' Andy one of its most widely circulated shows, announced that the program had been sold to two African countries, Kenya and Western Nigeria. Soon, an official of the Kenya government announced that the program would be banned in his country. In the summer of 1964, a Chicago station announced that it was resuming reruns. This announcement was met with widespread and bitter protests.

CBS found its market for the films suddenly disappearing, and in 1966 the program was withdrawn from sale, as quietly as possible. The show (72 episodes) is available once again through DVD and video release.

6. Melvin Patrick Ely, *The Adventures of Amos 'n' Andy: A Social History of an American Phenomenon* (New York: The Free Press, 1991), 208.

7. Mary E. Young, *Mules and Dragons: Popular Culture Images in the Selected Writings of African-American and Chinese-American Women Writers* (Westport, CT: Greenwood Press, 1993), 40.

8. Barbara Smith, "Doing Research on Black Women," *Women's Studies Newsletter* 4 (Spring 1976): 4.

9. Eldridge Cleaver, *Soul on Ice* (New York: Dell Publishing Company, 1968), 159. Biblical scholar, Peter T. Nash, notes that Cleaver's description resembles the description of the Hebrew women of Exodus (Personal note to the author).

10. Steven Fenton, "Ethnicity and Racism," *Echoes* vol. 17 (2000): 26.

11. Ibid., 24.

12. Ibid., 26.

13. Ibid., 27.

14. Fenton is not alone in arguing in this vein. See also K. Anthony Appiah's work *In My Father's House: Africa in the Philosophy of Culture* (New York: Oxford University Press, 1993) and *Color Conscious*, cowritten with Amy Gutman (Princeton: Princeton University Press, 1998). Appiah argues that any significant conception of race is really just culture in disguise. For him a truly nonracist world would be one in which ethnic identities that are based on racial difference would disappear over time. Further, what is now "racial identity" would become "ethnic identity." Ultimately for Appiah, culture can and should be the substitute for race. Although this position, like Fenton's, moves us away from various forms of inept biological determinism (race is only possessed by people of color, morality and intellect as inherited characteristics, nature no effort, inheritance always trumps learning), it ultimately fails to account for and develop models of resistance to entrenched forms of racism that are cultural, legal, social, and theological.

15. For a more thorough discussion of this and its particular manifestations within the Black communities of the United States see Emilie M. Townes, "Another Kind of Poetry: Identity and Colorism in Black Life" in *In a Blaze of Glory: Womanist Spirituality as Social Witness* (Nashville, TN: Abingdon Press, 1995).

16. Michael Omi and Howard Winant, *Racial Formation of the United States: From the 1960s to the 1990s*, 2E (New York: Routledge, 1994).

17. Other examples include the work of Jayne Choong-Soon Lee, "Navigating the Topology of Race" in *Critical Race Theory: The Key Writings That Formed the Movement*, ed. Kimberlé Crenshaw, Neil Kotanda, Gary Peller, and Kendall Thomas (New York: New Press, 1995), 441–448 and Martha Mahoney, "The Social Construction of Whiteness," in *Critical White Studies: Looking Behind the Mirror*, ed. Richard Delgado and Jean Stefancic (Philadelphia: Temple University Press, 1997), 330–333.

18. Mahoney, "The Social Construction of Whiteness," 330.

19. Ibid.

20. Colette Guillaumin, " 'I Know It's Not Nice, But . . . ': The Changing Face of 'Race' " in *Race, Identity, and Citizenship: A Reader*, ed. Rodolfo D. Torres, Louis F. Mirón, and Jonathan Xavier Inda (Malden, MA: Blackwell Publishers, 1999), 41.

21. For a comparative look at this shift, see Anthony W. Marx, *Making Race and Nation: A Comparison of the United States, South Africa, and Brazil* (New York: Cambridge University Press, 1998).

22. Guillaumin " 'I Know It's Not Nice, But . . . ,' " 41.

23. *Disrupting White Supremacy From Within: White People on What We Need to Do*, ed. Jennifer Harvey, Karin A. Case, and Robin Gorsline Hawley (Cleveland: Pilgrim Press, 2004). Joseph C. Hough, *Black Power and White Protestants: A Christian Response to the New Negro Pluralism* (New York: Oxford University Press, 1968). See also James N. Poling *Deliver Us From Evil: Resisting Racial and Gender Oppression* (Minneapolis: Fortress Press, 1996) and Mary Elizabeth Hobgood, *Dismantling Privilege: An Ethics of Accountability* (Cleveland: Pilgrim Press, 2000). As a Christian ethicist, I am focusing my critique on my own discipline's lack of engagement with racism as a theoethical category. As the persistent critique of Black theologian James H. Cone points out, the situation in Christian theology is little better. In both disciplines, those who do explore racism as a moral and theological problem tend to be those who are darker-skinned. See Cone's *God of the Oppressed* (New York: Seabury Press, 1975) and *Black Theology and Black Power* (Philadelphia: Lippincot, 1970). Black ethicists who have dealt with racism include Katie Geneva Cannon, *Black Womanist Ethics* (Atlanta: Scholar Press, 1988) and *Katie's Cannon: Womanism and the Soul of the Black Community* (New York: Continuum Publishing Company, 1995) and Victor Anderson, *Beyond Ontological Blackness* (New York: Continuum Publishing Company, 1995).

24. Ruth Frankenberg, *White Women, Race Matters: The Social Construction of Whiteness* (Minneapolis: University of Minnesota Press, 1993), 11.

25. David R. Roediger, *The Wages of Whiteness: Race and the Making of the American Working Class* (New York: Verso, 1991), 21.

26. Alastair Bonnett, "Constructions of Whiteness in European and American Anti-Racism" in Torres, Mirón, and Inda, eds, *Race Identity and Citizenship*, 200–201.

27. Frankenberg, *White Women, Race Matters*, 14–15.

28. Bonnett, "Constructions of Whiteness," 202.

29. Ibid.

30. For a more thorough discussion of these pseudosciences such as phrenology (reading of skulls) and physiognomy (reading faces), see Cornel West, *Prophesy Deliverance!: An Afro-American Revolutionary Christianity* (Philadelphia: Westminster Press, 1982). See also my *In a Blaze of Glory*, "Another Kind of Poetry: Identity and Colorism in Black Life," esp. 96–98.

31. "Miscegenation" is a late nineteenth century combination of the Latin words *miscere* (to mix) and *genus* (race). It was introduced in a 1863 pamphlet created by the Democrats to smear Republican opponents by implying that the Republican abolitionist position would lead to race mixing. For a more

complete discussion, see Kathleen Neal Cleaver, "The Antidemocratic Power of Whiteness" in *Critical White Studies*, 157–163.

32. K. Cleaver, "The Antidemocratic Power of Whiteness," 160–161.

33. Frankenberg, *White Women, Race Matters*, 139.

34. Bonnett, "Constructions of Whiteness," 206.

35. Ibid., 204.

36. Frankenberg, *White Women, Race Matters*, 142.

37. Aida Hurtado, "The Trickster's Play: Whiteness in the Subordination of Liberation Process," in *Race, Identity, and Citizenship*, 226.

38. Teun A. van Dijk has done a helpful study that points to the dangers of uninterrogated coloredness. He argues that elite groups in various societies often promulgate racist discourse. Van Dijk, who confines his study to western nations, notes that such language as "floods" or "massive invasions" of refugees, "illegal" immigration, "crime-riddled ghettos," "strange customs," and the like by mainstream media instills or confirms a xenophobic or antiminority resent among the white population at large. He identifies five elite discourses—political, corporate, academic, educational, and media—in which this is true. Teun A. van Dijk, *Elite Discourse and Racism* (Newbury Park, CA: Sage Publications, 1993). The work of Arthur K. Spears is also instructive at this juncture. See his introduction and afterword in *Race and Ideology: Language, Symbolism, and Popular Culture*, ed. Arthur K. Spears (Detroit: Wayne State University Press, 1999).

39. Spears, "Race and Ideology: An Introduction," 28–29.

40. Farai Chideya, *The Color of Our Future* (New York: William Morrow and Co., 1999), 17–19.

41. Adrienne D. Davis, "Identity Notes, Part One: Playing in the Light," *Critical White Studies*, 231.

42. "Ecopsychology and the Deconstruction of Whiteness: An Interview With Carl Anthony" in Ecopsychology: *Restoring the Earth, Healing the Mind*, ed. Theodore Roszak, Mary E. Gomes, Allen D. Kanner, James Hillman, and Lester O. Brown (San Francisco: Sierra Club Books, 1995), 265–276, esp. 265.

43. Ibid., 268.

44. Harris, "Whiteness as Property," 276–292, esp. 283–286.

45. bell hooks, "Representing Whiteness in the Black Imagination" in *Displacing Whiteness: Essays in Social and Cultural Criticism*, ed. Ruth Frankenberg (Durham, NC: Duke University Press, 1997), 168–169.

Chapter 5 Legends Are Memories Greater than Memories: Black Reparations in the United States as Subtext to Christian Triumphalism and Empire

1. Special Field Orders, No. 15, Headquarters Military Division of the Mississippi, January 16, 1865, Orders and Circulars, ser. 44, Adjutant General's Office,

Record Group 94, National Archives. Also published in *The Wartime Genesis of Free Labor: The Lower South*, ed. Ira Berlin, Thavolia Glymph, and Julie Saville (New York: Cambridge University Press, 1991), 338–340.

2. United States Constitution, Amendment Thirteen (1865). The complete text of the amendment is as follows:

> Section 1. Neither slavery nor involuntary servitude, except as a punishment for crime whereof the party shall have been duly convicted, shall exist within the United States, or any place subject to their jurisdiction.
>
> Section 2. Congress shall have power to enforce this article by appropriate legislation.

3. Published in *The Wartime Genesis of Free Labor: The Lower South*, 331–338; *Free at Last: A Documentary History of Slavery, Freedom, and the Civil War*, ed. Ira Berlin, Barbara J. Fields, and Steven Miller (New York: New Press, 1993), 310–318, and *Freedom's Soldiers: The Black Military Experience in the Civil War*, ed. Ira Berlin, Joseph Patrick Reidy, and Leslie S. Rowland (New York: Cambridge University Press, 1999), 149–153.

4. Ibid.

5. Ibid.

6. Ibid.

7. Ibid.

8. Ibid.

9. Ibid.

10. Du Bois, *Black Reconstruction*, 74.

11. Ibid.

12. Ibid., 274.

13. W.E.B. Du Bois, *The Souls of Black Folk* (New York: New American Library, 1969), 268–9.

14. Patrick Chamoiseau, *Texaco* (New York: Vintage Books, 1998), 53.

15. Ibid., 122.

16. Ibid., 176.

17. Ibid., 178.

18. Gary B. Nash, *Red, White, and Black: The Peoples of Early America* (New Jersey: Prentice-Hall, 1974), 289–290.

19. David Pilgrim, *The Tragic Mulatta Myth*, Jim Crow Museum of Racist Memorabilia, Ferris State University, Internet Article, www.ferris.edu/news/jimcrow/ mulatto/.

20. Quoted in George M. Fredrickson, *The Black Image in the White Mind: The Debate on Afro-American Character and Destiny 1817–1914* (New York: Harper & Row, 1971), 277.

21. Suzanne Bost, "Fluidity without Postmodernism: Michelle Cliff and the 'Tragic Mulatta' Tradition," *African American Review* vol. 32, no. 4 (Winter 1998): 675.

22. Bost, "Fluidity Without Postmodernism," 676.

23. Ibid.

24. Frederick Douglass was the senior Black statesmen and Black activist of the nineteenth century. Born a slave, Douglass learned to read and escaped to freedom in the North were he became a leading abolitionist and later advocate for women's rights. W.E.B. Du Bois is an intellectual giant of the twentieth century. As the first Black man to graduate from Harvard University, Du Bois went on to author such classics as *The Souls of Black Folk* (1903) and *Black Reconstruction* (1935). Mary Church Terrell was a leader in the nineteenth century Black women's club movement and Thurgood Marshall had a distinguished career as a trial lawyer and head of the NAACP Legal Defense Fund before being appointed to the Supreme Court in by. Malcolm X was a noted minister in the Nation of Islam and a Black activist in the North. Louis Farrakhan is the current leader of the Nation of Islam. Walter White was the former head of the NAACP. Adam Clayton Powell was an outspoken Congressman from Harlem and pastor of the historic Abyssinian Baptist Church of Harlem. Langston Hughes ("Good Morning, Revolution") and Jean Toomer (*Cane*, 1923) were noted writers of the Harlem Renaissance. Billy "Lady Day" Holiday lives on in record and CD collections all over the world.
25. Marcia Y. Riggs, *Awake, Arise and Act: A Womanist Call for Black Liberation* (Cleveland, OH: Pilgrim Press, 1993), 77.
26. Many thanks to ethicist Patricia-Ann Johnson for this marvelous turn of phrase.
27. Perry Miller, *The American Puritans: Their Prose and Poetry* (New York: Doubleday, 1956), 83.
28. Quoted in *God's New Israel: Religious Interpretations of American Destiny*, ed. Conrad Cherry (Englewood Cliffs: Prentice Hall, Inc., 1971), 65. Winthrop is quoted on 43; Whitaker is quoted on 33; Langdon is quoted on 99; Stiles is quoted on 88. The information about the Great Seal is found on 65.
29. See http://gbgm-umc.org/umw/joshua/nativeam.html. This web article is excerpted from by Roy H. May, Jr.'s *Joshua and the Promised Land* (New York: United Methodist Board of Global Ministries, 1997).
30. Exceptionalism is the belief that the United States has an exceptional way of life, institutions, and beliefs along with a mission to be, "like a city on a hill" or a model for other societies.
31. Social Darwinism is a quasi-philosophical, quasi-religious, quasi-sociological view based on the views of Herbert Spencer, an English philosopher in the 19th century. It did not achieve wide acceptance in England or Europe, but flourished in this country. Spencer popularized the theories of Charles Darwin in *Origin of Species* with the phrase, "survival of the fittest." Spencer opined that this applied to races as well as species and the coming Christian triumph would be Anglo-Saxon Protestant.
32. Kipling's poem:

> Take up the White Man's burden—
> Send forth the best ye breed—
> Go bind your sons to exile
> To serve your captives' need;
> To wait in heavy harness,

On fluttered folk and wild—
Your new-caught, sullen peoples,
Half-devil and half-child.

Take up the White Man's burden—
In patience to abide,
To veil the threat of terror
And check the show of pride;
By open speech and simple,
An hundred times made plain
To seek another's profit,
And work another's gain.

Take up the White Man's burden—
The savage wars of peace—
Fill full the mouth of Famine
And bid the sickness cease;
And when your goal is nearest
The end for others sought,
Watch sloth and heathen Folly
Bring all your hopes to nought.

Take up the White Man's burden—
No tawdry rule of kings,
But toil of serf and sweeper—
The tale of common things.
The ports ye shall not enter,
The roads ye shall not tread,
Go mark them with your living,
And mark them with your dead.

Take up the White Man's burden—
And reap his old reward:
The blame of those ye better,
The hate of those ye guard—
The cry of hosts ye humour
(Ah, slowly!) toward the light:—
"Why brought he us from bondage,

Our loved Egyptian night?"

Take up the White Man's burden—
Ye dare not stoop to less—
Nor call too loud on Freedom
To cloke your weariness;
By all ye cry or whisper,
By all ye leave or do,
The silent, sullen peoples
Shall weigh your gods and you.

> Take up the White Man's burden—
> Have done with childish days—
> The lightly proferred laurel,
> The easy, ungrudged praise.
> Comes now, to search your manhood
> Through all the thankless years
> Cold, edged with dear-bought wisdom,
> The judgment of your peers!

Rudyard Kipling was born in British India in 1865 and was educated in England before returning to India in 1882. His father was a museum director and authority on Indian arts and crafts there. By 1890, he had published in English about 80 stories and ballads previously unknown outside India. Between 1892–96, he wrote the two *Jungle Books* that became popular children's fiction. After returning to England, he published "The White Man's Burden" in 1899 as an appeal to the United States to assume the task of developing the Philippines that was won in the Spanish-American War.

33. Plutocracy is a government system where wealth is the principal basis of power. William Graham Sumner, "The Conquest of the United States By Spain," in *War and Other Essays*, ed. Albert Galloway Keller (New Haven: Yale University Press, 1911), 325–326.
34. Long, *Significations: Signs, Symbols, and Images*, 149.
35. Ibid.
36. Some things cannot be footnoted.
37. Michael Hardt and Antonio Negri, *Empire* (Cambridge: Harvard University Press, 2000), xii.
38. Paul Krugman, "Just Trust Us" nytimes.com, August 30, 2002.
39. Gopal Balakrishnan, "Virgilian Visions," *New Left Review* 5 (September– October 2000): 143.
40. Michael Hardt and Antonio Negri, *Empire* (Cambridge: Harvard University Press, 2000), 36.
41. Hardt and Negri, *Empire*, 294.
42. Ibid.
43. Ibid., xiii.
44. Erik Empson, "Anti-Capitalism with a Smiley Face," 63.
45. Hardt and Negri, *Empire*, 413.
46. Ibid., 18.
47. Ibid., 3. For a fuller treatment of Balakrishnan's critique, see his "Virgilian Visions" in *New Left Review*, September 5, 2000, 145–148.
48. Marcellus Andrews, *The Political Economy of Hope and Fear: Capitalism and the Black Condition in America* (New York: New York University Press, 1999), 139–140.
49. Michael Ignatieff, "The American Empire; The Burden," Magazine Desk, *The New York Times*, Internet article. nytimes.com.
50. Benedict Anderson, *Imagined Communities* (New York: Verso, 1991), 187–206.
51. Quoted in Ignatieff, "The American Empire."

52. Quoted in Ron Suskind's article "Without a Doubt" in *The New York Times Magazine*, Magazine Desk, October 17, 2004, 44ff.

53. For an excellent treatment of this see *Union Seminary Quarterly Review, New Testament and Empire*, vol. 5, no. 3–4 (2005).

54. Richard A. Horsley, "Introduction," in *Paul and Empire: Religion and Power in Roman Imperial Society*, ed. Richard A. Horsley (New York: Trinity Press International, 1997), 10.

55. Michael Ignatieff, "The American Empire; The Burden," nytimes.com, January 5, 2003.

56. Paul Krugman, "Things to Come," nytimes.com, March 18, 2003.

57. *New Hampshire Gazette*, "The Chickenhawks," http://nhgazette.com/chickenhawks.html.

58. Michael T. Klare, "The Generals' Revolt," April 2, 2003, http://www.thenation.com/doc.mhtml?i=20030421&=klare. Rumsfeld attended Princeton University on academic and NROTC scholarships (A.B., 1954) and served in the United States Navy (1954–57) as an aviator and flight instructor. In 1957, he transferred to the Ready Reserve and continued his Naval service in flying and administrative assignments as a drilling reservist until 1975. He transferred to the Standby Reserve when he became Secretary of Defense in 1975 and to the Retired Reserve with the rank of Captain in 1989. http://www.defenselink.mil/bios/rumsfeld.html.

59. U.S. Census Bureau, *Statistical Abstract of the United States: 2004–2005*.

60. Bernadette D. Proctor and Joseph Dalaker, U.S. Census Bureau, Current Population Reports, P60–222, *Poverty in the United States: 2002*, U.S. Government Printing Office, Washington, DC, 2003., 1–2.

61. The poverty line in 2004 was $19,307 for a family of four.

62. Quoted in Kathy Davis, "Headnote to Lydia Maria Child's 'The Quadroons' and 'Slavery's Pleasant Homes,' " Internet article, The Online Archive of Nineteenth-Century U.S. Women's Writings, ed. Glynis Carr, Posted Summer 1997, http://www.facstaff.bucknell.edu/gcarr/19cUSWW/LB/HNQSPH.html.

63. The call for reparations began with the early abolitionists in the eighteenth century. After the Civil War, antislavery leaders called for compensation to newly freed Blacks. At the 1865 Republican convention in Pennsylvania, Thaddeus Stevens called for giving slaves 400 million acres owned by their former masters. Reparations legislation appeared in Congress in 1866 and 1867. The debate died, however, after the southern oligarchy resumed control in the late 1870s. The modern reparations debate began with the Civil Rights movement in the 1960s. Martin Luther King, Jr., called for compensation for slavery, segregation, and continuous discrimination in 1963. In 1992, the Nation of Islam petitioned the United Nations for reparations for anti-Black racism and a dozen experts were selected by the Organization of African Unity to develop a campaign for African reparations like those provided by the German government to Nazi holocaust survivors. In March of 1996, the British House of Lords engaged in serious debate on the impact of slavery on Africa and Africans. A few members of that House proposed reparations to Africa from Britain and other colonial nations. Since 1989, Congressman John Conyers, Jr. (D-MI) has introduced a bill in Congress every year to set up

a commission to look into the continuing impact of slavery on Blacks and to examine the possibility of reparations for slavery. The key feature of this bill is to educate the public on the racist realities that are part of the core of the foundation of this republic. Although Conyers had not been able to secure hearings on the bill, he has 31 cosponsors.

Chapter 6   To Pick One's Own Cotton: Religious Values, Public Policy, and Women's Moral Autonomy

1. Sonia Sanchez, "haiku 6," in *Wounded in the House of a Friend* (Boston, MA: Beacon Press, 1995), 88.
2. For the purposes of this chapter, I adopt Thomas Dye's simple definition of public policy: whatever governments choose to do or not to do. Dye points out that this focuses on both government action and inaction. He notes that government inaction can have just as great an impact on society as government action. See Thomas R. Dye, *Understanding Public Policy*, 9E (Upper Saddle River, NJ: Prentice Hall, 1998), 3.
3. For an excellent discussion of this viewpoint, see Ivone Gebara, *Longing for Running Water: Ecofeminism and Liberation* (Minneapolis: Fortress Press, 1999), 23–64.
4. For further reading in womanist ethics, see, for example, Katie Geneva Cannon, *Black Womanist Ethics* (Atlanta, GA: Scholars Press, 1988) and *Katie's Canon: Womanism and the Soul of the Black Community* (New York: Continuum, 1995); Barbara A. Holmes, *Private Woman in Public Spaces: Barbara Jordan's Speeches on Ethics, Public Religion, and Law* (Harrisburg, PA: Trinity Press International, 2000) and *Race and the Cosmos: An Invitation to View the World Differently* (Harrisburg, PA: Trinity Press International, 2002); Cheryl A. Kirk-Duggan, *Exorcizing Evil: A Womanist Perspective on the Spirituals* (Maryknoll, NY: Orbis Books, 1997), *Misbegotten Anguish: A Theology and Ethics of Violence* (St. Louis: Chalice Press, 2001), and *Refiner's Fire: A Religious Engagement With Violence* (Minneapolis: Fortress Press, 2001); Joan M. Martin, *More Than Chains and Toil: A Christian Work Ethic of Enslaved Women* (Louisville: Westminster John Knox Press, 2000), Marcia Y. Riggs, *Awake, Arise, & Act: A Womanist Call for Black Liberation* (Cleveland: Pilgrim Press, 1994) and *Plenty Good Room: Women Versus Male Power in the Black Church* (Cleveland: Pilgrim Press, 2003) and Rosetta E. Ross, *Witnessing and Testifying: Black Women, Religion, and Civil Rights* (Minneapolis: Fortress Press, 2003).
5. Patricia Hill Collins, *Black Feminist Thought: Knowledge, Consciousness, and the Politics of Empowerment* (Boston, MA: Unwin Hyman, Inc., 1990), 202.
6. Collins, *Black Feminist Thought*, 202.
7. Ibid., 205.
8. Ibid.
9. Gebara, *Longing for Running Water*, 24.

10. Ibid., 54.

11. The key feature of a process epistemology is its dialogical character.

12. Robin Good, "The Blues: Breaking the Psychological Chains of Controlling Images" in *Dismantling White Privilege: Pedagogy, Politics, and Whiteness*, ed. Nelson M. Rodriguez and Leila E. Villaverde (New York: Peter Lang Publishing, Inc., 2000), 111.

13. Good, "The Blues," 112. Collins, *Black Feminist Thought*, 73–74.

14. Ibid., 74.

15. Collins, *Black Feminist Thought*, 75.

16. This study is commonly known as the Moynihan Report. See Daniel P. Moynihan, *The Negro Family: The Case for National Action* (Washington: Superintendent of Documents, U.S. Printing Office, 1965). Moynihan misappropriated E. Franklin Frazier's *The Negro Family in the United States* (Chicago: University of Chicago Press, 1939). The 1948 abridged edition of Frazier's work—the most widely available edition—paints a much more complex and rich description of the Black family and the roles of Black men and women in it. Moynihan did not include this material. It is important to note that the 1939 unabridged edition of Frazier's work contains more material than the 1948 edition. In short, Moynihan did a high selective and suspect reading of Black life. See Frazier, *The Negro Family in the United States*. See also W.E.B. Du Bois, *The Negro American Family* (Atlanta: The Atlanta University Press, 1908).

17. Cheryl Townsend Gilkes, "They Have Careers!: Women, Class, and Families in the Sociology of E. Franklin Frazier [or "Re: Reading" Frazier's Sociology of Women Through the *Black Bourgeoisie*]," 2000, TMs, 3.

18. Ibid., 7. See also Frazier, *The Negro in the United States* (New York: Macmillan Company, 1949).

19. E. Franklin Frazier, *Black Bourgeoisie: The Rise of a New Middle Class* (New York: The Free Press, 1957), 221.

20. Ibid.

21. Quoted in Gilkes, "They Have Careers!" 8.

22. Gilkes, "They Have Careers!" 9. See also Anthony Platt, *E. Franklin Frazier Reconsidered* (New Brunswick, NJ: Rutgers University Press, 1991), 17–19.

23. Frazier, *The Negro Family in the United States*, 14.

24. Quoted in Gilkes, "They Have Careers!" 11. W.E.B. Du Bois, "The Present Leadership Among American Negroes," in *W.E.B. Du Bois Reader*, ed. David Levering Lewis (New York: Henry Holt and Co., 1995 [1957]).

25. Personal correspondence with author. January 4, 2006.

26. Patricia Bell Scott, "Debunking Sapphire: Toward a Non-Racist and Non-Sexist Social Science" in *All the Women Are White, All the Blacks are Men, But Some of Us are Brave: Black Women's Studies*, ed. Gloria T. Hull, Patricia Bell Scott, and Barbara Smith (Old Westbury, NY: The Feminist Press, 1982), 87.

27. Quoted in Deborah Gray White, *Arn't I a Woman?: Female Slaves in the Plantation South* (New York: W.W. Norton and Co., 1985), 164.

28. Emilie M. Townes, *In A Blaze of Glory: Womanist Spirituality as Social Witness* (Nashville, TN: Abingdon Press, 1995) and *Womanist Justice, Womanist Hope* (Atlanta, GA: Scholars Press, 1993).

29. Mary Jo Bane, "Social Science, Christian Ethics and Democratic Politics: Issues of Poverty and Welfare," *The Annual of the Society of Christian Ethics* vol. 21 (2001): 25–37.

30. Alan Keith-Lucas, The *Poor You Have With You Always: Concepts of Aid to the Poor in the Western World from Biblical Times to the Present* (St. Davids, PA: North American Association of Christians in Social Work, 1989), 1. Keith-Lucas was a professor of social work at the University of North Carolina. He pioneered the integration of Christian faith and social work practice.

31. See John Calvin, *Institutes of the Christian Religion* vol.1, ed. John T. McNeill, trans. Ford Lewis Battles (Philadelphia, PA: Westminster Press, 1960), 724.

32. Joan M. Martin, *More Than Chains and Toil: A Christian Work Ethic of Enslaved Women* (Louisville: Westminster John Knox Press, 2000), 124.

33. Martin, *More Than Chains and Toil*, 124.

34. In an interesting twist, in a speech he made at Columbia University in September 2000, billionaire Warren Buffett pointed out the inequities of wealth.

> I hear friends talk about the debilitating effects of food stamps and the self-perpetuating nature of welfare and how terrible that is. These same people are leaving tons of money to their kids, whose main achievement in life had been to emerge from the right womb. And when they emerge from the womb, instead of a welfare officer, they have a trust fund officer. Instead of food stamps, they get dividends and interest.

Beth J. Harpaz, "Billionaire Buffett Takes a Swipe at Trust-Fund Kids," September 27, 2000, The Associated Press Archive, https://archive.ap.org/cgi-bin/display . . . . Name%3dAP%26publishingDocID% dD7795JV00.

35. Quoted by Sir Frederick Eden, *The State of the Poor; or, an History of the Labouring Classes, from the Conquest to the Present Period*, vol. I (London: np, 1797), 38.

36. Max Weber, *The Protestant Ethic and the Spirit of Capitalism*, trans. Talcott Parsons (Los Angeles: Roxbury Publishing Company, 1996 [1930]), 281, fn 103.

37. Frank M. North, "Where Cross the Crowded Ways of Life," 1903.

> Where cross the crowded ways of life,
> where sound the cries of race and clan,
> above the noise of selfish strife,
> we hear thy voice, O Son of Man.
> In haunts of wretchedness and need,
> on shadowed thresholds dark with fears,
> from paths where hide the lures of greed,
> we catch the vision of thy tears.
> From tender childhoods helplessness,
> from woman's grief, man's burdened toil,
> from famished souls, from sorrow's stress,

thy heart has never known recoil.
The cup of water given for thee
still holds the freshness of thy grace;
yet long these multitudes to see
the sweet compassion of thy face.
O Master, from the mountain side,
make haste to heal these hearts of pain;
among these restless throngs abide,
O tread the city's streets again;
Till all the world shall learn thy love,
and follow where thy feet have trod;
till glorious from thy heaven above,
shall come the city of our God.

38. Keith-Lucas, *The Poor You Have With You Always*, 37–39.
39. Katie Geneva Cannon, "Remembering What We Never Knew," *The Journal of Women and Religion* 16 (1998):167–177.
40. A further breakdown reveals that the top 1 percent own 38.1 percent of the wealth in the country, the next 4 percent owns 21.3 percent, and the next 5 percent owns 11.5 percent. See "U.S. Wealth Distribution: I Get $38, You Get 23 Cents—That's Fair, Right?: Distribution of Our Wealth Is Terribly Askew," *The Rational Radical*, www.therationalradical.com/dsep/wealth-distribution.htm, September 4, 2001. This is the last year for which statistics were available at the time of this writing.
41. Sharon Ladin, Sophia Murphy, Alexandra Spieldoch, and Steve Suppan, *Eye on America: Social Watch, 1997–2004* (Minneapolis, The Institute for Agriculture and Trade Policy, 2005), 21.
42. Keith-Lucas, *The Poor You Have With You Always*, 52.
43. "Income Stable, Poverty Rate Increases, Percentage of Americans Without Health Insurance Unchanged" (Washington, DC: U.S. Census Bureau News, Department of Commerce), www.census.gov/Press-Release/www/releases/archives/income_wealth/005647.html. Also found in the *Income Poverty, and Health Insurance Coverage in the United States: 2004* report, www.census.gov/prod/2005pubs/p60-229.pdf. Median income remained unchanged between 2003 and 2004 at $44,389. The poverty rate for the same period rose from 12.5 percent to 12.7 percent.
44. http://www.aflcio.org/corporatewatch/paywatch/.
In 1980, CEOs made 42 times the pay of average factory workers. In 1990, they made 85 times as much. By 1999, CEOs made 475 times as much as workers. The top CEOs can earn as much as small countries. The five most highly paid CEOs on the AFL-CIO 2004 Executive PayWatch were Yahoo's Terry S. Semel ($109,301,385), Coach's Lew Frankfort ($64,918,520), XTO Energy's Bob R. Simpson ($62,141,981), United Health Group's William W. McGuire ($58,784,102), and Viacom's Summer M. Redstone ($56,017,985).
45. Manning Marable, "Imprisoning Black Minds: Neoliberalism and Education Apartheid" *Metro Exchange*, July 2000, 8.
46. www.taipeitimes.com/News/worldbiz/archives/2005/04/06/2003249383

47. Stephen Labaton, "Now Who, Exactly God Us Into This?: Enron? Andersen? Shocking, Say Those Who Helped it along," *The New York Times*, February 3, 2002, Section 3, 1. Those who are in this group include Senator Christopher J. Dodd, D-CT, Representative Billy Tauzin, R-LA, Representative Michael Oxley, R-OH, and Harvey L. Pitt, the chair of the Securities and Exchange Commission.

48. Anne Larason Schneider and Helen Ingram, *Policy Design for Democracy* (Lawrence, KS: University of Kansas Press, 1997), 5.

49. Paul Krugman, "A Fiscal Fantasy," *The New York Times*, January 22, 2002, Section A, 19.

50. Krugman, "A Fiscal Fantasy," 19.

51. Editorial, "The New Year in Taxes," *The New York Times*, December 30, 2005, http://www.nytimes.com/2005/12/30/opinion/30fri1.html.

52. Schneider and Ingram, *Policy Design for Democracy*, 5.

53. For a more detailed discussion of this, see Emilie M. Townes, "Fragmented Efforts: Health Care in the United States" in *Breaking the Fine Rain of Death: African American Health Issues and a Womanist Ethic of Care* (New York: Continuum Books, 1998).

54. Schneider and Ingram, *Policy Design for Democracy*, 6.

55. This features a rise and fall motion. All the steps should be long. On the first step forward, the weight is taken on the heel, then on to the ball of the foot. A gradual rise to the toes should be started at the end of the first beat, and continued to the second and third beat of each bar of music. Lower to the normal position at the end of the third beat by lowering to the heel of the foot that is carrying the weight.

56. This ratio has more than doubled since 1977 when the top 1% had as much as the bottom 49 million.

57. Marx's understanding of religion, is summed up in a passage from the Introduction to his 1843–44 *Critique of Hegel's Philosophy of Right*: "Religious suffering is, at one and the same time, the expression of real suffering and a protest against real suffering. Religion is the sigh of the oppressed creature, the heart of a heartless world, and the soul of soulless conditions. It is the opium of the people." Marx's Gymnasium senior thesis of 1835 argued that the primary social function of religion was to promote solidarity. By 1843, Marx sees the social function as a way of expressing and coping with social inequality, thereby maintaining the status quo. Marx, *Critique of Hegel's Philosophy of Right*, ed. Joseph O'Malley (New York: Cambridge University Press, 1970).

58. Quoted in Markkula Center for Applied Ethics, Santa Clara University, "Common Good," www.scu.edu/SCU/Centers/Ethics/practicing/decision/commongood.html.

Chapter 7 Growing like Topsy: Solidarity in the Work of Dismantling Evil

1. Harriet Beecher Stowe, *Uncle Tom's Cabin; or Life Among the Lowly* (New York: A.L. Burt, Publisher, 1852), 250–251. Stowe brought the abolitionists'

message to the public conscience. She attempted to make Whites in the South and North see slaves human beings. Eliza Harris, a slave whose son is to be sold, escapes her beloved home on Shelby plantation in Kentucky and heads North and eludes the hired slave catchers by using the underground railroad. Another slave, Uncle Tom, is sent "down the river" for sale, and ultimately endures a martyr's death under the whips of Simon Legree's overseers. *Uncle Tom's Cabin* paints pictures of three plantations, each worse than the other, where even the best plantation leaves a slave at the mercy of fate or debt.

2. Tom shows were stage versions of *Uncle Tom's Cabin*. These shows were popular from the early 1850s until well into the twentieth century. The actors who performed in them were called Tommers. See Turner, *Ceramic Uncles and Celluloid Mammies*, 78.

3. Also spelled piccaninny or picanniny. The origin of pickaninny is most likely from the Spanish *pequeño*, which means small, and *niño*, which means child. It may also derive from Portuguese *pequenino*, the diminutive of *pequeno*, which means small. The word was used most often to refer to a Negro or mulatto infant in the United States and the West Indies. The Racial Slur Database (http://rsdb.fuck.org) notes three possible orgins for pickaninny. The first is when slave owners would "pick a nincompoop" from the lineup of slaves. The second is slave children who could not pick cotton "ain't pickaninny." Finally, in some parts of the South, breasts are referred to a ninnys, so pickaninny was a reference to Blacks used as wetnurses (women who used their own breast milk to provide nourishment for another woman's child).

4. Turner, *Ceramic Uncles and Celluloid Mammies*, 14.

5. Doris Y. Wilkinson, "The Toy Menagerie: Early Images of Blacks in Toys, Games, and Dolls," in *Images of Blacks in American Culture*, ed. Jessie Carney Smith (New York: Greenwood Press, 1988), 283.

6. Wilkinson, "The Toy Menagerie," 283.

7. Johana Gast Anderton, *The Collector's Encyclopedia of Cloth Dolls: From Rag Baby to Art Object* (Lombard, IL: Wallace-Homestead Book Company, 1984)

8. Wilkinson, "The Toy Menagerie," 283.

9. Elizabeth Closs Traugott, "Pidgens, Creoles, and the Origins of Vernacular Black English," in *Black English: A Seminar*, ed. Deborah Sears Harrison and Tom Trabasso (Hillsdale, NJ: Lawrence Erlbaum Associates, 1976), 97.

10. Traugott points out that words do not become functional unless the society in which they are located has an operational use for them. They raise the important question of why did the meaning change in the United States and in the original Portuguese or Spanish. They point out that there are many other paternalistic ways to say "Negro child" in Portuguese. Further, they conjecture that it may have been Black ladinos who were African enslaved in the Iberian peninsula who then acquired some Portuguese and Spanish language and customs, who transmitted the word. Traugott, "Pidgens, Creoles, and the Origins of Vernacular Black English," 97.

11. Light skinned pickannies are rare.

12. Turner, *Ceramic Uncles and Celluloid Mammies*, 15.

13. A pinback is similar to a brooch but it has a flat face to display an advertisement or other images.

14. Kern-Foxworth, *Aunt Jemima, Uncle Ben, and Rastus*, 31.
15. Jennifer Craig, "Cinematic Stereotypes in America: Outdated or Depressingly Current?" www.wwa.ufl.edu/~jdouglas/9.pdf.
16. For example, see William Smith, *The Color Line: A Brief in Behalf of the Unborn* (New York: np, 1905), x, 186–187, 190–191 and George Frederickson's discussion of these theories in *The Black Image in the White Mind: The Debate on Afro-American Character and Destiny, 1817–1914* (New York: Harper and Row, 1971), 71–164.
17. Turner, *Ceramic Uncles and Celluloid Mammies*, 15. David Pilgrim, "The Picaninny Caricature," www.ferris.edu/news/jimcrow/picaninny.
18. Turner, *Ceramic Uncles and Celluloid Mammies*, 15.
19. Eula's speech is from the film, *Daughters of the Dust* by the African American film maker, Julie Dash. Dash chronicles the story of a Black sea island or Gullah family preparing to come to the mainland at the turn of the twentieth century through the eyes of the Unborn Child who already loves her family, the Peazants, fiercely and who understands that she is traveling on a spiritual mission.

    Eula had been raped by a White man. The narrator, the Unborn Child, is her child. Only the audience knows that the child Eula carries is truly the one she conceived, in love, with her husband Eli. As Eula speaks, near the end of the movie, she calls the women to task for ostracizing Yellow Mary, a prostitute, who turned to this life after her own experience of rape. Yellow Mary had come home to the island to be with her family again and to heal. Eula reminds them all that the fate and hope of Yellow Mary is their own.

    > There's going to be all kinds of roads to take in life. . . . Let's not be afraid to take them. We deserve them, because we're all good women. Do you . . . do you understand who we are, and what we have become? We're the daughters of those old dusty things Nana carries in her tin can . . . We carry too many scars from the past. Our past owns us. We wear our scars like armor, . . . for protection. Our mother's scars, our sister's scars, our daughter's scars . . . Thick, hard, ugly scars that no one can pass through to ever hurt us again. Let's live our lives without living in the fold of old wounds.

20. Stowe, *Uncle Tom's Cabin*, 254–255. The scene ends: "St. Clare was leaning over the back of her chair. 'You find virgin soil there, Cousin; put in your own ideas,—you won't find many to pull up.' " In two places in this conversation, Jane, a maid in the household, interjects information about slave life. In the first is after Topsy says she was never born: "The child was evidently sincere, and Jane, breaking into a short laugh, said, 'Laws, Missis, there's heaps of 'em. Speculators buys 'em up cheap, when they's little, and gets 'em raised for market.' " The second is after Topsy tells Miss Ophelia that she does not know how long she lived with her previous owners: " 'Laws, Missis, those low negroes,—they can't tell; they don't know anything about time,' said Jane; 'they don't know what a year is; they don't know their own ages.' "
21. Katie Geneva Cannon discusses this in greater detail in her lecture, "Remembering What We Never Knew: The Epistemology of Womanist Ethics"

(paper presented at the Soul to Soul: Women and Religion in the 21st Century conference sponsored by the Center for Women and Religion, Graduate Theological Union, Berkeley, CA; February 27, 1998). James Melvin Washington discusses social amnesia in the Introduction to the his edited volume, *Conversations With God: Two Centuries of Prayers by African Americans* (New York: Harperperennial Library, 1995), xxvii–xlii. Washington goes on to note that "there are grave consequences when we cannot locate and integrate the memories of our forebears," for this can lead to soul murder (xxxvii). For Washington, we must look at the public and collective rage at injustice through an analytical procedure he calls historical demonology. This methodology assumes that demons are intelligent but thrive best when not exposed. Hence historical demonology unmasks the demons in our midst and names them with precision and clarity.

22. June Jordan, "Of Those so Close beside Me, Which Are You?" in *Technical Difficulties: African-American Notes on the State of the Union* (New York: Pantheon Books, 1992), 29.
23. Ibid., 28.
24. Robert Pear, "Bush's Aides Put Higher Price Tag on Medicare Law," *The New York Times*, January 30, 2004: A-1.

Chapter 8 Everydayness: Beginning Notes on Dismantling The Cultural Production of Evil

1. Howard Thurman, *With Head and Heart: The Autobiography of Howard Thurman* (New York: Harvest/HBJ Book, 1981).
2. Barbara Jordan, "Address to the House Judiciary Committee Over the Nixon Impeachment in 1974," The Barbara Jordan National Forum on Public Policy, LBJ School of Public Affairs, University of Texas-Austin, http://www.utexas.edu/lbj/barbarajordanforum/aboutbj_speeches.htm.
3. Peter J. Paris, *The Social Teachings of the Black Churches* (Philadelphia: Fortress Press, 1985), 14.
4. Chamoiseau, *Texaco*, 122.
5. Niebuhr, *The Responsible Self.*
6. This list includes my grandmother (Miss. Nora) and the men and women of her generation of Black folk in Southern Pines, North Carolina who helped raise me.
7. Pat Robertson made this remark. After calls from the left, right, and center for him to retract his remarks, Robertson first denied calling for the assassination of Venezuelan president Hugo Chavez. After transcripts of his remarks were made public, he then declared he was being taken out of context.
From the August 22, 2005 broadcast of Robertson's *The 700 Club*:

> There was a popular coup that overthrew him [Chavez]. And what did the United States State Department do about it? Virtually nothing. And as a

result, within about 48 hours that coup was broken; Chavez was back in power, but we had a chance to move in. He has destroyed the Venezuelan economy, and he's going to make that a launching pad for communist infiltration and Muslim extremism all over the continent.

You know, I don't know about this doctrine of assassination, but if he thinks we're trying to assassinate him, I think that we really ought to go ahead and do it. It's a whole lot cheaper than starting a war. And I don't think any oil shipments will stop. But this man is a terrific danger and the United . . . This is in our sphere of influence, so we can't let this happen. We have the Monroe Doctrine, we have other doctrines that we have announced. And without question, this is a dangerous enemy to our south,— controlling a huge pool of oil, that could hurt us very badly. We have the ability to take him out, and I think the time has come that we exercise that ability. We don't need another $200 billion war to get rid of one, you know, strong-arm dictator. It's a whole lot easier to have some of the covert operatives do the job and then get it over with.

Index